The Ritual Abuse Controversy
An Annotated Bibliography

The Ritual Abuse Controversy

An Annotated Bibliography

MARY DE YOUNG

McFarland & Company, Inc., Publishers
Jefferson, North Carolina, and London

Library of Congress Cataloguing-in-Publication Data

De Young, Mary, 1949–
    The ritual abuse controversy : an annotated bibliography /
Mary de Young.
        p.   cm.
    Includes bibliographical references and index.
    ISBN 0-7864-1259-3 (softcover : 50# alkaline paper)
    1. Ritual abuse — Bibliography.   I. Title.
    Z5703.4.O35D49   2002
    [HV6625]
    016.1334'22 — dc21   2002000735

British Library cataloguing data are available

Cover photograph ©2002 Art Today

Manufactured in the United States of America

*McFarland & Company, Inc., Publishers
    Box 611, Jefferson, North Carolina 28640
    www.mcfarlandpub.com*

To Dan, Kiri and Kaleigh ...
Now you *finally* have your
name in a book, too

Acknowledgments

I owe a substantial debt to an international cast of characters who, in almost Shakespearean roles—"tragedy, comedy, history, pastoral, pastoral-comical, historical-pastoral, tragical-historical, tragical-comical-historical-pastoral"—contributed to the writing of this book.

I am grateful to my colleagues in the Sociology Department at Grand Valley State University for supporting my sabbatical during which most of the writing took place, and for keeping the department just as I remembered it until my return. Over the years many people have supplied me with information on ritual abuse in the form of articles, transcripts and reports. My thanks for cluttering up my closet to Bill Ellis of Penn State Hazelton, James Richardson of the University of Nevada, Bill Bernet of Vanderbilt University, Jonathan Harris formerly of the Massachusetts Institute of Technology, Ken Lanning of the Federal Bureau of Investigation, and investigative journalist Debbie Nathan.

I owe a very special thanks to my international colleagues, and I promise to visit each one to personally give it. Sietske Dijkstra of the Netherlands kept me informed on the Oude Pekela case; investigative reporter David McLoughlin of New Zealand's *North and South Magazine* did the same for the Civic Creche case. Gary Clapton of Edinburgh, Scotland, sent me a copy of his book just because he thought I might find it interesting, and he was right—I did. Margaret Jervis and Madeline Greenhalgh of England showed me that it is possible to have a conversation about recovered memories and not come to fisticuffs, in fact to even have a few laughs. And a very special thanks to Joshua Fox for long London lunches and constructive criticism.

In addition, many mental health professionals, social workers, council members, law enforcement officers, judges and others, including alleged victims and perpetrators, who choose to remain anonymous have provided

vii

me with essential information, reports and transcripts on the various cases summarized in this book. I appreciate it.

The collection of data for this book has been greatly expedited by helpful staff members of the Grand Valley State University Library, the Cooley Law School Library, the British Library, the Mitchell Library in Glasgow, Scotland, the National Library in Dublin, Ireland, and the public libraries in Boston and Chicago, as well as in Liverpool and Manchester, England, where the provision of a "winding handle" was greatly appreciated.

One criticism a bibliographer always fearfully anticipates is that something was left out. To those whose contribution to the ritual abuse controversy somehow escaped me, my apologies.

Finally, I want to thank my siblings Karen, John and David and their families. We went through a bad patch during the writing of this book. We supported each other as we shared our grief; now we are finally able to laugh with each other as we share our fond and funny memories of our parents. Thanks.

Contents

Preface

Lillian Hellman, whose play *The Children's Hour* presaged many of the controversies found in the pages of this book, once said, "Despite many disillusions, I still cling obstinately to the belief that writing can be done with your left hand while your right is busy with something else." This annotated bibliography confirms that contumacious belief, compiled as it was with one hand while the other sorted through nearly two decades' accumulation of materials on ritual abuse.

In using the words "materials," I resist the more descriptive word "stuff." Much of what has been written on ritual abuse over the last twenty years or so is in the form of unpublished and endlessly reproduced "stuff," that is, epistles, marginalia and *obiter dicta* on satanism, cult symbols, rituals and roles, catalogues of ritual abuse indicators, signs and symptoms, and even satanic calendars that are said to reveal the days children are most at risk for ritual abuse. This "stuff"—a curious admixture of conjecture, folkloric and popular cultural representations of satanism, devil worship, occultism and witchcraft, as well as Christian Fundamentalist images of premillennarian evil—continues to this day to circulate through the labyrinthine communication network that links child protectionists around the world.

Despite its inimitable role in creating a synthetic demonology that lends both context and legitimacy to allegations of ritual abuse and responses to them, none of this "stuff" is cited in this annotated bibliography. For the reason that this "stuff"—empirically unverifiable, historically imprecise, confusingly contradictory—mystifies and obfuscates the very notion of ritual abuse, I was curious about what is left when it is set aside. So I turned to published articles, books and reports, legal opinions, and occasionally to thought-provoking newspaper and magazine articles for the materials of this annotated bibliography. It would be disingenuous to even suggest by my choice of using only published materials that each work cited in this bibliography represents rigorous scholarship or thorough investigation, but the point remains that anything published is more accessible and therefore more available for critical review by any scholar, researcher, practitioner or lay person whose interest is piqued by the subject of ritual abuse.

So what *is* left when all of the "stuff" is taken away? A fascinating body of international literature that lays bare the controversies surrounding ritual abuse. Is it a clandestine form of abuse only lately emerging into the harsh light of public scrutiny, a culture-bound fiction that symbolizes the anxieties and ambiguities peculiar to late-modern societies, or perhaps a contemporary reworking of ancient legends and myths about innocence and evil? What are the implications for justice when professionals and social institutions respond, or for that matter fail to respond, to allegations of ritual abuse? Should children's accounts and adults' recovered memories of it be believed, or are they formed in conversational partnership with their confidantes? What are the sequelae of such horrific abuse, and if allegations and memories of it are not genuine, then what are the consequences for children and adults of usurping their own autobiographies by believing they are? These and other questions are at the heart of this annotated bibliography, the compilation of which necessitated exercises in judgment that inevitably delimit, at least to some extent, the final product.

The first exercise of judgment has to do with the terms used to search various data bases for relevant materials. "Satanic ritual abuse," that provocative term coined in the United States in the early 1980s to describe the sexual abuse of children in satanic rituals that include such ghastly acts as cannibalism, blood-drinking and human sacrifice, fell out of favor just a few years later after repeated attempts to substantiate the satanic connection failed. It was replaced with "ritual abuse," its adjectival variations "ritualistic" and "ritualized," "cultic abuse," "multidimensional sex rings" and, in an apparent attempt to preserve the "SRA" acronym, "sadistic ritual abuse." European and Australasian child protectionists secularize the term even more. "Organized abuse" and "network abuse" often are used in their literature, although both also refer to other conspiratorial types of child abuse, and "satanist abuse," newly coined to describe a more secular threat to children, is gaining usage. I used each of these as a search term for the compilation of this book. The term "ritual abuse," however, is used consistently in the annotations.

Being spoiled for choice of terms does pose some problems, though. As search terms broaden and become more inclusive of other types of child abuse, the very idea of ritual abuse begins to blur and, in some ways, so does the controversy attending it. What enticed my interest in the topic in the first place is that it describes a form of horrific, repetitive, ceremonial abuse that was unheard of before the early 1980s and still resists mainstreaming twenty years later. I therefore used that description — I do not dare to call it a definition — as a basis for deciding whether the literature in question is really discussing the kind of abuse that is so contentiously debated.

The second exercise in judgment has to do with maintaining the book's focus on ritual abuse. One of the reasons why ritual abuse is so steeped in controversy is that it is inextricably entwined with quarrelsome clinical issues, such as repressed and recovered memories, dissociation, multiple personalities, traumatic stress, factitious disorders and iatrogenesis, as well as disputatious ideological issues like satanism and occultism. While many of the annotations touch *on* these issues, this book is not *about* them. I cited sources on these issues only if they shed some light on ritual abuse. I leave to some other bibliographer the onerous task of taking on those topics, and I look forward to perusing the final product.

The ritual abuse controversy is international in scope, and the compilation of this annotated bibliography was greatly assisted by colleagues around the world who generously shared sources for it, as well as by the opportunities to conduct research and interviews in many countries. That said, the third exercise in judgment has to do with my inability to confidently read languages other than my mother tongue. And because confidence is critical to the task of annotation, this book cites only those sources written in English, or translated into it by scholars more linguistically skilled than I. Unfortunately, that means that some foreign sources relevant to the international ritual abuse controversy are not cited in this annotated bibliography.

The creation of context also required an exercise in judgment on my part. Much of the ritual abuse literature focuses on specific cases, particularly the day care cases in the United States and what more often were the family and community-based cases in Europe and Australasia. Rather than risk compromising the contribution of these sources to the ritual abuse controversy, I have introduced each of these cases with a precis that contextualizes it. Each precis is derived from a thorough perusal of materials, many of which are not available to the public, including legal briefs, interview and court transcripts, and investigative reports. While I am grateful to all of the people who have given me access to those materials, I take responsibility for any factual errors in the precis.

The fifth exercise in judgment has to do with the internet where the ritual abuse controversy is alive and kicking on web pages, in chat rooms and on bulletin boards. Those electronic sources are not cited in this book, however, with the exception of articles from peer-reviewed web journals and postings of previously published materials.

Finally, my own scholarship on the ritual abuse controversy, which is cited in this annotated bibliography, is critical of both the notion of ritual abuse and the collective reactions to it. I have endeavored, however, to carefully and objectively annotate each cited source, regardless of its perspective, so that readers can decide for themselves, just as I have decided for myself, where they want to stand in this controversy.

When *The Children's Hour* opened on Broadway in the 1930s it was a smashing success. Its plot, centering around children's allegations of sexual impropriety, adult secrets, vicious rumors and volatile reactions, was believable to conservative post–Depression audiences. But the film version, produced thirty years later, was a critical failure. Why? The times had changed.

The times have changed, too, from the first allegations of ritual abuse in the early 1980's to the present. The passage of time is accompanied by a growing body of interdisciplinary and international literature on ritual abuse that is cited in this book. But what has not changed is the controversy that envelops ritual abuse. Over the last twenty years allegations were made and some retracted, memories were recovered and some lost again, reputations were made and some ruined, some convictions were overturned and some overturned convictions were reinstated, some communities never healed from the divisive impact of ritual abuse cases and others did. It is this kind of controversy about ritual abuse that this annotated bibliography seeks to dissect.

1

Definitions, Defense, and Denial

Coined in the early 1980s, the term "satanic ritual abuse" labeled what appeared to many to be a new and horrific type of childhood trauma. The term was so provocative, so imagistic, that it functioned both as label and description. To say the words "satanic ritual abuse" was to conjure up images of robed and hooded cultists sexually, physically and psychologically abusing young children in ghastly ceremonies performed in worship of the devil. There is no uncertainty in this image, no ambiguity in its definition; the victims and villains of satanic ritual abuse are distinct, and good and evil are well and separately situated.

Casting abuse in such morally absolute terms does not preclude disagreement, of course. From the moment the term "satanic ritual abuse" entered discourse, there were those who believed the images it evokes are more fantastical than real. But what could have been a rather quiet disagreement welled into a divisive international controversy when one investigation after another failed to find compelling and convincing evidence that those labeled and stigmatized as "satanic ritual abusers" had any allegiance to satanism at all.

In what critics certainly would call a rhetorical sleight of hand, the word "satanic" then slowly disappeared from usage. The term "ritual abuse" is left to stand in its place.

THE DEFINITIONAL CONTROVERSY

The term "ritual abuse" is not without its own controversies. It is still used to label abuse by alleged satanic cultists—indeed that is by far

5

its most common usage — but the unanticipated consequence of "de-satanizing" the term is its rather facile appropriation by those in search of a label for the abuse of children allegedly perpetrated by other organized groups, such as occultists, pedophile rings, pornographers, government agents, and Freemasons.

So just what exactly is ritual abuse, and how is it best defined? Nearly two decades after the term and the horrifying images it evokes became the subject of a divisive international debate, the answers to those questions are still elusive.

◆ 1   Featherstone, B., & Harlow, E. (1996). Organized abuse: Themes and issues. In B. Fawcett, B. Featherstone, J. Hern, & C. Toft (Eds.), *Violence and gender relations: Theories and interventions* (pp. 161–170). London: Sage.

Defining organized sexual abuse is problematic because it covers diverse areas, such as family and local sexual abuse rings, commercial sexual exploitation, and ritual abuse. Organized abuse operates in a context of secrecy and creates disbelief when it is made public. This is especially true of ritual abuse and as a result, children's disclosures often are dismissed as imaginary, and the ethics of proving them true create additional controversy.

◆ 2   Frude, N. (1996). Ritual abuse: Conceptions and reality. *Clinical Child Psychology and Psychiatry, 1,* 59–77.

The trend toward treating ritual abuse as a separate and distinct type of child abuse raises significant problems and should be resisted. Because ritual abuse is so difficult to define and conceptualize, it is nearly impossible to estimate its prevalence and effects and develop effective treatment strategies.

◆ 3   Gallagher, B. (2000). Ritual and child sexual abuse, but not ritual child sexual abuse. *Child Abuse Review, 9,* 321–327.

Two cases exemplify the problems in defining ritual abuse: a 15-year-old boy was lured into sexual abuse by his brother and his partner through occult rituals, and a mother who was a suspect in the sexual abuse of her 3-year-old daughter revealed she was a practicing witch and satanist. Although the cases have elements in common — sexual abuse and rituals — neither is a ritual abuse case because those elements occurred independently of each other. These types of cases demonstrate the need for a broader and more balanced debate about the definition and nature of ritual abuse.

◆ 4   Goodwin, J.M. (1993). Sadistic abuse: Definition, recognition, and treatment. *Dissociation, 6,* 181–187.

The term "sadistic abuse" is preferred over "ritual abuse" because it describes extremely adverse experiences in the similar contexts of satanic cults, prostitution and pornography rings, and the Holocaust. The abuse includes ritual participation, sexual and physical abuse, torture, terrorization, and emotional abuse. Patients reporting childhood histories of sadistic abuse often present with severe and complicated symptoms that require special treatment interventions, including safety and symptom control, biographical reconstruction, and relearning.

◆ 5   Jones, D.P.H. (1991). Ritualism and child sexual abuse. *Child Abuse & Neglect, 15,* 163–170.

There are commonalities in the descriptions children give of ritual abuse; they describe sexual penetration, forced drug ingestion, consumption of blood and urine, robed and hooded perpetrators, and ceremonies that involve the sacrifices of animals and infants and cannibalism. Despite these consistencies, no consensual definition yet has emerged and the very term "ritual abuse" only complicates the task with its suggestion that this is a form of abuse that has special or mystical significance. It is that perception that further impedes research and clinical intervention because it suggests that allegations of ritual abuse require a different and higher standard of proof than do allegations of other types of abuse. The use of the terms "ritual" or "satanic" abuse, therefore, appear unwarranted at this stage and actually may compromise the objectivity of professionals and prompt their overreaction to alleged cases of it.

♦ **6**   LaFontaine, J.S. (1997). The controversy over satanic ritual abuse. *Self and Society, 25,* 21–23.

Ritual abuse is controversial for many reasons, not least of which is its ambiguous definition. Its diverse meanings make it difficult for the various groups that intervene in alleged cases of it, such as the police, child protectionists and mental health professionals, to communicate with each other, and to develop policies and procedures to redress it.

♦ **7**   LaFontaine, J.S. (1996). Organized and ritual abuse. *Medicine, Science, and the Law, 36,* 109–117.

The terms "organized" and "ritual" abuse often are used interchangeably, but it is important to be more precise in their uses. Organized abuse has a conspiratorial nature and is acted out by multiple perpetrators on multiple victims. Accounts of ritual abuse, however, often have no clear conspiratorial dimension and may implicate lone perpetrators and single victims.

♦ **8**   LaFontaine, J.S. (1993). Defining organized sexual abuse. *Child Abuse Review, 2,* 223–231.

The label "organized abuse" is used with such a variety of meanings that it impedes communication between professionals, confounds research, and interferes with good practice and policy initiatives. Organized abuse is best defined as "abuse by multiple perpetrators who act together to abuse children." This definition excludes ritual abuse because reported cases in the United Kingdom have little in common with those in the United States, and all reported cases have little in common with each other: some allege multiple perpetrators while others do not, some allege multiple victims while others do not, and some implicate immediate and extended family members as abusers while others implicate day care providers and nursery school teachers.

♦ **9**   Lloyd, D.W. (1992). Ritual child abuse: Definitions and assumptions. *Journal of Child Sexual Abuse, 1,* 1–14.

Ritual abuse is best defined as the "intentional physical abuse, sexual abuse, or psychological abuse of a child by a person responsible for the child's welfare, when such abuse is repeated and/or stylized and is typified by such other acts as cruelty to animals, or threats of harm to the child, other persons, or animals, and is performed to reinforce the cult's religious cohesion."

♦ **10**   Lloyd, D.W. (1991). Ritual child abuse: Understanding the controversies. *Cultic Studies Journal, 5,* 122–133.

The lack of a clear definition of ritual abuse contributes to the controversy about it by hindering understanding and assessment. If ritual abuse is defined in terms of intentionally repetitive and stylized sexual, physical and psychological abuse of children that is carried out to reinforce a group's beliefs system, then data can be collected on its incidence and prevalence, information can be gathered on its dynamics, and assessment can be conducted on its sequelae.

♦ 11   Lloyd, D.W. (1991). Ritual child abuse: Where do we go from here? *Children's Legal Rights Journal, 12,* 12–18.

Ritual abuse is one of the most controversial issues to impact the child protection field. Part of its controversy certainly has to do with the lack of a consensual definition of it. All professions with a stake in ritual abuse are encouraged to work together to form that definition which, in turn, will inform research, practice and policy.

♦ 12   Lundgren, E. (1995). Matters of life and death. *Trouble and Strife, 31,* 33–39.

A working definition of ritual abuse must consider motive. Is ritual abuse really an expression of a belief system, such as satanism, or a strategy of individuals or groups for heightening sexual pleasure by exerting absolute control over their child victims?

♦ 13   McFadyen, A., Hanks, H., & James, C. (1993). Ritual abuse: A definition. *Child Abuse Review, 2,* 35–41.

The Ritualistic Abuse Study Group, a group of professionals from various fields who meet regularly in Leeds, England, proposes the following definition of ritual abuse: "Ritual abuse is the involvement of children in physical, psychological or sexual abuse associated with repeated activities ('ritual') which purport to relate the abuse to contexts of a religious, magical or supernatural kind." The definition aids assessment and diagnosis, and assists in recognition and detection.

♦ 14   Segerberg, M. (1997). Satanic abuse, with focus on the situation in Finland. *Journal of Clinical Forensic Medicine, 4,* 185–191.

There are four types of satanists that must be distinguished: intergenerational cultists, organized satanic church members, self-styled satanists and experimental satanists. The number of crimes committed by satanists has been increasing in Finland since 1990, but intergenerational cultists who are responsible for the ritual abuse of children still are rare.

DEFENSE OF THE DEFINITION

The definitional controversy aside for the moment, the term "ritual abuse" retains all of the denotative dignity of "satanic ritual abuse"— it has the same power to call up frightening images of sadistic abuse in the context of ghastly rituals, and the same power to generate controversy over whether there is any integrity to that image. For those who believe there is, the links between this contemporary image and its historical antecedents in all of their clever cultural disguises are convincing proof.

♦ 15   DeMause, L. (1994). Why cults terrorize and kill children. *Journal of Psychohistory, 21,* 505–518.

The assertion of critics that the pursuit of ritual abuse is nothing more than a witch hunt can be easily refuted. A survey of history reveals many examples of the ritual abuse of children by cults organized around the belief that the absorption of children's power through abuse, torture, and murder assures their own power and longevity. There is even evidence of ritual abuse in cave paintings that date back to the Paleolithic era, including depictions of the "devil's wand" used to rape children and of handprints with missing fingers, an image that represents the historical antecedent of the contemporary practice of satanists to amputate their own pinkie fingers. Regardless of its historical context, cult abuse is a sexual perversion that achieves sexual fulfillment by means of trauma reenactment.

◆ **16** Feldman, G.C. (1995). Satanic ritual abuse: A chapter in the history of human cruelty. *Journal of Psychohistory, 22,* 340–357.

Throughout recorded history, sadistic violence has been perpetrated against the powerless. In many cultures around the world humans have been sacrificed so their power or spirit can be absorbed; contemporary satanic cults continue that magical tradition. In the same vein, witchcraft is widely practiced around the world and throughout history; although not all witches are satanic, contemporary satanic cults use aspects of witchcraft in their rituals. Today's satanists fall into one of four categories: dabblers, self-styled, religious and cultic, and there are many cases around the world that illustrate each type. Yet, despite this historical and cross-cultural evidence, many professionals continue to deny that ritual abuse is real; in doing so, they serve the needs of the most powerful in society who want to maintain an old social order of denial and secrecy.

◆ **17** Hill, S., & Goodwin, J.M. (1993). Demonic possession as a consequence of childhood trauma. *Journal of Psychohistory, 20,* 399–411.

A 17th century case of demon possession and exorcism studied by Freud has parallels to a contemporary case of a 42-year-old woman whose demonic possession was the result of childhood ritual abuse by a satanic cult. Freud posited that on a symbolic level, the demons represent internalized abusers. The analysis of the contemporary case extends that understanding by suggesting that the demons also represent keepers of the secrecy of abuse, protectors of the patient, and substitutes for memory.

◆ **18** Hill, S., & Goodwin, J.M. (1989). Satanism: Similarities between patient accounts and pre–Inquisition historical sources. *Dissociation, 2,* 39–44.

Primary historical sources reveal 11 practices of 4th century satanic cults that are consistent with recovered memories of ritual abuse: orgiastic sex, nocturnal feasts, imitations and reversals of the Christian mass, ritual use of semen and blood, sacrifices of fetuses and infants, cannibalism, ritual uses of candles and torches, chanting, drug ingestion, dancing backward in circles, and dismemberment of corpses. The historical similarities give credence to the position that these recovered memories are accurate and should be believed.

◆ **19** Holmes, P.A. (1999). A look at the psychological, spiritual and legal aspects of ritual abuse: Recommendations for counselors. *Dissertation Abstracts International, 60* (3-A), 0659. (University Microfilms No. AAM99–23903)

A small sample of psychotherapists, pastoral counselors and legal professionals in the Puget Sound area of Washington was surveyed regarding their experiences in working with ritual abuse victims. Survey findings indicate that throughout history ritual abuse has occurred not only in satanic cults, but in a variety of cultural and religious settings. Regardless of the origin, disclosures of ritual abuse raise significant questions about the nature of memory, and the complications of giving voice to what was unspoken.

◆ **20**   Kent, S.A. (1993). Deviant scripturalism and ritual satanic abuse part one: Possible Judeo-Christian influences. *Religion, 23,* 229–241.

Readily accessible religious texts, central to Judeo-Christian culture, provide the inspiration and motive to those who want to worship Satan and engage in satanic practices, such as ritual abuse. Interviews with ritual abuse survivors and a review of their journal entries reveal that their accounts are consistent with historical accounts of ritual abuse perpetrated by those who distort Judeo-Christian principles for their own purposes.

◆ **21**   Kent, S.A. (1993). Deviant scripturalism and ritual satanic abuse part two: Possible Masonic, Mormon, magick, and pagan influences. *Religion, 23,* 355–367.

Interviews with ritual abuse survivors and a perusal of their journal entries find information that is consistent with the doctrinal precedents and justifications for ritual abuse found in deviant interpretations of Masonic, Mormon, magick, and pagan traditions.

◆ **22**   Noblitt, J.R., & Perskin, P.S. (1995). *Cult and ritual abuse: Its history, anthropology, and recent discovery in contemporary America.* Westport, CT: Praeger.

Published and unpublished accounts of ritual abuse demonstrate a convincing consistency with historical and anthropological accounts of ritual abuse. The evidence suggests that the practices of contemporary satanic cults can be traced to their African roots in voodoo, Santeria, and Palo Mayombe. Bringing together contemporary accounts of ritual abuse and cross-cultural studies on cults with identical practices supports the conclusion that multiple personality disorder, or dissociative identity disorder as it recently has come to be termed, with which most ritual abuse patients are diagnosed, is a Western version of demon possession.

The Price of Denial

The temptation to turn away from the disturbing images of ritual abuse lures even those who are convinced that it is a real and emergent threat to children. The exhortation to resist that temptation and, in doing so, to break an age-old pattern of indifference to the reality and the consequences of childhood trauma resounds through the literature.

◆ **23**   Borden, T.A., & LaTerz, J.D. (1991). Mother/daughter incest and ritual abuse: The ultimate taboos. *Treating Abuse Today, 3,* 5–8.

Ritual abuse and mother/daughter incest are topics that are in desperate need of more thorough research. What these types of abuse have in common is a cultural barrier to their recognition, and a professional barrier to researching them. They stand as illustrations of how a cultural taboo can infuse the practice of mental health professionals.

◆ **24**   Goodwin, J.M. (1994). Credibility problems in sadistic abuse. *Journal of Psychohistory, 21,* 478–496.

The primary credibility problem that obscures the study and understanding of ritual and other types of sadistic abuse is the simple unwillingness to believe it occurs despite evidence that it has throughout history. One strategy for overcoming this problem is to collect data on the epidemiology of ritual and sadistic abuse; another is to listen to the allegations of children and adult survivors, realizing that the very experience of ritual abuse — fragmenting, terrorizing, and disorienting as it is — will interfere with their ability to give a full, consistent, and credible account. History reveals that only a thin line separates "normal" people from sadistic perpetrators, as the cases of Gilles de Rais and the Marquis de Sade illustrate. Only when that final hurdle is cleared will the denial of ritual and sadistic abuse finally be overcome.

◆ **25** Gould, C. (1995). Denying ritual abuse of children. *Journal of Psychohistory, 22*, 329–339.

The evidence is quickly accumulating that ritual abuse is a problem of considerable scope and gravity, yet skeptics abound. There are two major factors in what has become an elaborate denial system: economic and sociocultural. Because cults are deeply involved in organized crime and program their victims to engage in profitable acts like prostitution, they are able to influence the media, derail investigations, and hire public officials to take the stance that ritual abuse does not occur. From a sociocultural point of view, Americans deny the reality of ritual abuse because it threatens their image as compassionate and responsive citizens. The price of raising awareness and coming to terms with the reality of ritual abuse will be very high, indeed, but the price of denying it and its impact on children is exorbitant.

2

Day Care Ritual Abuse Cases in the United States

Between 1983 and 1992, more than a hundred day centers and pre-schools in major cities and small towns across the United States were investigated for ritual abuse. Day care providers were accused of sexually abusing the young children entrusted to their care in the course of rituals that included such ghastly practices as blood-drinking, cannibalism and infant sacrifices. The day care investigations created deep and often irreparable fissures in the communities where they occurred and resulted in scores of arrests, often long and expensive criminal trials, many convictions, sometimes draconian prison sentences, blinding flurries of lawsuits and countersuits and, over recent years, many reversals of convictions upon appeal.

It is ironic that so many of these cases that exacted such a toll on the lives of the young children, the accused, the families of both, as well as the various intervening professionals escaped national attention, and more ironic yet that even some of those caught in the blinding light of national scrutiny still elude scholarly analysis. The American day care ritual abuse cases discussed in this chapter are constitutive of these ironies, as are the citations that annotate them. A few of the cited cases are so familiar as to be folkloric, some are lesser known but thoroughly scrutinized by local sources and others, familiar or not, are the subjects of scholarly analysis and debate.

The citations from local and national sources in this chapter are included only to flesh out the controversy and enliven the legalistic precis that introduces each case. Local newspaper reportage on the cases, although often excellent, is not cited with the exception of a Pulitzer Prize winning series. The scholarly citations are annotated to expose the heart or, perhaps more accurately *hearts,* of the ritual abuse controversy as it was played out in that most innocuous of American social institutions, the local day care center.

FOURTEEN DAY CARE RITUAL ABUSE CASES

McMartin Preschool

In 1983 a 2½-year-old child, an occasional attendee at the McMartin Preschool in Manhattan Beach, California, made comments suggestive of sexual abuse and named the center's only male provider, Raymond Buckey, as his abuser. The local police sent letters to 200 parents of current and past enrollees asking them to question their children about sexual abuse and naming Buckey as the suspect. Fifteen more children then accused him and named many other children as his victims. As the investigation accelerated, parents were referred to a child abuse assessment center to have their children evaluated, and over the next year 369 children were identified as victims and all seven of the providers as their abusers. Over the course of their interviews the children talked about the ingestion of feces and human flesh, disinterment of corpses, sacrifices of infants in tunnels under the center, and sexual abuse in airplanes, cemeteries, churches and hot air balloons. In 1986 the providers were indicted on a total of 135 counts of sexual assault and conspiracy; days later, the charges against five of them were dismissed for lack of evidence, leaving Buckey and his mother, Peggy McMartin Buckey, to stand trial.

◆ **26**   Carlson, P. (1984, April 16). A therapist uses puppets to help crack California's horrifying nursery school child abuse case. *People*, pp. 78–81.

Social worker Kee MacFarlane of the Children's Institute International uses puppets and dolls to coax out the "yucky secrets" of the young children in the McMartin Preschool ritual abuse case. She also spends considerable time comforting and consoling their distraught parents.

◆ **27**   Coleman, L. (1989). Learning from the McMartin hoax. *Issues in Child Abuse Accusations, 1.* Retrieved 4-March-01 from the World Wide Web: http://www.ipt-forensics.com/journal/volume1/j1_2_7.htm

The videotapes of the clinical interviews conducted with 46 of the children in the McMartin Preschool case show a pattern of suggestive, coercive and manipulative interactions that led to false allegations of ritual abuse. Transcripts from the interviews illustrate this conclusion.

◆ **28**   Earl, J. (1995). The dark truth about the "dark tunnels of McMartin." *Issues in Child Abuse Accusations, 7.* Retrieved 4-March-01 from the World Wide Web: http://www.ipt-forensics.com/journal/volume7/j7_2_1.htm

In 1990 consulting archaeologist Gary Stickle led a group of parents in a search for tunnels under the McMartin Preschool. Stickle reports they found 2 hand-dug underground passageways, a secret underground room and thousands of bones of small animals and fish, consistent with the children's accounts of animal sacrifices. The unpublished Stickle report contradicts the findings of a 1985 excavation by a professional archeological firm hired by the District Attorney that found no evidence of tunnels or rooms and that dismissed the bones as evidence of a trash scatter.

◆ **29**   Fischer, M.A. (1989, September 25). A case of dominoes? *Los Angeles Magazine*, pp. 126–136.

The actions of critical players in the McMartin Preschool ritual abuse case, including social worker Kee MacFarlane, reporter Wayne Satz, and District Attorney Ira Reiner, raise the real possibility that they invented the ritual abuse charges and fueled public uproar about them for their own personal and political reasons.

◆ **30**   Fischer, M.A. (1988, December). Flipflop: Why four years later, the press is taking a strikingly different approach to the McMartin Preschool scandal. *Los Angeles Magazine*, pp. 85–91.

Although the press fomented the mass hysteria about the McMartin Preschool ritual abuse case, it is now taking a critical stance and questioning the veracity of the children's allegations and the legal strength of the case.

◆ **31**   Fischer, M.A. (1988, May). In search of justice. *Life Magazine*, pp. 164–167.

Arrested in 1983, Raymond Buckey has spent more than 4 years in isolation in a county jail. Last December his bail was set at $3 million, an amount he has almost raised. Now he is about halfway into his criminal trial and admits to going through a "roller coaster of hope and despair." To date, the trial has cost $8 million, roughly twice the estimated cost to the taxpayers of the Iran-Contra Congressional hearings.

◆ **32**   Green, M. (1984, May 21). The McMartins: The "model family" down the block that ran California's nightmare nursery. *People*, pp. 109–115.

Biographical sketches of Virginia McMartin, the founder of the McMartin Preschool, her daughter Peggy McMartin Buckey, granddaughter Peggy Ann Buckey and grandson Raymond Buckey, all of whom are accused of ritually abusing over 300 young children in their care at the McMartin Preschool in southern California, are presented.

◆ **33**   Hackett, G. (1986, December 15). Child abuse or adult paranoia? *Newsweek*, p. 43.

As the allegations of the children become more bizarre and they name more people other than their providers as their abusers, doubts are growing about the veracity of the allegations of ritual abuse in the McMartin Preschool case.

◆ **34**   Lacayo, R. (1986, December 15). Hollywood tapes and testimony: A chilling sexual abuse case takes a strange turn. *Time Magazine*, p. 64.

As bizarre as the allegations of the children in the McMartin Preschool ritual abuse case are, even more bizarre is the prospect they are not true. Former prosecutor Glenn Stevens, who is working with producer Abby Mann on a film and book on the case, asserts in taped interviews that prosecutors behaved unethically by withholding evidence that exonerates Raymond Buckey and Peggy McMartin Buckey, including reports that the mother of the child who made the initial complaint is mentally ill and has made bizarre allegations of abuse against any number of other people.

♦ **35** Leo, J. (1984, April 23). Some day, I'll cry my eyes out. *Time Magazine*, pp. 72–74.

For years she was known as "Miss Virginia" who ran the best preschool in the city; now at age 76 she is facing charges of sexual abuse in the context of bizarre rituals. The allegations were coaxed from the children by social worker Kee MacFarlane who used hand-held puppets and anatomically correct dolls to uncover their secrets. If the case has any redeeming merits, it is to raise awareness of sexual abuse as a problem, urge the criminal justice system to be more responsive to it, and help parents and professionals identify its signs and symptoms.

♦ **36** Moss, D.C. (1987). Are the children lying? *ABA Journal, 73*, 58–62.

Several cases of reported ritual abuse, including the McMartin Preschool case, illustrate the problems inherent in deciding whether accusing children are telling the truth, lying, or engaging in fantasy.

♦ **37** Plummer, W. (1985, July 8). The young witnesses in the McMartin sex abuse case undergo a legal battering in court. *People*, pp. 26–28.

The experiences of the children testifying in the 19 month long preliminary hearing of the Martin Preschool ritual abuse case are discussed. The children find the experience extremely stressful, confusing and at times threatening, but most believe they are doing the right thing. One 10 year old child was on the witness stand for 16 days and was so relentlessly interrogated that many parents withdrew their children from the case.

♦ **38** Reese, M. (1986, January 27). A child abuse case implodes. *Newsweek*, p. 26.

The District Attorney drops all charges against 5 of the day care providers in the McMartin Preschool ritual abuse case, calling the evidence against them "incredibly weak."

♦ **39** Safian, R. (1989, October). McMartin madness. *The American Lawyer*, pp. 46–51.

A day-by-day account of 10 days towards the end of the trial of Raymond Buckey and his mother Peggy for ritually abusing children at the McMartin Preschool. Defense attorneys Danny Davis and Dean Gits are a study in contrast; the former is dramatic and flamboyant, the latter soft-spoken and meticulous, but both have based their defense on an elaborate witch hunt theory that implicates police, social workers, and prosecutors. During the 10 days, tempers are frayed, another juror is removed because of illness, the jurors and the reporters alternate between boredom and excitement, and Raymond Buckey finally testifies on his own behalf. He denies all charges against him and states he had never seen some of the child witnesses before the preliminary hearing. On cross-examination by prosecutor Lael Rubin, he admits he has a prior record for marijuana possession and drunk-driving and has a pornographic magazine collection.

♦ **40** Smith, S.B. (1987). The child witness. In L.F. Michaels (Ed.), *Representing children: Current issues in law, medicine, mental health, and protective services* (pp. 1–10). Denver, CO: National Association of Counsel for Children.

The McMartin Preschool ritual abuse case illustrates the problems inherent in cases involving children as witnesses in court. Although the case has multiple victims and defendants, its real complexity lies in the demands it makes on the criminal justice system to accommodate young witnesses. Court reforms, such as allowing children to testify via closed-circuit television, are long-overdue but pose their own problems. Nevertheless, courts must continue to develop ways of decreasing the trauma of testifying for child witnesses.

♦ **41**   Staver, S. (1985). In the wake of sexual abuse: Unraveling a nightmare. *American Medical News, 28*, 1–5.

The McMartin Preschool ritual abuse highlights the challenges to medical professionals of evaluating children for sexual abuse and for preparing testimony for what may become controversial criminal trials.

♦ **42**   Strasser, R. (1984, April 9). A sordid preschool "game." *Newsweek*, p. 38.

Children in the McMartin Preschool ritual abuse case describe the "Naked Movie Star" game in which they are stripped of their clothes and then filmed while being sexually abused by their providers and other adults. Their parents now realize they overlooked telltale signs of abuse, such as bedwetting and nightmares, and unwittingly sent their children to what authorities are describing as an outlet for child pornography and prostitution.

♦ **43**   Summit, R.C. (1994). Digging for the truth: The McMartin tunnel project versus trenchant disbelief. *Treating Abuse Today, 4*, 5–13.

In 1990 the parents of some of the children victimized in the McMartin ritual abuse case, led by archaeologist Gary Stickle, unearthed evidence of tunnels under the Preschool. The find confirms the accounts of many of the children, yet most skeptics are so firmly entrenched in their belief that nothing happened at the Preschool that even this compelling evidence fails to move them to reconsider their position.

♦ **44**   Summit, R.C. (1994). The dark tunnels of McMartin. *Journal of Psychohistory, 21*, 397–416.

Critics of the McMartin Preschool case cite the lack of physical evidence and the unbelievable accounts of the children as reasons for rejecting their claims of ritual abuse. The unearthing of evidence at the site of the Preschool by parents and an archaeologist require a public rethinking of the case. Tunnels discovered under the Preschool corroborate the accounts of many of the children that a network of tunnels leads to an underground room where the abuse took place.

♦ **45**   Timnick, L. (1984, September 10). Were tots molested at the McMartin Preschool? *National Law Journal*, p.1.

Three months into the McMartin Preschool ritual abuse case preliminary hearing, no children have yet testified. The hearing is being taken up by legal maneuvers, arguments over media access, and the fallout from the unexpected testimony of a jailhouse informant who stated that Raymond Buckey admitted to him that he had ritually abused the children in his care.

Post–McMartin Trials

The trial of Raymond Buckey and Peggy McMartin Buckey began in 1987 and lasted 28 months, the longest, and at $15 million, the most expensive criminal trial in American history. The jury listened to 124 witnesses, 13 of them children, and examined 974 exhibits before returning its verdict. It acquitted Peggy McMartin Buckey of all charges and Raymond Buckey of 39 charges, but deadlocked on the remaining 13. His second trial on 8 of those charges ended with a hung jury; a month later all charges against him were dismissed. The trial was dramatized in the 1995 HBO film, "Indictment: The McMartin Trial," aired just before Virginia McMartin died. Peggy McMartin Buckey died in 2000.

A decade after the verdicts, and nearly two decades after the first allegation, the McMartin ritual abuse case continues to raise questions about the legal merit of ritual abuse cases, the methods of interviewing young children, the proper role of the media, and the consequences of ritual abuse — whether real or imagined — for the accusing children, the accused and even the culture.

(Legal Issues)

♦ **46** Anderson, D.D. (1996). Assessing the reliability of children's testimony in sexual abuse cases. *Southern California Law Review, 69,* 2117–2161.

In multi-victim cases like McMartin Preschool and Wee Care Nursery, many children who never disclose or exhibit symptoms of abuse will be vigorously interviewed, often by interviewers who already are certain they have been abused. Skepticism by courts about the reliability of children's statements under these conditions is warranted, but should be tempered by a concentrated approach to reliability assessment in either a hearsay or a taint hearing context.

♦ **47** Askowitz, L.R., & Graham, M.H. (1994). The reliability of expert psychological testimony in child sexual abuse prosecutions. *Cardozo Law Review, 15,* 2027–2101.

Notorious cases such as the McMartin Preschool ritual abuse case often are set in a context of mass hysteria that increases the likelihood that false allegations will be made. While expert testimony plays an important and legitimate role in child sexual abuse trials, courts must take an active role in ensuring its reliability. High profile ritual abuse cases like McMartin show how easy it is for public abhorrence of a crime to compromise reliability standards.

♦ **48** Besharov, D. (1990, February 19). The McMartin case: Protecting the innocent. *National Review,* pp. 44–46.

The only evidence presented at the McMartin Preschool defendants' criminal trial was the testimony of the children; their statements and their credibility as witnesses were undermined during cross-examination and summation. The unique problems of using young children as witnesses require creative strategies for protecting them without abusing the law.

♦ **49** DeBenedictus, D.J. (1990). McMartin Preschool's lessons. *ABA Journal, 76,* 28–30.

A review of the criminal trial of the McMartin Preschool defendants reveals that the police investigation was shoddily conducted, the defendants were tried on too many counts, and the unrelenting media coverage of the trial contributed to its length and expense.

♦ **50**   Dunn, A.R. (1995). Questioning the reliability of children's testimony: An examination of the problematic elements. *Law and Psychology Review, 19,* 203–215.

The McMartin Preschool and the Wee Care Nursery ritual abuse cases show how factors such as repetitive and suggestive interviewing can influence children's testimony. Although the courts have considerable discretion in evaluating the truthfulness of children's testimony, including taint hearings, better and more consistent procedures for doing so are still needed.

♦ **51**   Eberle, P., & Eberle, S. (1993). *Abuse of innocence.* Buffalo, NY: Prometheus.

An exposé of the McMartin Preschool ritual abuse case trial with special attention to the role of the legal system, mental health experts, and the media in sensationalizing the case. Trial transcripts illustrate the conclusion that the trial was a witch hunt and the charges in the case were baseless.

♦ **52**   Fukurai, H., Butler, E.W., & Krooth, R. (1994). Sociologists in action: The McMartin sexual abuse case, litigation, justice, and mass hysteria. *American Sociologist, 25,* 2–44.

Jury consultants to the defense attorneys in the McMartin Preschool ritual abuse trial explain the process of "scientific defense *voir dire*" they used to seat an impartial jury. The 12 jurors and 6 alternates met the basic demographic, socioeconomic and attitudinal criteria derived from the statistical analyses of community survey data, *voir dire* questionnaires, and observational data. Jury composition certainly can be credited in the acquittals of Raymond Buckey and Peggy McMartin Buckey.

♦ **53**   Lacayo, R. (1990, August 6). The longest mistrial. *Time Magazine,* p. 28.

The decision to dismiss all charges against Raymond Buckey after the jury deadlocked in his second trial was legally wise but publicly foolish. The McMartin Preschool ritual abuse case is prompting a reexamination of the methods for investigating allegations, but the dismissal of charges leaves the accusing children and their parents bitter that justice was not done.

♦ **54**   Mann, A. (1993). *Shocking true story of the McMartin child abuse trial.* NY: Random House.

An exposé of the McMartin Preschool ritual abuse trial, discussing the prosecution in the absence of evidence and the original prosecutor's doubt that the children had been sexually abused, let alone ritually abused.

♦ **55**   Mason, M.A. (1991). The McMartin case revisited: The conflict between social work and criminal justice. *Social Work, 36,* 391–395.

There is a fundamental conflict between the goal of the social work system to protect and treat children, and the goal of the criminal justice system to prosecute defendants. That irreconcilable conflict is evident in the McMartin Preschool ritual abuse case in which social workers often acted as investigators to aide the prosecution's case.

♦ **56**   McGough, L.S. (1994). *Child witnesses: Fragile voices in the American legal system.* New Haven, CT: Yale University Press.

The problems inherent in using children as witnesses are evident in the McMartin Preschool, Wee Care Nursery and Craig's Country Preschool ritual abuse cases. These cases demonstrate how child witnesses are more prone to suggestibility, memory fade and fantasy than are adult witnesses. Three basic principles of reform should be considered: videotaping of children's testimony according to strict rules that will ensure objectivity and reliability; streamlining the criminal investigation process so that children are not subjected to protracted and multiple interviews; and revising existing evidentiary barriers to the admission of out-of-court statements.

◆ **57**   Montoya, J. (1993). Something not so funny happened on the way to conviction: The pretrial interrogation of child witnesses. *Arizona Law Review, 35*, 927–987.

All children's out-of-court statements should be subject to a trustworthiness inquiry that would guide the trial court's determinations, as the McMartin Preschool, Wee Care Nursery and Craig's Country cases attest. Both children and the fact-finding process need protection from relentless reinterviewing. The current videotape legislation, which only invites adult abuses by rehearsing children's testimony, fails to do that. Consequently, only an adversarial testing of children's stories will achieve that goal.

◆ **58**   Salthe, E. (1989/1990). Statutory immunity. *Journal of Family Law, 28*, 847–850.

The 1989 decision in the *McMartin v. Children's Institute International* suit is in favor of the defendant. The injuries to the McMartin Preschool and to its 7 providers arising out of the reports of ritual abuse made by the Children's Institute International, the agency contracted by Los Angeles County to assess the preschoolers, are not recoverable because the agency is statutorily immune.

(Interviewing Young Children)

◆ **59**   Garven, S., Wood, J.M., & Malpass, R.S. (2000). Allegations of wrongdoing: The effects of reinforcement on children's mundane and fantastic claims. *Journal of Applied Psychology, 85*, 38–50.

Reinforcement, a specific component of the McMartin Preschool ritual abuse case interviews, is examined with a sample of 120 children between the ages of 5 and 7. Reinforcement elicits 3 times more false allegations against a classroom visitor than simple questions alone, and 10 times more agreement that a fantastic event occurred, in this case being taken from school in a helicopter, than simple questions alone. The findings indicate that reinforcement can swiftly induce children to make persistent false allegations as it did in the McMartin Preschool case.

◆ **60**   Garven, S., Wood, J.M., Malpass, R.S., & Shaw, J.S. (1998). More than suggestion: The effect of interviewing techniques from the McMartin Preschool case. *Journal of Applied Psychology, 83*, 347–359.

Child interviewing techniques derived from the interview transcripts of the children in the McMartin Preschool ritual abuse case elicit almost 4 times more false allegations from preschool children about a classroom visitor than simple suggestive questions alone. An "SIRR model" is set out to explain how false statements are elicited through the kinds of suggestive questions, social influence, reinforcement, and removal from direct experience used in the McMartin interviews.

◆ **61**   Ronan, W.J. (1993). Memory, suggestion and truth. *Issues in Child Abuse Accusations, 5*. Retrieved 4-March-01 from the World Wide Web: http://www.ipt-forensics.com/journal/volume5/j5_2_5.htm.

The transcripts of the interviews conducted with the children in the McMartin Preschool case illustrate how leading questions from social workers acting as investigators produce false memories of ritual abuse for children who are socialized to obey the expectations of authority figures.

♦ **62**   Waller, P. (1991). The politics of child abuse. *Society, 28,* 6–13.

Political and ideological agendas undermine the credibility of the mental health and social work professions in child abuse cases, as the McMartin Preschool ritual abuse case demonstrates. That case brings to light examples of clinical practice previously not scrutinized, including how interviewer bias and beliefs shape children's accounts.

(Role of the Media)

♦ **63**   McConnell, F. (1990, March 23). The trials of television — The McMartin case. *Commonweal,* pp. 189–191.

The media fomented public reactions to the McMartin Preschool ritual abuse case by biased, pro-prosecution reporting.

♦ **64**   Shaw, D. (1990, January 22). McMartin coverage was biased, critics charge. *Los Angeles Times,* p. A-1.

Part III of the Pulitzer Prize winning exposé focuses on the *Los Angeles Times* coverage of the McMartin Preschool ritual abuse case and the charges of critics that it was pro-prosecution in its reportage. An analysis of the coverage shows a more balanced approach than critics claim, although in the early months of the story the newspaper certainly participated in the "feeding frenzy" that characterized much of the local and national reportage on the case.

♦ **65**   Shaw, D. (1990, January 20). Reporter's early exclusives trigger a media frenzy. *Los Angeles Times,* p. A-1.

Part II of the Pulitzer Prize winning exposé focuses on KABC reporter Wayne Satz who broke the McMartin Preschool ritual abuse case story. His coverage of the story earned him several awards, kudos from the parents of the children, criticism from his colleagues for biased reporting, and raised questions about ethical misconduct for the affair he had with social worker Kee MacFarlane while she was interviewing the children and he was reporting on the case.

♦ **66**   Shaw, D. (1990, January 19). Where was skepticism in the media? Pack journalism and hysteria marked early coverage of the McMartin case. *Los Angeles Times,* p. A-1.

Part I of the Pulitzer Prize winning exposé of the role of the media in the McMartin Preschool ritual abuse case covers the initial rush to uncover details of the ritual abuse, the sensationalized reporting and the rumor-mongering role of the press.

(Accusers, Accused, and Culture At-Large)

♦ **67**   Billingsley, K. (1993, November). Abuse of the child abuse war. *The World & I,* pp. 429–439.

The McMartin case, where sensational charges diverted attention from the reliability of the accuser, is the best example of how the war on child abuse is wreaking havoc on innocent people. Judy Johnson, the mother of the young boy who supposedly made the first allegation, not only accused Raymond Buckey of ritual abuse but

5 other men including her husband, and a Los Angeles School Board member. The only remedies to cases built upon such unreliable allegations as this is to drop the immunity clause so that police and prosecutors will be held legally accountable for their actions, and to cut off federal funding to states that deprive suspects of their due process rights.

♦ **68**   Buckey, P., Buckey, R., & Buckey, P.A. (1990). After the McMartin trials: Some reflections from the Buckeys. *Issues in Child Abuse Accusations, 2*. Retrieved 4-March-01 from the World Wide Web: http://www.ipt-forensics.com/journal/volume2/j2_4_6.htm

Raymond Buckey, his mother Peggy and sister Peggy Ann discuss the toll the McMartin Preschool ritual abuse case took on them and their family. For Raymond and his mother, the years in jail awaiting trial were particularly difficult; each was assaulted by other inmates, shunned by neighbors and friends, and demoralized by the increasingly bizarre accounts of ritual abuse made by a growing number of children. Peggy Ann lost her license to teach and had to initiate a civil suit for its restoration. They take comfort in their religious beliefs and in their knowledge that they are innocent of all charges.

♦ **69**   Carlson, M., Beatty, J., & Lafferty, E. (1990, January 29). Six years of trial by torture. *Time Magazine*, pp. 26–28.

The 6 year long McMartin Preschool ritual abuse case leaves a trail of victims, including the children and their parents, the defendants, the jurors who sat through the longest criminal trial in United States history, the community and the nation.

♦ **70**   Cockburn, A. (1990, January 26). Abused imaginings. *New Statesman and Society*, pp. 19–20.

The hysteria over ritual abuse, which began with the McMartin Preschool case and spread across the United States, is a product of greatly exaggerated fears, fanned by mental health professionals, prosecuting attorneys and the media, about the vulnerability of children to sexual abuse.

♦ **71**   deYoung, M. (1997). The devil goes to day care: McMartin and the making of a moral panic. *Journal of American Culture, 20*, 19–25.

The McMartin Preschool ritual abuse case was set in a cultural context rife with fears about sexual and satanic threats to children, and with middle class guilt about sending children to day care. Once the initial allegation was made, interest groups such as the social workers and the media, played on those fears and guilt, fueling a moral panic that swept across the country. The panic brought in its wake some modest changes in day care that alleviated parental fear and guilt.

♦ **72**   Fischer, M.A. (1993, October). Instant karma: Aftermath of the McMartin Preschool child molestation prosecutions. *Los Angeles Magazine*, pp. 48–55.

Profiles of those involved in the McMartin Preschool case — defendants, police, prosecuting and defense attorneys, social workers and children and their parents — are examined a decade after the first allegation of ritual abuse was made.

♦ **73**   Fischer, M.A. (1990, April). Ray Buckey: An exclusive interview. *Los Angeles Magzine*, pp. 90–100.

Raymond Buckey shares his plans for the future upon his acquittal in the McMartin Preschool ritual abuse case. He plans to reenroll in college and eventually to study law. Although he and his family have been devastated by the case, he believes the real victims are the children who were led into making false allegations.

◆ **74**   Nathan, D. (1990, June 12). What McMartin started: The ritual abuse hoax. *Village Voice,* pp. 36–38, 40–44.

The ritual abuse allegations in the McMartin Preschool case set off similar allegations in dozens of other day care centers across the United States. These allegations are the product of overzealous interviewers and frantic parents who have a bias to find ritual abuse and are given credence by a culture filled with irrational fear about satanic menaces to children. The harm this hysteria is wreaking on civil liberties, women's rights and even on the children who are the alleged ritual abuse victims is simply inestimable.

◆ **75**   Schindehette, S., Kelly, J., Bacon, D., Wohlfert, L, Micheli, R., & Tamarkin, C. (1990, February 5). After the verdict, solace for none. *People,* pp. 70–71, 73–76, 78, 80.

The acquittals of Raymond Buckey and Peggy McMartin Buckey stun the children who testified and leaves them feeling betrayed by the system. Several of the profiled children are experiencing nightmares and intrusive memories of their ritual abuse. Their parents will start a letter-writing campaign to get Raymond Buckey retried on the deadlocked charges, and with their children will appear on television talk shows to rally national support. Although 7 of the jurors appearing at a post-trial press conference believe the children were sexually abused at the center, none of them believes the prosecution proved the charges. The McMartin defendants will file a multi-million dollar suit against Kee MacFarlane who interviewed the children, the Children's Institute International, the police and Los Angeles County for malicious prosecution, defamation of character, and violation of civil rights.

◆ **76**   Waterman, J., Kelly, R.J., Oliveri, M.K., & McCord, J. (1993). *Behind the playground walls.* NY: Guilford Press.

The short- and long-term effects of reported ritual abuse on the children in the McMartin Preschool case are examined and compared to those for children sexually abused in a day care center, and children with no history of abuse. At initial assessment, the ritually abused children show significantly higher scores on all levels of distress, more school problems, more symptoms of post-traumatic stress disorder, less social competency, and more body image dissatisfaction than do the sexually abused and nonabused children. Symptoms tend to dissipate over time, with 17% of the children exhibiting clinically significant symptoms after 5 years. The parents of ritually abused children report significant stress, with mothers more likely to blame themselves, and to experience depression. At the peak of their involvement with the ritually abused children, 78% of their psychotherapists met the diagnostic criteria for post-traumatic stress disorder.

Country Walk Day Care Center

In 1984 a 3 year old disclosed that Ileana Fuster, his day care provider, had kissed his body. The unlicensed Miami, Florida, home day care center quickly became the focus of an investigation that identified 15 victims, including Ileana's husband Frank's 6 year old son. The children alleged they were forced to pray to Satan, eat human flesh and sacrifice animals, and were filmed while having sex with the Fusters and each other. Ileana, 17 years old, eventually pled guilty and agreed to testify against her husband. In return for her plea, she received a 10 year prison sentence; she served three years and then was deported to her native Honduras. She retracted her confession the following year. That retraction can be found at the internet URL: http://www.geocities.com/CapitolHill/Embassy/9062/ileanatxt.html.

Frank Fuster was tried and found guilty in 1985 of 14 counts of rape against the children who testified via closed circuit television. He was sentenced to six consecutive life sentences. All attempts to appeal his conviction have been unsuccessful. He remains in prison.

◆ **77**   Cockburn, A. (1993, Sept. 20). Reno's victim. *The Nation*, pp. 272–274.

Frank Fuster, recovering from a prison attack that left a ballpoint pen lodged in his neck near an artery, is one of Janet Reno's victims. As Dade County District Attorney, she was so desperate for a successful prosecution in the Country Walk ritual abuse case that she visited Ileana Fuster in jail over 30 times to persuade her to confess and testify against her husband. Ileana, who was being held naked in solitary confinement, eventually agreed.

◆ **78**   Cockburn, A. (1993, March). Legal abuse in Dade County. *New Statesman and Society*, pp. 12–13.

The case against the Fusters was weak but the atmosphere was hysterical. Months of brainwashing techniques were used by prosecution psychologists to convince Ileana that her husband was a ritual abuser and that she should testify against him. Dade County District Attorney Janet Reno endorsed questionable prosecution methods to secure a conviction that would assure her reelection.

◆ **79**   Hollingsworth, J. (1986). *Unspeakable acts.* Chicago, IL: Congdon and Weed.

A freelance journalist's account of the Country Walk ritual abuse case in Miami, Florida, beginning with the initial allegation, the roles played by Drs. Laurie and Joseph Braga as interviewers, the activism of the parents who formed the Justice for Children Group and lobbied for the creation of a Department of Children's Services in Florida, the backgrounds of the Fusters, and the trial and its outcome. The book was made into the 1990 made-for-television movie, *Unspeakable Acts.*

◆ **80**   Nathan, D. (1993). Revisiting Country Walk. *Issues in Child Abuse Allegations, 5.* Retrieved 4-March-01 from the World Wide Web: http://www.ipt-forensics.com/journal/volume5/j5_1_1.htm

The Country Walk case often is cited as a corroborated ritual abuse case; one child tested positive for gonorrhea of the throat, and Ileana Fuster confessed to ritually abusing the children. These pieces of corroborating evidence are disputable. The gonorrhea test proves to be unreliable and no evidence was presented that Fuster ever had gonorrhea. Ileana's confession was coerced through isolation and repeated interrogation, alternating with relaxation and visualization exercises and promises of a light sentence.

◆ **81**   Surette, R. (1999). Media echoes: Systemic effects of news coverage. *Justice Quarterly, 16,* 601–631.

The effects of media coverage on the Miami, Florida, judicial system are analyzed by comparing over 3,000 felony cases tried in the 5 years after the sensational Country Walk ritual abuse trial to cases tried 5 years before. Findings indicate that high profile case publicity tends to echo through the judicial system so that similarly charged but nonpublicized cases are tried and sentenced differently than were those cases before the high profile case occurred.

Fells Acres Day Care

In 1984 a 5 year old, questioned about his sexual play with another child, disclosed he had been molested in a magic room in the Fells Acres Day Care Center by Gerald Amirault, the son of the owner. Malden, Massachusetts police and state social workers met with parents of the enrollees and asked them to question their children and note any symptoms of sexual abuse, such as bedwetting and nightmares. Eventually 40 children claimed Amirault, his sister Cheryl LeFave, and their mother Violet Amirault had sexually abused them in rituals that included rape with butter knives and magic wands, animal torture and infant sacrifices. Each was arrested and charged with multiple counts of indecent assault.

Gerald Amirault's trial began in 1986 with six of the child witnesses testifying in court and one via closed-circuit television. He was convicted of 15 counts of indecent assault and sentenced to 30 to 40 years. Violet Amirault and Cheryl LeFave were tried together and convicted of indecent assault; each was sentenced to 8 to 20 years. After serving the minimum, parole was denied because both refused to admit guilt. In 1995 they filed for a new trial citing their 6th Amendment confrontation rights had been violated by the courtroom seating arrangement that had the children seated at a small table facing the jury with their backs to the defendants. The motion was granted and they were released from prison pending a new trial, but the Supreme Judicial Court then reinstated their convictions, although also continuing their bail. The following year, the lower court granted another motion for a new trial on the basis that they had received ineffective counsel, and that new scientific evidence about the suggestibility of children raised questions about the reliability of the allegations in this case. That decision can be found at the internet URL: http://www.socialaw.com.superior/Amirault.html.

In 1999, while awaiting a new trial, Violet Amirault died at the age of 74. That same year the Supreme Judicial Court once again overruled the lower court and reinstated the convictions of LaFave on the grounds that the ineffective counsel had been waived and the scientific information about children's suggestibility was neither new nor significant. That ruling can be found at the internet URL: http://www.lawyersweekly.com/sjc/1018099.htm. Prosecutors did not seek to return LeFave to prison; instead, she was placed on probation after agreeing not to pursue further legal action, not to have unsupervised contact with children or contact with her accusers, and not to give televised interviews.

Gerald Amirault had a commutation hearing in September 2000. The hearing board unanimously recommended commutation, but Acting Governor Swift overruled the recommendation in 2002. Amirault remains in prison.

◆ **82**   Draddy, G.C. (1998). Special courtroom seating arrangement fails to meet confrontation clause requirements—*Commonwealth v. Amirault*, 677 N.E. 2d 652 (Mass, 1997). *Suffolk University Law Review, 32,* 161–168.

In the Fells Acres ritual abuse trial, child witnesses were allowed to sit at a small table, facing the jury. Because they had their backs to the defendants, the defendants were unable to see their facial expressions and successfully argued that their right to confrontation was denied.

◆ **83**   Harshbarger, S. (1995, May 12). The Amiraults are not the victims [Letter to the Editor]. *Wall Street Journal,* p. A-13.

The State Attorney General who brought charges in the Fells Acres ritual abuse case criticizes reporter Rabinowitz (see citations 92–94) for a misleading and selective portrayal of the defendants as the real victims in this case.

◆ **84**   Juliar, D.S., & Harshbarger, S. (1996). *Report on the Fells Acres day care cases.* Boston, MA: Office of the Attorney General.

The trials of Gerald Amirault, Violet Amirault and Cheryl LeFave in the Fells Acres ritual abuse case, the decision to have the children sit in the courtroom with their backs to the defendants, and the challenges that seating arrangement poses to the defendants' 6th Amendment confrontation rights are explained.

◆ **85**   Kelley, S.J. (1993). Ritualistic abuse of children in day-care centers. In M.D. Langone (Ed.), *Recovery from cults: Help for victims of psychological and spiritual abuse* (pp. 343–355). NY: W.W. Norton.

The results of the Parent-Child Behavior Checklist for 35 children ritually abused in day care centers, including Fells Acres, were compared to those for 32 children sexually abused in day care centers, as well as to those of 67 nonabused children. Ritually abused children score significantly higher in behavior problems than either sexually abused or nonabused children; they also have higher scores for social withdrawal, depression, somatic complaints and sex problems.

◆ **86**   Kelley, S.J. (1992). Stress responses of children and parents to sexual abuse and ritualistic abuse in day care settings. In A.W. Burgess (Ed.), *Child trauma I: Issues and research* (pp. 231–257). NY: Garland.

The parents of 134 children who were ritually abused at Fells Acres, sexually abused, or not abused in other day care settings completed the Parent-Child Behavior Checklist to assess the stress responses of their children, the Symptom Checklist-90-R, and the Impact of Event Scale to assess their own stress. The results show that the ritually abused children experience the most behavior problems, and their parents experience the most psychological distress.

◆ **87**   Kelley, S.J. (1990). Parental stress response to sexual abuse and ritualistic abuse of children in day-care centers. *Nursing Research, 39,* 25–29.

The parents of children ritually abused at Fells Acres, or sexually abused in other day care settings were administered the Symptom Checklist-90-R, a measure of psychological distress, and the Impact of Event Scale, a measure of symptoms of posttraumatic stress disorder. Their scores were compared to a matched comparison group of parents of children who had not been abused. The parents of ritually abused children display the most severe psychological distress, followed by the parents of sexually abused children.

◆ **88**   Kelley, S.J. (1989). Stress responses of children to sexual abuse and ritualistic abuse in day care centers. *Journal of Interpersonal Violence, 4,* 505–513.

The results of the Parent-Child Behavior Checklist for 35 children ritually abused at Fells Acres are compared to those for 32 children sexually abused in day care centers, as well as to those of 67 nonabused children. Ritually abused children score significantly higher in behavior problems than either sexually abused or nonabused children; they also have higher scores for social withdrawal, depression, somatic complaints and sex problems than either sexually abused or nonabused children.

◆ **89**   Kelley, S.J. (1988). Responses of children and parents to sexual abuse and satanic ritualistic abuse in day care centers. *Dissertation Abstracts International, 49* (12-B), 5521. (University Microfilm No. AAG89–04202)

A sample of 67 children, 35 of whom had been ritually abused in the Fells Acres day care center and 32 who had been sexually abused in other day care centers, was compared to 67 nonabused children. The findings indicate that both children and parents are severely traumatized by sexual abuse in day care settings. The ritually abused children have significantly more behavior problems than the sexually abused and the nonabused children, and the parents of ritually abused children score significantly higher on measures of stress than do the parents of the sexually abused and nonabused children.

◆ **90**   Pollit, K. (1999, October 18). Subject to debate: Finality of justice? *Nation,* p. 10.

The Fells Acres ritual abuse case is a textbook example of injustice fueled by political ambition.

◆ **91**   Rabinowitz, D. (1995, October). Unspeakable acts. *Good Housekeeping,* pp. 128–137.

At 72, Violet Amirault is the oldest inmate in the Massachusetts prison. Kept separate from her daughter, she spends her days reading and taking college classes, and like both her daughter and son, she adamantly maintains her innocence in the ritual abuse case that devastated the day care center that began in a room in her house 20 years ago when her first husband left her, and grew into a successful business that had "graduated" almost 5,000 children.

◆ **92**   Rabinowitz, D. (1995, May 12). A darkness in Massachusetts, Part III. *Wall Street Journal*, p. A-12.

The Fells Acres case was tried in an atmosphere of mass hysteria over the ritual abuse of children in day care. Like the other cases that preceded it, the defendants were convicted on the words of children and without corroborating evidence. The Massachusetts Governor should commute the sentences of all of the defendants.

◆ **93**   Rabinowitz, D. (1995, March 14). A darkness in Massachusetts, Part II. *Wall Street Journal*, p. A-14.

The Fells Acres ritual abuse case is the product of leading and suggestive interviews conducted with the children by doctoral student Susan J. Kelley, and behind-the-scenes political machinations by local politicians and prosecutors.

◆ **94**   Rabinowitz, D. (1995, January 30). A darkness in Massachusetts, Part I. *Wall Street Journal*, p. A-20.

The allegations made in the Fells Acres ritual abuse case resemble those made in other day care cases across the United States. This time the mass hysteria about ritual abuse targets Violet Amirault, a 61 year old woman who turned the center into a profitable business and who aggressively took on state authorities in an effort to keep her day care license and defend her innocence.

◆ **95**   Shalit, R. (1995, June 19). Witch hunt. *New Republic*, pp. 14–16.

The Amiraults were accused and convicted at the peak of mass hysteria over ritual abuse in day care. The case was contaminated from its start when the parents were encouraged to question their own children, and the problem was compounded by the suggestive and leading interviews conducted by pediatric nurse and doctoral student, Susan J. Kelley, as transcripts from the interviews illustrate. Despite prosecutors' contention that the case should not be reexamined to protect the children and their parents from reliving the trauma, the real victims in this case are the Amiraults.

Small World Preschool

In 1984 a woman reported her daughter had been molested by Richard Barkman, a teacher's aide and the husband of the owner of the Small World Preschool in Niles, Michigan. Police and social workers began interviewing the enrollees; eventually 50 of them accused Barkman, his wife and the seven other providers of ritual abuse. The children alleged that Barkman had filmed their sexual abuse, forced them to ingest hallucinatory drugs, and sacrificed animals and infants. Barkman was charged with 19 counts of sexual abuse on 9 children; charges against his wife were later dismissed and no charges were filed against the other providers. Barkman was tried in 1985 on three counts of criminal sexual conduct on a four year old boy who testified against him for three hours on the witness stand. He was convicted of all charges and sentenced to 50 to 75 years, but his conviction was overturned in 1988 on the grounds that the trial judge had excluded evidence that indicated the child had fabricated the allegation. Facing retrial, Barkman entered a no contest plea to a lesser charge of assault on another child at the preschool, agreed not to pursue a civil suit, and was placed on five years probation.

♦ **96**	Bybee, D., & Mowbray, C.T. (1993). An analysis of allegations of sexual abuse in a multivictim day care center case. *Child Abuse & Neglect, 17,* 767–783.

Data were gathered from the case records of agencies involved in the Small World Preschool ritual abuse case. Criteria derived from the Statement Validity Analysis (SVA) protocol were used to assess the veridicality of the abuse allegations. The data analysis reveals there was consistency, logical structure and spontaneity in the children's allegations, all evidence of truthfulness.

♦ **97**	Bybee, D., & Mowbray, C.T. (1993). Community response to child sexual abuse in daycare settings. *Families in Society, 74,* 268–281.

The results of a national survey reveal the factors, all evident in the illustrative Small World case, that complicate community response to ritual abuse cases. These include: the young age of the children, the ritualistic and extraordinary elements of the allegations, and the large number of alleged victims and perpetrators. Recommendations for improving community responses include increasing resources for day care licensing, educating children about abuse, and making treatment available to children.

♦ **98**	Lengel, A. (1985, May 19). A nightmare in Niles. *Michigan: The Magazine of the Detroit News,* pp. 13–14, 16, 18, 20, 22.

The ritual abuse charges in the Small World case have devastated families, ruined the reputations of Richard Barkman and his wife, and divided the small rural community of Niles, Michigan. The parents of 39 of the children, in 24 different civil suits, are suing the Barkmans, the teachers' aides and Small World Board of Directors. The Barkmans, in turn, filed a multimillion dollar federal civil suit against the state police, the Department of Social Services, the Riverwood Community Mental Health Center, and Prosecuting Attorney Dennis Wiley for willful and malicious false accusations.

♦ **99**	Mowbray, C.T., & Bybee, D. (1995). Treatment of children sexually abused in a day care setting. *Journal of Child Sexual Abuse, 4,* 31–54.

The problems presented by 56 children who disclosed ritual abuse at the Small World Preschool are complex, and include fears, nightmares, self-esteem problems, and acting out. Therapists who treat the children use a wide variety of psychotherapeutic and educational techniques. The duration of the therapy is related to family dynamics, the presence of a treatment goal of fear reduction, and family income.

♦ **100**	Mowbray, C.T., & Bybee, D. (1990). *Sexual abuse in a day care setting: The community investigation response.* Lansing, MI: State of Michigan Department of Mental Health.

An investigation conducted in Niles, Michigan, to assess community response to the Small World ritual abuse case shows that this small, rural, conservative community, although deeply divided over the truthfulness of the allegations, responded to them with the provision of a wide range of services and support for the accusing children and their families. Recommendations for improving community and agency responses to allegations of ritual abuse in day care settings are presented.

Rogers Park Jewish Community Day Care Center

In 1984 a woman in Chicago, Illinois questioned her 4 year old daughter about the embrace she witnessed Deloartic Parks, the day care center's janitor, giving her. The girl eventually alleged that Parks had fondled her, an allegation confirmed by another child enrolled in the center. A team comprised of local police and state social workers was formed to investigate the allegations and determine if there were any other victims among the 88 enrollees. One of the children interviewed, a 3 year old girl, alleged that Parks and 8 other center staff killed animals and boiled a baby in water and forced the children to eat the body. In subsequent interviews, other children confirmed her account. Parks then was charged with 246 counts of sexual abuse on 35 children and was indicted on 6 counts involving three girls. His bench trial on one of those counts involving the girl who made the initial complaint began in 1985. The girl testified for more than two hours, but under cross-examination said she had made up the stories about sexual and ritual abuse. Parks was acquitted.

◆ **101**   Hill, J. (1996). Believing Rachel. *Journal of Psychohistory, 24,* 132–146.

The pseudonymous mother of a 4 year old girl who disclosed she was ritually abused by the janitor and some of the day care providers at the Rogers Park Jewish Community Child Care Center offers her account of the case. Her child experienced severe emotional and behavioral problems after disclosure; the problems were exacerbated by her initial unwillingness to believe her daughter had been ritually abused. She reluctantly changed her mind when other enrollees at the center confirmed her daughter's account. Her belief in her daughter was a significant factor in her recovery.

Wee Care Nursery School

In 1985 a four year old stated that his day care provider, Kelly Michaels, took his temperature rectally. Suspicious that he was really disclosing sexual abuse, his mother brought him to be interviewed by a state social worker and a county prosecutor. He told the interviewers that Michaels sexually abused him and other children in her care during their nap time at the Wee Care Nursery School in Maplewood, New Jersey. As the investigation proceeded, 31 children alleged that Michaels had inserted knives and forks into their vaginas or rectums, made them drink urine, smeared them with peanut butter and licked it off, and forced them to have sex with her while she was menstruating. She was indicted on 235 counts of sexual assault and endangering the welfare of a child and tried on 131 of those counts. The children testified against her via closed-circuit television. She was convicted of 115 counts and sentenced to 47 years in prison.

◆ **102**   Crowley, P. (1990). *Not my child: A mother confronts her child's sexual abuse.* NY: Doubleday.

The mother of one of the children who accused Kelly Michaels of ritually abusing her at the Wee Care Nursery School describes the impact of the abuse and the trial on her daughter, and the devastating effects the case had on her family.

◆ **103**   Manshel, L. (1990). *Nap time.* NY: William Morrow.

An account of the Wee Care case from the initial allegation, the investigation, to the growing horror of the parents and the community as the ritual abuse elements of the case unfolded. The stories of several children illustrate the psychological and social effects of ritual abuse on both them and their parents. The children's ordeal of testifying in the 10 month long, $3 million trial was considerable, as evidenced by the trial transcripts.

WEE CARE AND THE PRESS

The Wee Care case is one of only a few day care ritual abuse cases that became a *cause célèbre*. The mission of securing Michaels' release from prison was taken up by a number of prominent journalists who formed the Kelly Michaels Defense Committee, and used the prestige and popular press to champion their cause, as did Michaels, herself.

◆ **104**   Hass, N. (1995, September 10). Margaret Kelly Michaels wants her innocence back. *New York Times Magazine,* pp. 37–41.

Kelly Michaels will file a $10 million federal civil suit for malicious prosecution against the county, the state, and various professionals involved in the Wee Care ritual abuse case, and may write a book about her experience. She hopes her case will cause the public to be more skeptical about allegations of ritual abuse.

◆ **105**   Hentoff, N. (1993, April 27). Can the children always be believed? *Village Voice,* pp. 18–19.

The transcripts of the interviews of the children in the Wee Care ritual abuse case show that children can be manipulated and led into making false allegations and concocting bizarre stories. It is quite possible that whatever traumas these children still struggle with are the result of their relentless interrogation by state social workers and psychotherapists.

◆ **106**   Hentoff, N. (1992, June 9). Cotton Mather in Maplewood, New Jersey. *Village Voice,* pp. 22–23.

The analogies between the 17th century Salem witch trials and the Wee Care ritual abuse case are striking. Both are characterized by the total abdication of reason and fairness, and the relentless pursuit of a single hypothesis.

◆ **107**   Lowry, R. (1994, December 5). Creating victims. *National Review,* pp. 66–67.

Bogus charges of ritual abuse, as exemplified in the Wee Care case, are modern psychology's original sin. The transcripts of the interviews with the children illustrate the paucity of psychological understanding about the suggestibility of children.

◆ **108**   Manshel, L. (1991, July-August). Reporters for the defense in a child abuse case. *Washington Journalism Review,* pp. 17–21.

Partisan media reporters are discounting young child witnesses and building a flawed defense of Kelly Michaels in the Wee Care Nursery ritual abuse case.

◆ **109**   Michaels, M.K. (1993, November). I am not a monster. *Mademoiselle,* pp. 126–133.

Kelly Michaels protests her innocence in the Wee Care ritual abuse case. She describes herself as a naïve, trusting young woman who believed, when she was arrested, that the police had made a terrible mistake and that she would be completely vindicated at trial. Disillusioned after her conviction, she spent several years in solitary confinement before her conviction was overturned. Although the prosecutor intends to retry her, she is confident she will be completely exonerated once the jury understands how the children were browbeaten by their interviewers into making the bizarre ritual abuse allegations against her.

◆ **110**   Michaels, M. K. (1993, Sept. 6). Eight years in Kafkaland. *National Review,* pp. 36–37.

Kelly Michaels gives her personal account of her 8 year legal battle in the Wee Care ritual abuse case and her amazement that an ordinary person like herself could be the target of such an irrational moral panic over ritual abuse.

◆ **111**   Nathan, D. (1995, June). Sweet justice: My fight to free Kelly Michaels. *Redbook,* pp. 84–87, 122, 124.

The author, a freelance reporter, first met Kelly Michaels in 1988 when she was awaiting sentencing on her conviction in the Wee Care ritual abuse case. Although she was shunned by other reporters who referred to Michaels as "The Demon Seed," and by the parents of the Wee Care children, she did review the evidence in the case and listened to the tapes of the interviews with the children. Convinced that Michaels was innocent, she began a campaign that led to the formation of the Kelly Michaels Defense Committee, and culminated in the overturning of Michaels' convictions.

◆ **112**   Nathan, D. (1988, August 2). Victim or victimizer? *Village Voice,* p. 31.

Kelly Michaels insists she is innocent of the ritual abuse charges against her and that she is the victim of witch-hunt that is targeting day care providers.

◆ **113**   Rabinowitz, D. (1990, May). From the mouth of babes to a jail cell. *Harper's Magazine,* pp. 52–64.

The Wee Care ritual abuse case is the tragic product of the kind of paroxysm of virtue that the United States periodically experiences when it attempts to purge itself of real and imagined enemies. In this case, the imagined enemy is Kelly Michaels and state social workers and psychotherapists set out to prove her guilty by shaping and molding children's stories. Transcripts from those interviews illustrate that contention.

◆ **114**   Taylor, J. (1993, April 12). Salem revisited. *New York,* pp. 1–11.

The Wee Care case occurred in the midst of nationwide hysteria about the ritual abuse of children in day care. It is one more expression of the culture of victimization being created in the United States by social workers and psychotherapists who find it in their best interests to create a nation of victims in need of therapy. That culture creates real victims, such as Kelly Michaels, in the name of protecting manufactured ones.

STATE OF NEW JERSEY V. MICHAELS

In 1994 Michaels' conviction was reversed on the grounds that the trial court had failed to make specific, individualized findings about the child witnesses' fear and trauma before deciding they could testify via closed circuit television. The Court also cited the suggestive and coercive interview methods described in an *amicus curiae* brief submitted by the Committee of Concerned Social Scientists as sufficient reason to call into question the reliability of the children's testimony. The brief can be found at the internet URL: http://falseallegations.com/amicus.htm. The Court ruled that should the state retry Michaels, a pretrial hearing must be conducted to assess the reliability of the children's statements. That ruling can be found at the internet URL: http://www.geocities.com/CapitolHill/Embassy/9062/witchhunt/Wee_Care/supreme.txt. In late 1994, at the request of the children's parents, prosecutors decided not to retry Michaels, but the issue of the so-called "taint hearing" became the subject of considerable debate among legal scholars.

♦ **115**   Anderson, D.D. (1996). Assessing the reliability of children's testimony in sexual abuse cases. *Southern California Law Review, 69,* 2117–2161.

In multivictim cases like McMartin Preschool and Wee Care Nursery, many children who never disclose or exhibit symptoms of abuse will be vigorously interviewed, often by interviewers who already are certain they have been abused. Skepticism by courts about the reliability of children's statements under these conditions is warranted, but should be tempered by a concentrated approach to reliability assessment in either a hearsay or a taint hearing context.

♦ **116**   Bruck, M., & Ceci, S.J. (1995). *Amicus* brief for the case of *State of New Jersey v. Michaels* presented by a Committee of Concerned Social Scientists. *Psychology, Public Policy, and Law, 1,* 272–322.

The *amicus brief* submitted to the New Jersey Supreme Court by 46 members of the Committee of Concerned Social Scientists in the case of Kelly Michaels contends that the interviews conducted with the children were suggestive, leading and coercive. Empirical research shows interviews of this type actually shape children's accounts and decrease their reliability and veracity as witnesses. Transcripts of the interviews illustrate these points.

♦ **117**   Ceci, S.J., Bruck, M., & Rosenthal, R. (1995). Children's allegations of sexual abuse: Forensic and scientific issues. *Psychology, Public Policy, and Law, 1,* 494–520.

The intent of *amicus brief* submitted by a Committee of Concerned Social Scientists in *Michaels,* is to summarize the findings of well designed and well controlled empirical research on children's suggestibility, and to use those research findings to analyze the interviews conducted with the children in the Wee Care ritual abuse case. The state of knowledge about suggestibility is now so valid and reliable that interviews conducted with children in ritual abuse cases can be weighed against it in pretrial taint hearings.

◆ **118**   Dugas, C.M. (1995). *State of New Jersey v. Michaels* 642 A.2d 1372 (N.J. 1994). *Louisiana Law Review, 55,* 1205–1234.

Evidence from interviews such as those conducted in the Wee Care ritual abuse case should be admitted into trial if found reliable because precedent demonstrates that regardless of how it is obtained, reliable evidence can result in a fair trial.

◆ **119**   Jablonski, J.A. (1998). Where has *Michaels* taken us? Assessing the future of taint hearings. *Suffolk Journal of Trial and Appellate Advocacy, 3,* 49–63.

The *Michaels* decision began a nationwide trend in allowing pretrial "taint hearings" to assess child witnesses' reliability before they testify in sexual abuse trials. Those jurisdictions that have declined to allow taint hearings ground their arguments in weak reasoning and fail to follow precedent.

◆ **120**   Lyon, T.D. (1995). False allegations and false denials in child sexual abuse. *Psychology, Public Policy, and Law, 1,* 429–437.

The *amicus brief* in *Michaels* ignores the likelihood that abused children will fail to disclose and discuss their abuse unless they are asked direct and even leading questions. The brief overstates the occurrence of false allegations by overlooking the complicated aspects of the *Michaels* case that make it unlike most other sexual abuse cases.

◆ **121**   Manshel, L. (1994). The child witness and the presumption of authenticity after *State v. Michaels. Seton Hall Law Review, 26,* 685–763.

Michaels reintroduces archaic stereotypes about children as "the most dangerous of all witnesses." The decision stigmatizes children as a class of citizens especially vulnerable to victimization, and does so with the imprimatur of the state's highest court. By permitting defendants to overcome the presumption of the authenticity of child witnesses, *Michaels* risks closing the doors to many child victims of sex crimes.

◆ **122**   Marxsen, D., Yuille, J.C., & Nisbet, M. (1995). The complexities of eliciting and assessing children's statements. *Psychology, Public Policy, and Law, 1,* 450–460.

Several specific areas of sexual abuse investigations require more examination than what they are afforded in the *amicus curiae* brief submitted in *Michaels*: the complexities of assessment in alleged multivictim ritual abuse cases; the types of remedial actions needed to minimize the problems associated with children's suggestibility; and the types of interview techniques that elicit the most reliable and accurate information. Nineteen criteria for determining the truthfulness of children's allegations are presented.

◆ **123**   Mason, M.A. (1995). The child sex abuse syndrome: The other major issue in *State of New Jersey v. Margaret Kelly Michaels. Psychology, Public Policy, and Law, 1,* 399–410.

Testimony from prosecution and defense expert witnesses in the Wee Care ritual abuse case shows the danger of admitting evidence about the socalled "child sexual abuse accommodation syndrome" into trial. The appeals court quite properly rejected that testimony as unscientific.

◆ 124 McGough, L.S. (1995). For the record: Videotaping investigative interviews. *Psychology, Public Policy, and Law, 1,* 370–386.

The prospects for videotaping interviews with child witnesses in the light of the *Michaels* decision must be considered. While there may be no constitutional imperative to preserve records of interviews conducted or authorized by the prosecution, state legislatures may decide to require their videotaping. While professionals often fear the abuse of videotaped interviews, the success of a California pilot program may prove those fears unfounded.

◆ 125 Myers, J.E.B. (1996). Taint hearings to attack investigative interviews: A further assault on children's credibility. *Child Maltreatment, 1,* 213–222.

The attack on interviews in cases of ritual and sexual abuse assumed new dimensions with the *Michaels* decision in which the court created a procedure that allows defense attorneys to request pretrial taint hearings to challenge the investigative interviews conducted with the child witnesses. In these kinds of cases, qualified professionals who can testify as expert witnesses in defense of competent interview practices are urgently needed.

◆ 126 Myers, J.E.B. (1995). New era of skepticism regarding children's credibility. *Psychology, Public Policy, and Law, 1,* 387–398.

Three sources of the growing skepticism about the credibility of children's allegations of abuse are the popular media's skeptical coverage of the ritual abuse day care cases of the 1980s, the writings of some social scientists who portray children in a negative light, and the *Michaels* decision that exaggerates doubts about children's memory and suggestibility.

◆ 127 Myers, J.E.B. (1994). Taint hearings for child witnesses? A step in the wrong direction. *Baylor Law Review, 46,* 873–946.

The *Michaels* decision that allows the use of taint hearings to challenge the investigative interviews conducted with children damages the credibility of child witnesses, creates additional options for appeal, and makes the prosecution of ritual and sexual abuse more difficult to prove. It is recommended that the appropriateness of taint hearings be analyzed under the 6th Amendment confrontation clause rather than the 14th Amendment due process clause.

◆ 128 Rosenthal, R. (1995). *State of New Jersey v. Margaret Kelly Michaels:* An overview. *Psychology, Public Policy, and Law, 1,* 246–271.

The history of the Wee Care ritual abuse case is laid out by the attorney who successfully appealed Kelly Michaels' conviction and secured her release from prison after 5 years. The two points of error which reversed her conviction upon appeal — the misuse of expert testimony and the abuses of closed-circuit television testimony by the children — are central issues in many of the ritual abuse cases that followed this one.

◆ 129 Ross, K.L. (1999). *State v. Michaels* 625 A.2d 489 (N.J. 1993): A New Jersey Supreme Court ruling with national implications. *Michigan Bar Journal, 78,* 32–35.

Suggestive and coercive interviewing of children can lead them into giving false accounts of abuse, as the Wee Care ritual abuse case demonstrates. The New Jersey Supreme Court recognized this problem in a recent ruling on the Michaels case by requiring pretrial taint hearings to establish if potential child witnesses had been properly interviewed.

◆ **130**   Ross, K.L. (1997). *State v. Michaels:* A New Jersey Supreme Court prescription for the rest of the country. *Issues in Child Abuse Accusations, 9.* Retrieved 4-March-01 from the World Wide Web: http://www.ipt-forensics.com/journal/volume9/j9_1_1.htm

The New Jersey Supreme Court in *Michaels* determined that suggestive and coercive interviews can lead children to give false accounts of abuse. By requiring pretrial taint hearings to determine if children have been interviewed properly, the Court sets a precedence that should be adopted throughout the country.

◆ **131**   Weineman, A. (1995). The use and misuse of anatomically correct dolls in child sexual abuse evaluations: Uncovering fact...or fantasy? *Women's Law Reporter, 16,* 347–360.

The Wee Care ritual abuse case illustrates the controversy over whether interviewers' use of anatomically correct dolls elicit accurate accounts of ritual abuse from young children, or encourage fantasy and confabulation.

Craig's Country Day Care

In 1985 a child stated she had been molested by Jamal Craig whose mother, Sandra, owned Craig's Country Day Care in Clarksville, Maryland. Months later the suspicion arose that another child also had been sexually abused at the center. Her mother, concerned there were more victims, took the story to the local newspaper and organized meetings between parents of the center's enrollees, police and state social workers. As a result, many enrollees were referred for interviews to a local sexual assault center. One of them, after several interviews, alleged she had been ritually abused by Craig and Jamal. Over the next several months, 11 children confirmed her account that Craig had filmed and photographed them being sexually abused by her son, inserted screwdrivers and thumbtacks into their vaginas, confined them in cages, sacrificed animals and buried children alive in the woods. Craig and Jamal were charged with 70 counts of sexual assault and perverted sexual practices.

Craig's trial on six counts involving one child began in 1987. The child testified via closed-circuit television and Craig was convicted and sentenced to 10 years. She still faced a second trial on 19 charges involving other children. Jamal's trial started later in 1987 but a mistrial was declared when the child witness, also testifying via closed-circuit television, could not remember any abuse and was declared incompetent to testify. All charges against him were later dismissed.

Craig's conviction was overturned in 1989 on the grounds that her 6th Amendment confrontation right was violated by the use of closed circuit television testimony. Prosecutors appealed that decision to the United States Supreme Court, attaching an *amicus curiae* brief by the American

Psychological Association in support of closed-circuit television testimony by children. A summary of the brief can be found at the internet URL: http://www.psyclaw.org/maryland.html. In 1990, in a 5–4 decision, the Supreme Court ruled that the 6th Amendment confrontation clause does not guarantee defendants an absolute right to face their accusers in court. It further stated that the state's interest in the protection of children may supercede the defendants' right to confront their accusers.

◆ **132**   Goodman, G.S., Levine, M., & Ogden, D.W. (1991). Child witnesses and the confrontation clause: The American Psychological Association brief in *Maryland v. Craig. Law and Human Behavior, 15,* 13–29.

The *amicus curiae* brief to the U.S. Supreme Court in *Craig* is based on empirical research that finds that children can be so traumatized by face-to-face confrontation with defendants as to diminish their ability to communicate in a court of law. The brief urges the Court to consider a broader definition of face-to-face confrontation and allow child witnesses to testify via closed-circuit television or videotape.

◆ **133**   Goodman, G.S., Levine, M., & Melton, G.B. (1992). The best evidence produces the best law. *Law and Human Behavior, 16,* 244–251.

Contrary to the position taken by Underwager and Wakefield (see citation 136), the *amicus curiae* brief submitted by the American Psychological Association in *Craig* recognizes both the seriousness of defendants' interest in confronting their accusers, and the importance of protecting child witnesses from harm. The psychological evidence, as the studies cited in the brief demonstrate, supports the conclusion that children may be so traumatized by testifying in the presence of defendants as to render their testimony unreliable.

◆ **134**   Murphy, W.H. (1989). Appeal brief, Court of Appeals of Maryland: *Maryland v. Craig. Issues in Child Abuse Accusations, 1.* Retrieved 4-March-01 from the World Wide Web: http://www.ipt-forensics.com/journal/volume1/j1_3_3.htm.

The brief presented before the Maryland Court of Appeals in the case of Sandra Craig is summarized by her attorney.

◆ **135**   Roesch, R., Golding, S.L., Hans, V.P., & Reppucci, N.D. (1991). Social science and the courts: The role of *amicus curiae* briefs. *Law and Human Behavior, 15,* 1–11.

The American Psychological Association's brief in the *Craig* case illustrates the strengths and weaknesses of *amicus curiae* briefs submitted to courts by social scientists.

◆ **136**   Underwager, R., & Wakefield, H. (1992). Poor psychology produces poor law. *Law and Human Behavior, 16,* 233–243.

The American Psychological Association's *amicus curiae* brief to the U.S. Supreme Court in the case of *Craig v. Maryland* is "poor psychology" based on unconvincing and unscientific findings. To protect children from the alleged trauma of in-court testimony, the Court responded by creating "bad law" that allows children to testify via closed-circuit television.

MARYLAND V. CRAIG

The United States Supreme Court ordered the Maryland Court of Appeals to reexamine the Craig case. It did so and concluded that although the Constitution may not mandate that the judge hold pretrial interviews with children to gauge their capacity to testify in front of defendants, such an interview under Maryland law should be the rule, not the exception. It therefore reversed Craig's conviction a second time and remanded her for another trial. The lower court decided not to retry her, however, at the request of the accusing child's parents. All charges against Craig were dismissed in 1991, but the debate over the balance between a defendant's confrontation right and a child witness's right to be shielded from additional trauma waged for many years.

◆ **137**   Barry, K.A. (1990). Witness shield laws and child sexual abuse prosecutions: A presumption of guilt. *Southern Illinois University Law Journal, 15,* 99–121.

   Craig prompts both a consideration of other ways that courts can alleviate the trauma of testifying for children, and a call for further research to identity exactly what parts of the trial process are most distressing to child witnesses. Only if actual face-to-face confrontation is identified as the stressor should defendants' 6th Amendment rights be compromised, and then only as a last option.

◆ **138**   Bayardi, M. (1990). Balancing the defendant's confrontation clause rights with the state's public policy of protecting child witnesses from undue traumatization. *Arizona Law Review, 32,* 1029–1050.

   Craig raises the basic question of whether defendants have an absolute right to physically confront adverse witnesses and, if they do not, under what circumstances that right must yield to other considerations. It is important to realize that the confrontation clause gives the right to confront, not to intimidate. Because abused children are easily intimidated by the presence of their abusers in court, the available technology of closed-circuit television and videotaped testimony affords a unique opportunity to secure the public policy goal of protecting children and doing so without significant harm to the rights of defendants.

◆ **139**   Besnyl, G. (1991). *Maryland v. Craig*: Defendants' confrontation rights not violated by the use of one-way closed circuit television testimony in child abuse cases. *Western State University Law Review, 18,* 861–872.

   Craig demonstrates that widespread public concern about an issue can influence judicial decision-making. The U.S. Supreme Court was wise in choosing to balance the right of face-to-face confrontation with the mandate to protect child witnesses from trauma. Children are uniquely vulnerable, as the public realizes, and deserve the benefits afforded by modern technology in rendering their testimony.

◆ **140**   Bloe, R. (1991). *Maryland v. Craig. Southern University Law Review, 18,* 275–291.

   Craig is vulnerable to attack by defense attorneys because of its broad interpretation of constitutional standards. In the decision, the U.S. Supreme Court should have set out specific guidelines for defining the nature and the extent of trauma child witnesses must experience to trigger any exception to the confrontation clause.

◆ **141**   Brannon, L.C. (1994). The trauma of testifying in court for child victims of sexual assault v. the accused's right to confrontation. *Law and Psychology Review, 18,* 439–460.

The *Craig* decision raises significant questions about predicting and characterizing the emotional effects of testifying against the accused for child witnesses in the light of defendants' 6th Amendment rights. Developments in the law after the *Craig* decision are discussed, with special reference to the enactment of the Child Victims' and Child Witnesses' Rights statute.

◆ **142**   Cecchettini-Whaley, G.D. (1992). Children as witnesses after *Maryland v. Craig. Southern California Law Review, 65,* 1993–2037.

The psychological evidence in support of *Craig* that child witnesses are harmed by face-to-face confrontations with defendants in court is unconvincing. A greater degree of proof of considerable trauma to children must be demonstrated before alternative procedures for children's testimony are put into place.

◆ **143**   Chase, C.A. (1993). Confronting supreme confusion: Balancing defendants' confrontation clause rights against the need to protect child abuse victims. *Utah Law Review, 1993,* 407–427.

The 6th Amendment confrontation clause is intended to ensure the reliability of evidence. *Craig* is logically consistent with legal precedent and with the rules of evidence, and will promote the efficient resolution of abuse cases.

◆ **144**   Cotton, T.A. (1994). *Maryland v. Craig:* The Supreme Court clarifies when a child protective statute which allows a child witness to testify outside the presence of the accused will violate the confrontation clause. *Thurgood Marshall Law review, 19,* 309–332.

As both reports of child abuse and the prospect of more criminal trials with children as witnesses increase, taking away defendants' rights to confront their accusers, as *Craig* does, is a grave travesty of justice.

◆ **145**   Cullen, T.F. (1993). *Maryland v. Craig:* The collision of policy and history. *New England Journal on Criminal and Civil Confinement, 19,* 141–173.

Although *Craig* is criticized for infringing on the confrontation rights of defendants, the decision is consistent with the historical and ideological trajectory of U.S. Supreme Court decisions on the 6th Amendment.

◆ **146**   Cusik, T. (1991). Televised justice: Toward a new definition of confrontation under *Maryland v. Craig. Catholic University Law Review, 40,* 967–1000.

Craig leaves many crucial questions unanswered about the level of evidence needed to invoke an exception to face-to-face confrontation and about the characteristics of the class entitled to protection. The exception actually may overreach its limited purpose of protecting child witnesses from trauma.

◆ **147**   Delaney, H.J. (1990). Witnesses: Child sexual abuse victims not categorically prohibited by confrontation clause from testifying via one-way closed circuit television. *North Dakota Law Review, 66,* 735–741.

The *Craig* decision is sensitive to the special vulnerabilities of children who must testify in court to their own victimization. The used of closed-circuit television as a means of testimony does not severely jeopardize defendants' 6th Amendment confrontation rights.

♦ **148** Emerson, P.K. (1990). Protecting sexually abused children: *Maryland v. Craig. Thurgood Marshall Law Review, 16,* 109–125.

Craig raises the question as to whether the 6th Amendment requires an actual face-to-face meeting between a child witness and a defendant before a closed circuit television procedure is used. The importance of *Craig* is its acknowledgement that affirmative exceptions to confrontation do exist.

♦ **149** Evans, S.H. (1991). Criminal procedure — Closed circuit television in child sexual abuse cases: Keeping the balance between realism and idealism —*Maryland v. Craig. Wake Forest Law Review, 26,* 471–502.

There are problematic areas in *Craig,* including the lack of guidelines as to when closed circuit television procedure should be invoked, the defendant's right to presence, and the presumption of innocence. While the closed circuit television procedure is not perfect, it does balance the traditional purpose of the confrontation clause with the state's interest in protecting child witnesses from trauma.

♦ **150** Fields, B.J. (1990). *Maryland v. Craig*: The constitutionality of closed circuit testimony in child sexual abuse cases. *Georgia Law Review, 25,* 167–197.

In *Craig,* the majority opinion held that face-to-face confrontation is not an absolute guarantee under the 6th Amendment. The exception recognized in *Craig* is a departure from the U.S. Supreme Court's previous focus on the truth-finding function of the clause. By locating the confrontation clause exception in the state's interest in protecting child witnesses, the Court risks undermining its purpose.

♦ **151** Fields, G.A. (1992). *Maryland v. Craig*: Suffering children to testify via closed circuit television. *Howard Law Journal, 35,* 285–301.

In permitting children to testify via closed circuit television, *Craig* balances the scales of justice by assuring that young victims, who otherwise would not have a voice in the court system, will be allowed to testify in such a way that they do not suffer further emotional trauma.

♦ **152** Fisher, G.P. (1991). Constitutional law — Restricting an accused's Sixth Amendment right to confront child witnesses in child abuse cases— *Maryland v. Craig,* 110 S. Ct. 3157 (1990). *Suffolk University Law Review, 25,* 1224–1232.

The U.S. Supreme Court's ruling in *Craig* is consistent with the philosophy underlying previous rulings on the 6th Amendment, but in the face of a growing number of child sexual abuse cases being heard in courts across the country, is destined to raise major questions about defendants' confrontation rights.

♦ **153** Francis, K.A. (1992). To hide in plain sight: Child abuse, closed circuit television, and the confrontation clause. *University of Cincinnati Law Review, 60,* 827–856.

The protections guaranteed by the confrontation clause and the implications posed by *Craig* are in conflict. The decision risks undermining the original purpose of the confrontation clause.

♦ **154**   Gambela, F.A., & Serritella, W.J. (1992). Three recent United States Supreme Court decisions for professionals who testify in child sexual abuse cases. *Journal of Child Sexual Abuse, 1,* 15–30.

It is imperative that professionals who are called upon to testify in child sexual abuse trials be familiar with 3 recent U.S. Supreme Court cases, *Maryland v. Craig, Idaho v. Wright* and *White v. Illinois*. These opinions set out the nature and the scope of expert testimony.

♦ **155**   Gassner, S. (1993). Child witness statutes. *Journal of Juvenile Law, 14,* 227–233.

In light of *Craig,* state laws may override federal laws regarding the degree of confrontation rights.

♦ **156**   Goodhue, G.K. (1991). *Maryland v. Craig*: Balancing the Sixth Amendment confrontation rights with the rights of child witnesses in sexual abuse trials. *New England Law Review, 26,* 497–528.

Provided the reliability of a child's testimony is otherwise assured and the court makes an early and specific finding that the child will be emotionally traumatized by face-to-face testimony, the use of alternative methods for taking the child's testimony, such as that set out in *Craig,* does not violate the defendant's 6th Amendment confrontation rights.

♦ **157**   Goodman, A.C. (1995). Two critical evidentiary issues in child sexual abuse cases: Closed circuit testimony by child victims and exceptions to the hearsay rule. *American Criminal Law Review, 32,* 855–882.

Craig is an example of a tough case making bad law by jeopardizing defendants' constitutionally protected 6th Amendment confrontation rights.

♦ **158**   Gordon, D.S. (1991). "Jug Jug" to "Dirty Ears:" *Maryland v. Craig* through a literary lens. *New York University Law Review, 66,* 1404–1455.

The *Maryland v. Craig* decision illustrates how the literary contrivances of diction, narrative and metaphor can enhance judicial opinion writing and make facts, law and the intersection of the two come alive for the various audiences that will be affected by the decision. The decision, itself, lacks these literary qualities, thus it fails to communicate adequately with readers. The dissent, however, is rich in these qualities and is a much more powerful and persuasive presentation of fact and law.

♦ **159**   Kamego, A.L. (1991). The confrontation clause does not prohibit a child witness in a child abuse case from testifying via one-way closed circuit television when face-to-face confrontation would cause trauma to the witness. *University of Detroit Law Review, 68,* 555–564.

Craig overlooks the fact that there are few empirical studies that conclusively prove that children are traumatized by the experience of testifying in court; exceptions to face-to-face testimony must be considered in some cases, and the use of closed circuit television is only one of several alternative methods that should be considered.

♦ **160**   Kiefer, L. (1990). Confrontation clause revisited: Supreme Court decisions *Idaho v. Wright,* and *Craig v. Maryland.* An attorney's response. *Issues in Child Abuse Accusations, 2.* Retrieved from the World Wide Web 4-March-01: http://www.ipt-forensics.com/journal/volume2/j2_3_7.htm

Two recent decisions, *Idaho v. Wright* and *Maryland v. Craig* allow for alternatives to children's in-court testimony, but to protect the rights of defendants all investigative interviews with children should be videotaped, and qualified experts should question children in the presence of defendants to determine if they will be too traumatized to give testimony in court.

◆ **161** King, R.H. (1992). The molested child witness and the Constitution: Should the Bill of Rights be transformed into the bill of preferences? *Ohio State Law Journal, 53,* 49–99.

Craig is the most recent of a several U.S. Supreme Court decisions on the confrontation clause, but it is inconsistent with the legal logic informing previous decisions.

◆ **162** Kohlmann, R.H. (1996). The presumption of innocence: Patching the tattered cloak after *Maryland v. Craig. St. Mary's Law Journal, 27,* 389–421.

The special treatment *Craig* affords child witnesses sends an unspoken but compelling message to juries that judges have determined child witnesses need protection from defendants. This message erodes the practical value of the presumption of innocence.

◆ **163** McCarvill, T.J., & Steinberg, J.M. (1992). Have we gone far enough? Children who are sexually abused and the judicial and legislative means of prosecuting the abuser. *St. John's Journal of Legal Commentary, 8,* 339–368.

Despite recent judicial and legislative initiatives, barriers to the successful prosecution of child sex abusers remain. The kind of flexible approach to the confrontation clause afforded by *Craig* is not enough to ensure successful prosecution. What still is needed is uniform legislation that tolls the statute of limitations when the victim is 23 years old.

◆ **164** McNeil, W.K. (1991). *Maryland v. Craig:* The demise of face-to-face confrontation. *Loyola Law Review, 36,* 1137–1155.

In its zeal to protect children, the U.S. Supreme Court in *Craig* eliminates the historically recognized safeguard of face-to-face confrontation.

◆ **165** Metz, J.K. (1995). Child molestation and the confrontation clause: Has the Supreme Court gone too far? *Journal of Juvenile Law, 16,* 15–168.

In *Craig,* the U.S. Supreme Court fails to consider recent research on the psychological benefits to children who face defendants in court and testify against them, as well as research on the difficulties in accurately predicting whether children will be traumatized by testifying in front of defendants.

◆ **166** Miller, L.R. (1990). Allowing a child abuse victim to testify via one-way closed-circuit television does not violate a criminal defendant's Sixth Amendment confrontation clause right if the trial court specifically finds such a procedure necessary to protect the child's welfare. *St. Mary's Law Journal, 22,* 555–577.

The confrontation right is not absolute, as the U.S. Supreme Court correctly ruled in *Craig.* The closed circuit television procedure for children's testimony, therefore, is a perfectly logical way to address an exception to the clause in that it protects children without completely denying defendants' confrontation rights.

◆ **167** Montoya, J. (1992). On truth and shielding in child abuse trials. *Hastings Law Journal, 43,* 1259–1319.

The social science data offered in support of *Craig* is compelling, but the implications of compromising courtroom confrontations between child witnesses and defendants are insufficiently considered by the U.S. Supreme Court.

◆ **168** Moore, E.A., Howitt, P.S., & Grier, T. (1991). Child witness testimony: Is it sufficiently reliable to justify the protective procedures sanctioned by *Maryland v. Craig? Juvenile and Family Court Journal, 42,* 1–9.

Psychological studies uphold the *Craig* decision, showing that children are sufficiently reliable witnesses as a class to justify the use of protective measures.

◆ **169** National Center for the Prosecution of Child Abuse (1991). *State legislation regarding the use of closed-circuit television testimony in criminal child abuse proceedings.* Alexandria, VA: American Prosecutors Research Institute.

Craig brings attention to alternative methods for the presentation of children's testimony in abuse cases. State statutes allowing or mandating the use of closed circuit television testimony are summarized according to the crimes specifically listed by the statute, the specified age of the victim, the factors courts must consider in determining the need for closed circuit television testimony, and the individuals who may be present during the testimony.

◆ **170** Parise, A.S. (1991). *Maryland v. Craig:* Ignoring the letter and purpose of the confrontation clause. *Brigham Young University Law Review, 2,* 1093–1106.

Videotapes of sessions between children and their counselors should be used as an alternative to closed circuit testimony when children are unable to testify in the presence of defendants. The tapes would provide accurate information while protecting defendants from coached testimony.

◆ **171** Pershkow, B.I. (1991). *Maryland v. Craig:* A child witness need not view the defendant during testimony in child abuse cases. *Tulane Law Review, 65,* 935–943.

In *Craig,* the U.S. Supreme Court properly allows an exception to defendants' right to physical confrontation with their accusers, and in doing so protects child witnesses from further trauma.

◆ **172** Rittershaus, M.A. (1991). *Maryland v. Craig:* Balancing the interests of a child victim against the defendant's right to confront his accuser. *South Dakota Law Review, 36,* 104–119.

The *Craig* decision is consistent with both the spirit of the confrontation clause and legal precedent.

◆ **173** Ruddock, E.M. (1991). Confrontation clause. *Thomas M. Cooley Law Review, 8,* 389–409.

In trying to balance the welfare of child witnesses against the clearly established constitutional right of defendants, *Craig* harkens the beginning of a well-intentioned reconstruction of the Star Chamber.

◆ **174** Sanders, J. (1991). Protecting the child victim of sexual abuse while preserving the Sixth Amendment confrontation rights of the accused: *Maryland v. Craig. Saint Louis University Law Journal, 35,* 495–509.

There is well documented legal precedence for partially denying defendants' face-to-face confrontations with their accusers. *Craig* is consistent with those cases.

◆ **175**   Schwalb, B.L. (1991). Child abuse trials and the confrontation of traumatized witnesses: Defining confrontation to protect both children and defendants. *Harvard Civil Rights–Civil Liberties Law Review, 26,* 185–217.

There are compelling questions as to whether *Craig* convincingly proves that testimony via closed circuit television advances the protection of child witnesses. The decision inadequately considers the impact of closed circuit television on a trial's ability to fairly and reliably pursue the truth. *Craig* may become a springboard from which the confrontation clause can be used to test the qualitative fairness of criminal trials.

◆ **176**   Small, M.A. (1994). Constitutional challenges to child witness protection legislation: An update. *Violence and Victims, 9,* 369–377.

The U.S. Supreme Court's landmark *Craig* decision creates uncertainty about the state constitutionality of child witness protection legislation.

◆ **177**   Small, M.A., & Melton, G.B. (1994). Evaluation of child witnesses for confrontation by criminal defendants. *Professional Psychology: Research and Practice, 25,* 228–233.

In *Craig,* the U.S. Supreme Court leaves it to psychologists and other clinicians to evaluate the potential trauma any given child witness will face in court as a result of face-to-face confrontation with a defendant. Research relevant to this assessment is reviewed, and it is suggested that psychologists may be helpful in preparing children to testify. Psychologists are admonished to pay careful attention to the ethical and legal issues involved in each case, and to not overstep the limits of their expertise.

◆ **178**   Stokes, J.B. (1990/1991). *Maryland v. Craig* and the conflict clause: When does "confront" mean confront? *American Journal of Trial Advocacy, 14,* 363–387.

U.S. Supreme Court Justice Scalia was correct in his scathing dissent in *Craig* when he asserted that current beliefs about the terrible consequences of child abuse hardly justify a retreat from 200 years of constitutional law.

◆ **179**   Tomlinson, K.L. (1991). *Maryland v. Craig*: Televised testimony and an evolving concept of confrontation. *Villanova Law Review, 36,* 1569–1610.

Over the years, the U.S. Supreme Court has struggled with the protections that should be given under the confrontation clause, taking into consideration the changing times, circumstances and purposes served by the right to confront. *Craig* is consistent with the evolving concept of face-to-face confrontation.

◆ **180**   Underwager, R.C. (1990). Confrontation clause revisited: Supreme Court decisions. *Idaho v. Wright,* and *Craig v. Maryland.* A Psychologist's Response. *Issues in Child Abuse Accusations, 2.* Retrieved from the World Wide Web 4-March-01: http://www.ipt-forensics.com/journal/volume2/j2_3_8.htm

No mental health professional is able to predict with accuracy whether any given child will be traumatized by giving testimony in court in the presence of a defendant. The *Craig* decision is bad law in that it establishes requirements for the assessment of children that psychologists simply cannot meet.

◆ **181**   Walton, E. (1994). The confrontation clause and the child victim of sexual abuse. *Child and Adolescent Social Work Journal, 11,* 195–207.

For social workers interested in the testimony of children, *Craig* foregrounds the clash between the 6th Amendment rights of those accused of sexual abuse and the state's interest in protecting child witnesses from trauma, and reveals the necessity of improving social workers' interactions with children before they testify.

◆ **182**   Wendel, P.T. (1993). A law and economic analysis of the right to face-to-face confrontation post *Maryland v. Craig*: Distinguishing the forest from the trees. *Hofstra Law Review, 22,* 405–494.

A macro-analysis of *Craig* suggests that at some point the benefits of face-to-face confrontation in terms of the low possibility of erroneous conviction will be exceeded by the greater possibility of erroneous conviction due to the high cost of witness refusal to testify because of anticipated trauma. In the light of that analysis, *Craig* poses only a narrow intrusion on the right to face-to-face confrontation, and one that is necessary to achieve the efficient and effective enforcement of child abuse laws.

◆ **183**   Whitlock, C.A. (1991). Admissibility of video-taped testimony: What is the standard after *Maryland v. Craig* and how will the practicing defense attorney be affected? *Mercer Law Review, 42,* 883–905.

A total of 37 states now permit closed circuit testimony in child abuse cases, but possible infringements on the rights of defendants still must be considered, especially by defense attorneys.

◆ **184**   Wolf, M.J. (1991). *Maryland v. Craig*: Electronic testimony and the confrontation clause. *Journal of Juvenile Law, 12,* 145–150.

The conflict between trial procedures designed to lessen the trauma of testimony for child witnesses and protect the rights of defendants to confront their accusers at trial is difficult to resolve, although the *Craig* decision makes some progress towards resolution.

East Valley YMCA Day Care Center

In 1985 a three year old accused his providers at the East Valley YMCA Day Care Center in El Paso, Texas of fondling him. In the absence of corroborating evidence and any other allegations, the police closed the investigation. Parents continued to question their children and the investigation was reopened after a three year old disclosed she also had been molested by providers Michelle Noble and Gayle Dove. During subsequent investigative interviews with police and state social workers, eight more children were identified as victims and claims of ritual abuse, including infant sacrifices, the removal and replacement of eyeballs, and the filming of pornography, were made. Noble and Dove were arrested and charged. Noble's trial began in 1986; the children, who testified on videotape, were never present in the courtroom. She was convicted of 18 counts of sexual assault and sentenced to life plus 311 years; her conviction was overturned two years later on the grounds that the children's videotaped testimony violated her 6th Amendment confrontation rights. She was retried with the children now testifying in open court and acquitted of all charges. In a separate trial, Dove was found guilty of 6 counts of sexual assault and sentenced to life plus 60 years. A mistrial was declared, however, when a juror revealed she had voted guilty only so she would not be perceived as condoning child abuse. Dove was retried on one count, convicted, and sentenced to 20 years. Her conviction was overturned on the grounds that testimony by the parents on the sequelae of abuse had been improperly admitted. All charges against her were later dismissed.

♦ **185**   Nathan, D. (1988, April 26). Day care witch trials. *Village Voice*, p. 17.

Michelle Noble is the first provider to be acquitted in a day care ritual abuse case in the United States, but is unlikely to be the last provider accused in this wave of hysteria over ritual abuse.

♦ **186**   Nathan, D. (1988, March 1). Justice abuse. *Village Voice*, pp. 16, 19.

Michelle Noble is awaiting a retrial in the East Valley YMCA ritual abuse case after the Texas Court of Criminal Appeals outlawed videotaped testimony and overturned her conviction. Prosecutors will have the children testify in court in the retrial so the jury can see how they react to her.

♦ **187**   Nathan, D. (1987, September 29). The making of a modern witch trial. *Village Voice*, pp. 19–32.

Mass hysteria about the ritual abuse of children in day care has been sweeping across the United States. It is a product of unsettling changes in both the structure of the family and in women's roles that led to an increased demand for day care and turned providers, like Michelle Noble and Gayle Dove who are profiled, into scapegoats for larger social ills. The ritual abuse case against Noble and Dove only makes sense if special attention is paid to a small group of parents who, seeking to make sense of their children's behavioral and emotional changes, successfully pressured officials to keep the case open until prosecuting attorney Debra Kanof, who also is profiled, could file charges.

Presidio Army Base
Child Development Center

In 1986, a three year old accused his teacher at the Presidio Army Base Child Development Center in San Francisco, California of fondling him. The subsequent medical examination raised the suspicion that the child had been sodomized. The Army immediately sent letters to the parents of the 220 enrollees, encouraging them to bring their children to the Medical

Center for medical examinations and interviews. Over the year, 59 additional children were identified as victims of Gary Hambright, the center's civilian teacher. Hambright was arrested, but the charges were later dismissed. Parents pressured the Army to continue its investigation and over the next few months another 12 children were identified as victims, and many described ritual abuse. One of them also named Michael Aquino as her ritual abuser. An Army Lieutenant Colonel, Aquino is also a High Priest of the Temple of Set, a satanic church in San Francisco. The investigation turned up no evidence to substantiate the allegation, and because Aquino was in Washington D.C. the month the accusing child was in day care, no charges were filed against him. The District Attorney, however, reindicted Hambright on 12 charges against 10 children, but later dismissed the charges for lack of evidence. Hambright died of AIDS in 1990.

♦ **188**   Adler, J. (1987, November 16). The 2nd beast of the revelation: Claims of satanism and child molesting. *Newsweek*, p. 73.

The allegations of ritual abuse against Michael Aquino, an officer in the United States Army, are examined. A practicing satanist and High Priest in the Temple of Set, Aquino holds high rank in the Army and has top-security clearance. His wife Lilith is a priestess in the Order of the Vampyre of the Temple of Set.

♦ **189**   Ehresaft, D. (1992). Preschool child sexual abuse: The aftermath of the Presidio case. *American Journal of Orthopsychiatry, 62,* 234–244.

Using process notes and evaluation records from the assessment and treatment of 2 young girls allegedly victimized at the Presidio Child Development Center, the sequelae of ritual abuse for the children, their parents and the family systems are examined. Both of the children present with sleep disturbances, sexually inappropriate behaviors, temper outbursts, magical thinking and sudden mood shifts. The reactions of their parents diverge along gender role lines: their mothers report reactive depression and pervasive feelings of failure in their maternal role; the fathers report rage and feelings of emasculation for failing to protect their daughters. The sense of betrayal by the military is pervasive both in family systems and the larger community.

Faith Chapel Day Care Center

In 1989, Dale Akiki, a developmentally delayed provider at the Faith Chapel Day Care Center in San Diego, California was accused by a three year old of exposing himself to her. The church hired a counselor to interview other children in Akiki's care and one of them confirmed her disclosure. The accusations were announced to the 3,000 members of the charismatic church, and parents were encouraged to question their children and meet with detectives to discuss their concerns. That meeting was held the day after the airing of *Do You Know the Muffin Man*, a television movie about day care ritual abuse. The detectives gave some credence to the parents' fear that this was a ritual abuse case, but without corroborating evidence of any kind of abuse no charges could be filed. Members of the city's Ritual Abuse Task Force were influential in getting the investigation reopened. Children were then referred for interviews with local psychotherapists and over the next year, dozens began talking about drinking "red oil" and participating in the murder of a baby and the sacrifices of an elephant and a giraffe. They named Akiki and others, some of them church officials, as their ritual abusers. Akiki was arrested and charged. His trial began in 1993 and lasted over seven months, the longest and, at $2.3 million, one of the most expensive, trials in the city's history. The children who testified against him did so in open court. During the trial 17 charges were dismissed for lack of evidence, and Akiki was acquitted of the 35 remaining charges.

♦ **190**   Fine, J. (1994, July). Seeking evil: The hell of prosecuting satanic ritual abuse. *California Lawyer,* pp. 50–55, 90–92.

The entire case against Akiki rests on reports from mental health professionals involved with the children, and these professionals are ideologically disposed to believe that ritual abuse is widespread and perpetrated by satanists who have infiltrated day care centers. Akiki's acquittal means that the jury's decision was not influenced by that same ideology and is in line with research that shows that children can be pressured and led into telling complicated stories about events that never occurred. That research, in turn, puts special demands on prosecutors to determine the credibility of children's allegations and the conditions under which they were made before using them as witnesses in trial.

♦ **191**   Gleick, E. (1993, December 13). Free at last: A deformed man, jailed 30 months, is acquitted of child abuse charges. *People,* pp. 83–86.

Akiki is acquitted of all charges of ritual abuse in the controversial Faith Chapel case. He has always asserted his innocence and is relieved that the jury believed him. The children who testified against him are disappointed and confused as are their parents who feel betrayed by the system they trusted. Faith Chapel officials are committed to doing whatever they can to heal the rifts within their congregation.

♦ **192**   Montoya, J. (1995). Lessons from *Akiki* and *Michaels* on shielding child witnesses. *Psychology, Public Policy and Law, 1,* 340–369.

The Akiki (Faith Chapel) and Michaels (Wee Care) ritual abuse trials were based on different assumptions about both the value of incourt testimony from children and the value children can accrue from actually confronting their alleged abusers in court. In *Michaels,* the shielding of children impaired the defendant's legal right to confront her accusers, and the court's decision to do so was based on the testimony of parents and mental health professionals who, it can be argued, usually will be biased in the direction of shielding.

♦ **193**   Sauer, M., & Okerblom, J. (1993, September 6). Trial by therapy. *National Review,* pp. 30–39.

The Faith Chapel ritual abuse case is yet another product of the dubious therapy and interviewing techniques, widely touted during the 1980s, that led, manipulated and coerced young children into making false allegations.

♦ **194**   Wright, L. (1994, October 3). Child care demons. *New Yorker,* pp. 5–6.

The ritual abuses case against Akiki is another example of the libel that society is imposing on those who are entrusted to care for young children. Collective guilt for giving up children to strangers to rear is causing society to scapegoat providers and to use abusive methods to elicit horrible stories from the very children it wishes to protect.

Breezy Point Day School

In 1989 a four year old alleged that her provider at the Breezy Point Day School in Langhorne, Pennsylvania, rubbed "cinnamon cream" in her vagina. Although a subsequent medical exam was negative for sexual penetration, an investigation ensued. The child disclosed little to investigators, but told her mother that she had been raped and beaten by her provider, and named several other children as victims. Two of those children confirmed her story, but none of the other 30 enrollees disclosed any abuse to investigators. The airing of the television movie about day care ritual abuse, *Do You Know the Muffin Man*, caused the parents of the three accusing children to wonder if this was a ritual abuse case. They hired a consultant to look into it. His investigation concluded that the provider and her aide were members of a secret satanic church, that a song they gave the children to sing at the center contained satanic messages, and that a Cabbage Patch doll in the playroom was a satanic token. In subsequent interviews now focusing on ritual abuse the children began talking about the consumption of urine and feces, the mutilation of animals, sexual orgies and human sacrifices. A year long intensive investigation, however, failed to turn up any evidence to corroborate their allegations or the results of the private inquiry. No criminal charges were filed.

♦ **195**   Conroy, T. (1991, April 19). The Devil in Bucks County. *Philadelphia,* pp.81–83, 136–137, 139–140.

The first complaint in the Breezy Point ritual abuse case set off an investigation that divided the parents of other enrollees, investigators from various agencies, and the community into believers and disbelievers. The parents of the 3 accusing children, confident they are telling the truth, distressed over their behavioral changes, and frustrated with the lack of momentum in the investigation, filed multimillion dollar civil suits against the 2 accused providers. The investigation failed to find evidence to corroborate the children's ritual abuse allegations and as their accounts become more bizarre over time, both investigators and the district attorney became more skeptical. Meanwhile, enrollment at the exclusive Breezy Point Day School dropped by one-third, and the accused providers and the owners of the center have filed countersuits against the parents for defamation and deliberate infliction of emotional distress.

♦ **196**   Fox, M.E. (1994, December 5). Insurer need not defend in civil child abuse suit. *Pennsylvania Law Weekly,* p. 1.

Refining the case law on insurers' duty to defend, the Pennsylvania Superior Court finds that insurance companies cannot be forced to defend policyholders sued for child sexual abuse under homeowners' policies. As a result of the ruling, Aetna Insurance Company refused the request of former teachers at the Breezy Point Day School to defend them in the civil suit brought against them by 3 sets of parents who claim they ritually abused their children.

◆ **197** Rubenstein, A.M. (1990). *Report: Investigation into Breezy Point Day School.* Doylestown, PA: Office of the District Attorney.

A report filed by the Bucks County District Attorney on the year long investigation into the Breezy Point ritual abuse case chronicles the case, examines the children's allegations and the findings of their medical and psychological examinations, looks into the backgrounds of the 2 accused providers, and into the dubious credentials and criminal record of James Stillwell, founder of the National Agency Against the Organized Exploitation of Children and consultant to the parents. The report details the process and the rationale for the decision to not prefer criminal charges against the 2 accused providers.

Old Cutler Presbyterian Church Day Care

In 1989 a psychologist reported the sexual abuse of a three year old by Bobby Fijnje, a 14 year old provider at the Old Cutler Presbyterian Church Day Care Center in Miami, Florida. Although the investigation failed to turn up enough evidence to file charges, church officials barred Fijnje from working in the center. Rumors circulated through the church and over the next several months three more children accused him of sexual abuse. Fijnje was arrested and charged with eight counts of sexual battery. Fijnje, a diabetic who was in the first stage of insulin shock during his five hour interrogation, confessed to accidentally touching the vagina of a child he had taken to the bathroom. He later retracted that confession. He remained in isolation in a juvenile detention center for two years while the investigation proceeded and identified 16 more victims who, during their many interviews, talked about eating the flesh of sacrificed infants, drinking blood, and posing for pornography. Fijnje, who refused a plea bargain, was tried as an adult in 1991 and acquitted of all charges.

When Dade County District Attorney Janet Reno, who pursued the case against Fijnje, was nominated for U.S. Attorney General, Fijnje's father wrote an open letter to the American people and to the U.S. Senate Judiciary Committee, in protest. The letter can be found at the internet URL: http://www.ags.uci.edu/~dehill/witchhunt/ccla/pages/fijnje.htm.

◆ **198** Armbrister, T. (1994, January). Justice gone crazy. *Reader's Digest*, pp. 33–40.

The Fijnje trial was the longest and most expensive in the history of Dade County and was the culmination of a well-orchestrated witchhunt. Prominent among those involved it are Judith Wilson, president of Justice for Sexually Abused Children, who along with WCIX-TV news anchor Giselle Fernandez pursued and publicized the theory that Fijnje and his family were satanists involved in an international child pornography ring. The role of Dade County District Attorney Janet Reno in pursuing the case against Fijnje even when police and the FBI failed to find any evidence to corroborate the allegations, is also significant. The Fijnjes moved back to the Netherlands after the trial.

♦ **199**   Cockburn, A. (1993, April 16). Reno's dirty linen. *New Statesman and Society,* pp. 10–11.

The newly confirmed U.S. Attorney General Janet Reno has a career stake in child abuse prosecutions, but her involvement in the Old Cutler ritual abuse case when she was the Dade County District Attorney shows a callous disregard for the welfare of the defendant, Bobby Fijnje, who was only 14 years old.

♦ **200**   Cockburn, A. (1993, April 5). Tales out of school: More on Reno. *The Nation,* pp. 438–439.

The Old Cutler ritual abuse case is another blunder by Janet Reno, then Dade County District Attorney, and now U.S. Attorney General. The prosecution of Bobby Fijnje was malicious and based solely on the stories of young children who were coaxed and coerced by zealous interviewers.

Little Rascals Day Care Center

In 1989 a woman whose son had been slapped by Robert Kelly, husband of the owner of the Little Rascals Day Care Center in Edenton, North Carolina, contacted other parents to find out if they had heard anything unusual about the center. One had — her son said he had seen Kelly playing doctor with some of the children. Now suspicious that her son had been abused, she had him assessed by a psychiatric nurse who confirmed her suspicion. As rumors spread through the small community, parents began questioning their children and a local detective, state social workers and local psychotherapists were called in to conduct interviews. Over months of questioning, 90 children alleged they had been ritually abused by Kelly, his wife, the three other providers, a provider at another day care center, and a local video store owner. The children described the insertion of knives into their vaginas and rectums, being locked in freezers and cooked in microwave ovens, participating in the sacrifices of animals and infants, and being sexually abused by their providers and strangers dressed as clowns and witches on boats, in private homes and on a space ship. The seven accused were arrested in 1989 and charged with over 400 counts of sexual assault, indecent liberties and conspiracy.

Kelly's eight month long trial ended in 1992 with his conviction on 99 counts involving 12 children. He was sentenced to 12 consecutive life terms; the children jeered him as he was led from the courtroom. His conviction was overturned in 1995, however, due to the improper admission of the parents' testimony about sequelae of abuse, the judge's failure to examine the notes of the children's therapists, and the improper admission of testimony by his original defense attorney who resigned when his own son revealed Kelly had abused him. The appellate brief can be found at the internet URL: http://www.geocities.com/CapitolHill/Embassy/ 9062/bobkelly-_ToC.html. At the parents' request, the state did not retry Kelly, and all charges against him were dismissed two years later. Dawn Wilson, the center's cook, was convicted in 1993 of five counts of indecent liberties and sentenced to life in prison. Her conviction was overturned two years later on the grounds that flagrant violations of courtroom rules and procedures had denied her a fair trial. All charges against her were dismissed in 1997. Betsy Kelly pled no contest in 1994 and was released on parole after spending three years in jail awaiting trial. Willard Privott, the video store owner, also pled no contest, was given a 10 year suspended sentence and placed on probation after spending three years in jail awaiting trial. The charges against the other three providers, who had remained free on bail, were dismissed in 1996.

A three-part PBS *Frontline* documentary, produced by Ofra Bikel, raised the decibel level of public debate over ritual abuse. Part one, "Innocence Lost," aired in 1991. It examines the divisive effect the ritual abuse allegations had on the community, the parents of the accusing children, and the defendants. Part two, "Innocence Lost: The Verdict," aired in 1993; focusing on the trials of Kelly and Wilson, it exposes serious jury misconduct. Part three, "Innocence Lost: The Plea," aired in 1997 and examines Betsy Kelly's choice to plead no contest to charges she denies in return for release from jail.

◆ **201**   Abbott, J.S. (1994). Little Rascals' Day Care Center case: The bitter lesson, a healthy reminder. *Journal of Child Sexual Abuse, 3,* 125–131.

   The author, a social worker who evaluated and treated 19 children who accused the Little Rascals defendants of ritual abuse, describes the therapist's responsibilities in complex cases like this one, the challenges posed by the intense scrutiny of the legal community on assessment, and approaches for dealing with the backlash that inevitably comes when society has to confront the reality of a problem it has chosen to ignore.

◆ **202**   Bruck, M. (1998). The trials and tribulations of a novice expert witness. In S. J. Ceci & H. Hembrooke (Eds.), *Expert witnesses in child abuse cases* (pp. 85–104). Washington, D.C.: American Psychological Association Press.

   The author, an experimental psychologist, served as a defense expert witness in the Little Rascals ritual abuse trial in Edenton, North Carolina and the Sterling Day Care ritual abuse trial in Martensville, Canada. She had not fully anticipated the effects the adversarial trial process has on an expert witness: the attempts to impeach credibility, the attacks on the science of psychology, the barrage of questions on topics unrelated to stated expertise, and the long periods on the witness stand of fear, confusion, boredom and fatigue. Despite all that, experts should make themselves available for testimony in controversial cases such as these. In this era of pseudoscience and anti-science, expert court testimony in ritual abuse cases is urgently needed.

♦ **203**   Dobie, K. (1992, June). Little town of horrors. *McCalls,* pp. 85–86, 88, 90–93, 95.

Edenton, North Carolina is a family-oriented, close-knit community of 6,000 that is being overrun by journalists and tourists who are fascinated with the Little Rascals ritual abuse case that received national attention with the 1991 airing of the PBS documentary, *Innocence Lost.* The documentary also brought in a flood of letters and phone calls critical of the parents of the accusing children and of the town itself. The difficulties of maintaining community cohesion and social ties in the face of both criticism and fears that the criticism is warranted are considerable.

♦ **204**   Duffy, T. (1997, January 2). No easy answers. *People,* p. 18.

Documentary producer Ofra Bikel spent 7 years investigating and reporting on ritual abuse charges in the Little Rascals case. Her work culminated in the 3-part PBS series *Innocence Lost.* She now believes it is impossible to determine what, if anything, happened at that day care center, and she is left with more questions than answers.

♦ **205**   Durkin, M. (1992, July). Day care operator convicted: Defense blunders, independent therapists, credible witnesses aid prosecution. *ABA Journal,* p. 78.

Although the Little Rascals ritual abuse case is similar to the McMartin Preschool case, the trial of Robert Kelly resulted in his conviction while that of Raymond Buckey ended in his acquittal. Why did the trials end differently? The success of the Little Rascals trial was due to the fact that the prosecutors learned from the mistakes of the McMartin trial: they brought fewer charges involving a smaller number of children, had some of the children evaluated by independent therapists, used credible expert witnesses, and kept the trial as short as possible.

♦ **206**   Geltz, R.M. (1994). The Little Rascals' Day Care Center case: A prosecutor's perspective. *Journal of Child Sexual Abuse, 3,* 103–106.

The Little Rascals trial clearly demonstrates that trial preparation is the key area in which prosecuting attorneys, physicians and psychotherapists should work most closely together.

♦ **207**   Hentoff, N. (1992, June 30). Guilty until proven guilty. *Village Voice,* pp. 22–23.

The Little Rascals' ritual abuse case is a classic case of children being manipulated by frightened parents, controlling psychotherapists, prosecutors and police, and academics. The context of growing mass hysteria in Edenton, North Carolina, is contrasted with the prevailing national opinion that children always must be believed.

♦ **208**   Hentoff, N. (1992, June 16). Pay no attention to the man behind the curtain. *Village Voice,* pp. 22–24.

The legal machinations and proceedings that brought Robert Kelly to trial in the Little Rascals ritual abuse case are strikingly similar to those in other high profile cases that were the product of an American witch hunt.

◆ **209**   Lamb, N.B. (1994). The Little Rascals' Day Care Center case: The ingredients of two successful prosecutions. *Journal of Child Sexual Abuse*, 3, 107–116.

The attorney who prosecuted Kelly and Wilson in the Little Rascals ritual abuse case describes successful prosecution strategies: each defendant was tried separately, even though that delayed the trials; the venue of Kelly's trial was changed, despite the stress that travel added to the children and families; the parents were kept informed of progress and supported in the face of the defense strategy to depict the charges as products of mass hysteria; the children were prepared for incourt testimony by participating in a "court school" that familiarized them with the courtroom setting, the roles of court officials, and the importance of testimony; and each child was worked with individually before giving testimony. In cases like these, it is critical that prosecutors organize multidisciplinary teams that will see the case through its investigation and prosecution.

◆ **210**   McCann, J. (1994). Lessons learned from the Little Rascals' Day Care Center case: A commentary. *Journal of Child Sexual Abuse*, 3, 137–139.

As Abbott (see citation 201) points out, there are challenges facing mental health professionals by complex multiperpetrator/multivictim cases. They are called upon to function as investigators and to provide information in an adversarial judicial system. The dual role of mental health professional and investigator is uncomfortable and at times untenable. The traditional role of the former is being altered significantly by these controversial cases.

◆ **211**   Reichard, R.D. (1994). The "Little Rascals" cases: A judge's perspective. *Journal of Child Sexual Abuse*, 3, 117–120.

A response to the Lamb article (see citation 209) by a judge who recommends that complicated ritual abuse cases like Little Rascals be placed on an accelerated docketing system in order to reduce victim attrition and witness contamination, and increase the chance of a fair trial. The use of multidisciplinary teams is strongly recommended so as to avoid unnecessary duplication of effort and repeated interviewing. A "court school" in which children roleplay court testimony can prepare them for their court appearance.

◆ **212**   Rubins, D.M. (1994). Molests in daycare environments. *Journal of Child Sexual Abuse*, 3, 121–123.

The successful prosecutions of 2 of the providers in the Little Rascals ritual abuse case must be weighed against the acquittals of defendants in other high profile ritual abuse trials. Although the difference between successful and unsuccessful prosecution strategies is difficult to pinpoint, case presentation is critical. Prosecutors must search for new ways to present these complicated cases in trial.

◆ **213**   Smith, J.C., Runyan, D.K., & Fredrickson, D.D. (1994). The Little Rascals' Day Care Center Case: A perspective on medical testimony in a prominent public trial. *Journal of Child Sexual Abuse*, 3, 89–97.

The authors, physicians at an outpatient child abuse evaluation clinic, medically assessed more than 50 children in the Little Rascals ritual abuse case. Their medical evaluation procedure is highly individualized, but generally entails one visit with history-taking and physical examination; follow-up interviews, if needed, are arranged with a hospital social worker or mental health professional in the community. They review findings with both prosecuting and defense attorneys, and in the Kelly and Wilson trials, assumed the role of educators, teaching the judge and the jury about the medical aspects of sexual abuse, and the role of consultants to the prosecuting attorneys.

♦ **214**   Summit, R.C. (1994). The Little Rascals Day Care Center case: Commentary on clinical testimony in prominent public trials. *Journal of Child Sexual Abuse, 3,* 99–102.

Expert clinical testimony is both the backbone and the bone of contention in sexual abuse trials. Clinical experts must become more familiar with the legal limitations on their testimony and better trained in giving it. The Little Rascals case exemplifies these points and also illustrates the dilemma of trying defendants on accusations of ritual abuse that are both unprovable and unimaginable.

Fran's Day Care

In 1991 a three year old accused her day care provider, Fran Keller, and her husband Dan of molesting her. Told about the accusation, another parent questioned her son and he eventually stated the Kellers had sexually abused him, threatened to decapitate him, and taught him to insert his fingers into a cat's anus. His mother called a friend who recently had recovered memories of childhood ritual abuse to ask if this was evidence of ritual abuse; she confirmed it was. Under further questioning by his mother, the child said the Kellers read a satanic bible, baptized children with blood, decapitated a baby, skinned a person alive, and filmed children in orgies with adults costumed as monsters. His mother then called the parent of another enrollee at the Austin, Texas, center and asked her to question her son about ritual abuse. He denied any abuse but insisted he knew a secret about the Kellers he could not tell. A formal investigation began and all three children were referred to psychotherapists hired by the Sheriff's Department for further interviews; over the next several months, all began disclosing ritual abuse. The Kellers, were indicted but fled the state, only to turn themselves in three months later. Their trial began in 1992; each was charged with one count of sexual assault against the child who made the initial complaint. While on the witness stand, Fran Keller revealed that other children also had accused her of ritual abuse; that disclosure allowed the prosecutors to introduce the allegations of the two boys, one of whom testified via closed circuit television. The Kellers were convicted and sentenced to 48 years. They remain in prison.

♦ **215**   Cartwright, G. (1994, April). The innocent and the damned. *Texas Monthly,* pp. 100–105, 145–156.

Set in the context of recent reversals of other ritual abuse cases, this investigative report examines the allegations 3 children made in the Fran's Day Care case, and their parents' conviction they were ritually abused as part of an international pornography ring and brainwashed to respond dissociatively to satanic triggers, such as a Ninja Turtle doll. The distressed parents witnessed their children's psychological deterioration during the investigation and testified to it at the trial. In the trial, the child who made the initial complaint denied she knew the Kellers and that she ever attended the center; prosecution expert witness Dr. Randy Noblitt hypothesized that her denial was in response to hand signals from Dan Keller that triggered an alternate personality programmed by the ritual abuse. The second child testified via closed-circuit television and gave lurid details of the ritual abuse. Although the guilty verdicts vindicated the parents' belief their children were ritually abused, they did not resolve the children's psychological problems: all 3 still are in therapy and 2 are diagnosed with multiple personality disorder.

OTHER CITATIONS ON
DAY CARE RITUAL ABUSE

One more irony about the day care cases is that the unique opportunity they afford for the examination of "trauma echoes," that is, the reverberation of ritual abuse throughout the life courses of children, their families, the accused, their communities and even the culture has not been enthusiastically seized. The studies that have taken the opportunity, though, resonate with the distressing consequences of day care ritual abuse.

◆ **216**   Ben-Meir, S.L. (1989). Emotional functioning in children alleging ritualistic sexual abuse in preschool. *Dissertation Abstracts International, 50*(12-B), 5873. (University Microfilms No. AAG90–05174)
The emotional sequelae of ritual abuse in preschool were assessed for 55 children between the ages of 6 and 11; their responses to a battery of psychological tests were compared to a matched group of 28 nonabused children. The ritually abused children show significantly more emotional problems, including pervasive anxiety and fearfulness, aggressive acting out, depression, extreme defensiveness and avoidant coping.

◆ **217**   Burgess, A.W., Hartman, C. R., Kelley, S. J., Grant, C. A., & Gray, E. B. (1990). Parental response to child sexual abuse trials involving day care settings. *Journal of Traumatic Stress, 3*, 395–405.
Parents' stress responses to the decision as to whether their children should testify in a day care ritual abuse trial are examined. The results of the Symptom Checklist-90-R and the Impact of Event Scale were compared for the parents of 17 testifying children and the parents of 50 nontestifying children. The parents of the testifying children present greater symptoms of psychological distress; the reported stress is higher for fathers than mothers. These parents also report more stressful life events after their children's disclosures of ritual abuse, including loss of income, marital problems, and periods of separation. The motives underlying the parents' decision to permit their children to testify are analyzed, and the need for trauma-specific interventions for parents in cases like this is emphasized.

◆ **218** deYoung, M. (1998). Another look at moral panics: The case of satanic day care centers. *Deviant Behavior, 19,* 257–278.

A sample of 15 American day care ritual abuse cases illustrates how a moral panic foments and spreads, and what kind of often contradictory and largely symbolic social and legal changes it can bring about. The day care ritual abuse moral panic also reveals that the providers use whatever power available to them to resist their stigmatization as ritual abusers, and the battle to restore their reputations further divides the public, professionals, and communities into believers, skeptics and disbelievers.

◆ **219** deYoung, M. (1997). Satanic ritual abuse in day care: An analysis of 12 American cases. *Child Abuse Review, 6,* 84–93.

An analysis of a sample of 12 American day care ritual abuse cases reveals that each began when a child made a complaint vaguely suggestive of sexual abuse; ritual abuse details only emerged during the investigative interviews that followed. Although some features of ritual abuse, such as infant and animal sacrifices, were reported in all 12 cases, each also featured highly idiosyncratic details, such as rape by space aliens and being cooked in a microwave oven. The 28 day care providers accused in the 12 sample cases ranged in age from 14 to 61 years old; 17 were female and 11 male. Twenty-two of the providers were tried in court; 15 were found guilty, but the verdicts of 12 of them have since been overturned. The day care cases are so controversial that they contribute little to the debate about whether ritual abuse is real or rumor, but they do set an agenda for the international child abuse professional community for research, practice and discussion.

◆ **220** Finkelhor, D., Williams, L.M., Burns, N., & Kalinowski, M. (1988). *Nursery crimes: Sexual abuse in day care.* Newbury Park, CA: Sage.

A 2 year nationwide investigation of sexual abuse in day care finds that about 15% of reported cases involve allegations of ritual abuse. These cases are more likely to involve multiple perpetrators, female perpetrators, and bizarre and coercive elements, than do sexual abuse cases. Ritually abused children score higher than sexually abused children on all measures of psychological distress. The policy implications of day care ritual abuse include increasing the awareness of ritual abuse, training investigators in its dynamics, forming multidisciplinary teams to deal with allegations, educating parents on its signs and symptoms, and providing counseling and support services for children and their parents.

◆ **221** Fisher, C.B. (1995). American Psychological Association's (1992) Ethics Code and the validation of sexual abuse in daycare settings. *Psychology, Public Policy, and Law, 1,* 461–478.

The activities of psychologists who validate ritual abuse accusations in day care settings raise pressing ethical concerns. A review of these activities uncovers many disturbing instances of violations of the American Psychological Association's (1992) Ethics Code that prohibits the establishment of multiple relationships with clients and their families, the use of assessment techniques not grounded in psychological science, the reliance on untested theories, misleading court testimony, and advocacy in the name of assessment.

◆ **222** Hartman, C.R., Burgess, A.G., Burgess, A.W., & Kelley, S.J. (1992). Extrafamilial child sexual abuse: Family-focused intervention. In A.W. Burgess (Ed.), *Child trauma I: Issues and research* (pp. 307–333). NY: Garland.

The parents of 41 children either ritually or sexually abused in day care submitted to a battery of psychological tests to measure their level of stress. Parents of ritually abused children experience significantly more stress than the parents of sexually abused children, with fathers exhibiting more stress than mothers. A strong interaction between the stress of the parents and the symptomatic reaction to the abuse of the children in both groups is noted. A family-focused intervention program is needed.

◆ **223**   Hunt, P., & Baird, M. (1990). Children of sex rings. *Child Welfare, 69*, 195–207.

A sex ring is a group of adults, males and/or females, who gather for the express purpose of sexually exploiting children. Ten children, ranging in age from 3 to 5 years, who were victimized in either a day care or family-based ring are the subjects of this study. All report a wide range of sexual abuse, pornography, bondage, bestiality, death threats, "snuff" films, animal mutilation and infant sacrifices. They differ from sexually abused children in terms of gender confusion, inconsistency in reporting, and leakage of trauma material into daily life. All of the children in this study require longterm therapy to reestablish trust, negate the effects of mind control or brainwashing, and reestablish a sense of self. Parents also need help in maintaining normalcy in their relations with their children.

◆ **224**   Isaac, R.J. (1997, June 30). Abusive justice. *National Review*, pp. 31–36.

January 14, 1997, is the 300th anniversary of the Day of Contrition, a day set aside to express remorse for the public hysteria that led to the Salem witch trials. Joining the over 200 people who gathered in Salem, Massachusetts, were some of the day care providers who were the victims of the modern ritual abuse witch hunt. Raymond Buckey, Violet Amirault, Cheryl LeFave and Kelly Michaels asked the audience to remember the providers who are still imprisoned, as well as those who have been personally and financially ruined by false allegations of ritual abuse.

◆ **225**   Kelley, S.J. (1994). Abuse of children in day care centres: Characteristics and consequences. *Child Abuse Review, 3*, 15–25.

The characteristics of abuse in day care settings merit special attention because of their ritualistic nature, the extreme abuse described, and the large number of victims and perpetrators alleged. The sequelae of ritual abuse in day care include anxiety, excessive fearfulness, behavioral disturbances, sexual acting out and sleep disorders. The parents of the children also experience psychological distress that often meets the diagnostic standards of post-traumatic stress disorder.

◆ **226**   Kelley, S.J. (1988). Ritualistic abuse of children: Dynamics and impact. *Cultic Studies Journal, 5*, 228–236.

Ritualistic abuse may occur in families or outside of them, as they have in the American day care cases. In both settings, the dynamics are similar: children are physically, emotionally and sexually abused in ceremonies that involve blood-drinking and animal sacrifice. The sequelae of ritual abuse include fear, anxiety and dissociation.

◆ **227**   Kelley, S.J., Brant, R., & Waterman, J. (1993). Sexual abuse of children in day care centers. *Child Abuse & Neglect, 17*, 71–89.

Allegations of sexual abuse in day care pose unique challenges to mental health professionals because they typically allege multiple victims, multiple perpetrators, bizarre ritualistic acts and severe threats to prevent disclosure. Ritually abused children experience more and more severe symptoms than do sexually abused children, and their parents experience more stress than do parents of sexually abused children. Ritually abused children also are more reluctant to disclose the details of their abuse and often do not have the kind of language and memory development necessary for full and convincing disclosure. The implications of all of this for clinical intervention with ritually abused children and their families are considerable.

♦ **228**   Schumacher, R.B., & Carlson, R.S. (1999). Variables and risk factors associated with child abuse in daycare settings. *Child Abuse & Neglect, 23*, 891–898.

In addition to sexual and physical abuse, ritual abuse also occurs in day care, usually in the context of satanic or quasisatanic activity involving human sacrifices, the ingestion of blood and semen, animal mutilations and death threats. Ritually abused children experience more sexual acts than sexually abused children and more forms of penetration; they also experience more psychological sequelae. Risk factors for day care ritual abuse include a small day care staff, small town or rural setting, access of non-caregivers to the children, parental ignorance of signs and symptoms of abuse, and disbelief of disclosures. Increased risk factors for children are an inability to withstand threats against the family and the self, young age, and capacity to dissociate. An unawareness of ritual abuse and its sequelae are risk factors for regulatory agencies and professionals.

♦ **229**   Stickland, J. (1999). Where are they now? An update on defendants. Part 3 — High profile sexual abuse in child care cases. *Child Care Information Exchange, 127*, 80–84.

The allegations against the defendants in the controversial McMartin Preschool, Fells Acres, Wee Care Nursery, Little Rascals and Breezy Point Day School ritual abuse cases have left many of them bitter, bankrupt, yet determined to restore their reputations.

♦ **230**   Victor, J.S. (1998). Moral panics and the social construction of deviant behavior: A theory and application to the case of ritual abuse. *Sociological Perspectives, 41*, 541–565.

The American day care ritual abuse cases illustrate the nature of the moral panic that swept over the United States in the 1980's. Originating in the unsettling changes in the nature of the family, women's roles and the economy, the moral panic was spread by child-savers whose claims were legitimated by various social institutions.

3

The American Family and Neighborhood Ritual Abuse Cases

While no less controversial than the day care cases, the American family and community-based cases only broadly resemble them. The accusing children do offer similar accounts of sexual abuse within the context of rituals performed by groups of perpetrators, but that similitude aside, there are significant sociological differences between the two types of cases that deserve comment.

First, the accusing children in the family and community-based ritual abuse cases tend to be older, in fact sometimes much older, than the three and four year olds in the day care cases. That age difference immediately vests them with credibility, thus the investigations into the family and community-based cases tend to proceed at a much brisker pace than do the day care investigations, for which it may be said with a turn of phrase, haste is only slowly and deliberately made. Second, the accused in these cases are parents, family members, neighbors and sometimes local officials. That relationship of accuser to accused means that children are pitted against their own families and communities, an adversarial posture that persists long after the cases are closed. The cases in which parents are the accused, as a matter of fact, often culminate in dramatic courtroom confrontations with their children who, for their own protection, often were taken out of the family and placed in foster or institutional care. That confrontation has a public face as well. While in many of the day care cases parents form advocacy groups to support their children, in many of the family and community-based cases parents join advocacy groups to protect them *from* their children. So while the day care parents march under the banner, "We Believe Our Children!" the parents in these cases carry signs that declare, "Witch Hunt!" Finally, the family and community-based ritual abuse cases often prompt the kind of official inquiries that the day care cases never could generate. While the purpose of these various official inquiries is the same — to end, once and for all, the controversy the case generated — with their speculation that some innocent people were accused and some guilty people overlooked, and their charges of official malfeasance and public hysteria — none really did.

As in Chapter 2 on the day care ritual abuse cases, each family and community-based case is introduced by a legalistic precis. Both scholarly and national news sources are cited for their ability to add analysis and/or to personalize the cases. Once again, local newspaper reportage is not cited, with the exception of a Bosch Award winning series.

SIX FAMILY AND COMMUNITY-BASED RITUAL ABUSE CASES

Jordan, Minnesota

In 1983 a woman reported James Rud, her live-in boyfriend and convicted child molester, for sexually abusing her nine year old daughter. Rud confessed and implicated her and five other adults in the abuse. All were arrested.

Police questioned the friends of the children Rud admitted abusing, but none disclosed anything. The Scott County District Attorney then took over the interviewing and eventually 37 children named their parents and other adults as their abusers. Rud, allowed to read the police reports on the suspects, confirmed in a 113-page statement he later retracted, that they were part of a sex ring abusing local children. Twenty-five of the interviewed children then were removed from their families and placed in foster care while continuing their interviews. By 1984, 24 adults had been arrested.

Robert and Lois Bentz were the first to go to trial. Their two youngest sons testified against them but retracted their allegations under cross-examination. Rud, who agreed to be the chief witness against them in exchange for a 40 year sentence, could not identify them in a court line-up. The Bentzes were acquitted of all 24 counts and eventually reunited with their sons.

During their trial, the district attorney prevented defense attorneys from obtaining notes that detailed allegations of sexual mutilation, pornography and ritual murder by some of the children. Facing a court order to release the notes, she dropped all charges against the remaining defendants, citing the ongoing investigation into the ritualistic abuse and murders of children as having prosecution priority.

When a joint police and FBI investigation failed to find evidence corroborating these allegations, the Minnesota Attorney General began an investigation. Most of the accusing children then retracted when questioned and in the absence of any corroborating evidence, the Attorney General concluded that no charges would be re-filed because the investigation had been compromised from the start.

In the wake of the Jordan case, the organization VOCAL (Victims of Child Abuse Laws) was formed, and now has branch offices in many cities across the United States.

♦ **231**   Carlson, P. (1984, October 22). Divided by multiple charges of child abuse, a Minnesota town seethes with anger. *People*, pp. 34–38.

Jordan is a town of 2900 with 3 streets, 4 churches, and an atmosphere rife with rumors about ritual abuse and witch hunts. People shun each other, children are forbidden to enter the homes of neighbors, parents have stopped taking their children to babysitters, and some even are afraid to show affection to their own children. Much of the community's anger is directed at District Attorney Kathleen Morris. Critics charge that she went after the Bentzes because they had criticized her handling of another child abuse case. The acquittal of the Bentzes does not resolve the controversy.

♦ **232**   Feher, T.L. (1987). The alleged molestation victim, the rules of evidence, and the Constitution: Should children really be seen and not heard? *American Journal of Criminal Law, 14*, 227–255.

The Jordan ritual abuse case shows how a sexual abuse investigation can go terribly wrong; not only were people falsely accused, they were criminally charged on the words of children alone. Once a sex abuse case comes to trial, the defendant's ability to cross-examine a child witness is inhibited by Rule 608 of the Federal Rules of Evidence. The testimony of children should be excluded at trial under Federal and State rules of evidence because, as the Jordan case proves, they are suggestible and can be quite easily led into making false allegations.

♦ **233**   Lamar, J.V. (1985, February 25). Disturbing end of a nightmare. *Time Magazine*, p. 22.

The idyllic image of the small town of Jordan is shattered by allegations of sex rings and ritual abuse. Adults were charged, children removed from their homes, and the investigation broadened as some of the children alleged they witnessed ritual murders. The failure of state and federal investigators to find any evidence of the murders, and the state Attorney General's carefully worded but damning report, only add to the tarnish.

♦ **234**   Nikiforuk, A. (1984, September 16). A small town's nightmare. *Maclean's*, pp. 62, 64.

The town of Jordan is ferociously split over District Attorney Kathleen Morris's decision to dismiss charges against 21 remaining defendants in the ritual abuse case. Some citizens are relieved the witch hunt is over and support those of the accused who had their children taken away; others fear that ritual abusers and perhaps murderers are roaming the town. No one in Jordan knows who is innocent and who is guilty, but everyone agrees that the local judicial system bungled the case.

♦ **235**   Peters, J.M. (1991). Specialists a definite advantage in child sexual abuse cases. *Police Chief, 58,* 21–23.

The Jordan ritual abuse case demonstrates the importance of thorough, competent investigations using the skills and assistance of specialists. The case shows that law enforcement officers, conventionally trained in investigative methods, do not have the skills to investigate complex ritual abuse rings. Multidisciplinary teams, comprised of social workers, police and prosecutors are needed.

♦ **236**   Robson, B. (1991, March). The scars of Scott County. *MPLS–St. Paul,* pp. 48–53, 123, 125–131.

Marlin Bentz was 12 when his parents were arrested. He endured a year of isolation and coercion by District Attorney Kathleen Morris and others in their unsuccessful attempt to make him testify against his parents. Although his younger brothers were persuaded to do so, Marlin testified in their defense. He was unable to re-establish his relationship with them upon their acquittal, however, and attributes his drug problems and antagonism towards women to the trauma of the experience. Andy Myers was taken into care with his siblings when his stepfather was arrested for sexual abuse. He initially denied any abuse but after 45 sessions with therapist Thomas Price and 29 interviews with the district attorney and others, he began to have visions of abuse that he was told were really memories. Over subsequent interviews, he named his mother and 7 others as his abusers, and described orgies in which children were sexually assaulted, tortured, castrated and murdered. Scheduled as a key prosecution witness in 11 trials, Andy recanted his allegations to the state Attorney General's investigators. He then spent several months in a psychiatric facility diagnosed with post-traumatic stress disorder before returning home.

♦ **237**   Wimberly, L. (1994). The perspective from Victims of Child Abuse Laws. In J.E.B. Myers (Ed.), *The backlash: Child protection under fire* (pp. 47–59). Thousand Oaks, CA: Sage.

VOCAL (Victims of Child Abuse Laws) was founded by parents who were falsely accused in the Jordan ritual abuse case. VOCAL supports the goals of child protection but believes that child abuse laws are too vague and that child protection workers are not sufficiently trained to handle most cases. As is evident in the Jordan ritual abuse case, the false allegations have a shattering impact on families, children who often are placed in state care, and society in general. Child protection can be improved through in-depth training, provision of services to at-risk families, and consistent focus on corroborative cases rather than illusory cases like the Jordan ritual abuse case proves itself to be.

IN REGARD TO MORAL ENTREPRENEURS

In many ways, Scott County District Attorney Kathleen Morris is typical of the moral entrepreneurs, as sociologists refer to them, who assume leadership roles in controversial ritual abuse cases. Venerated by some as champions for abused children, vilified by others as zealots, moral entrepreneurs serve as lightning rods for all of the highly charged emotions sparked by ritual abuse cases, regardless of their *loci delicti.*

◆ **238**   Blodgett, N. (1985). Sex ring fallout. *ABA Journal, 71,* 17–18.

Six parents accused in the Jordan ritual abuse case have filed suit against Scott County District Attorney Kathleen Morris, other county officials, and some of the mental health professionals involved in the initial proceedings. The parents assert their children were coerced into accusing them of ritual abuse.

◆ **239**   Kaibel, E. (1990, January). Twin citizens of the decade: Ten people who made the biggest difference in a big-change decade. *MPLS–St. Paul,* pp. 52–58.

Scott County District Attorney Kathleen Morris is one of the Twin Cities citizens of the decade for her vigorous prosecution in the Jordan ritual abuse case. The kudos she originally received for championing the rights of children turned to criticism when the case fell apart, leaving people baffled by her motives, put off by her abrasive personality and awed by her zeal. She is the most enigmatic of the citizens who defined the decade.

◆ **240**   Mach, T. (1984, October). A tough prosecutor for a heinous crime. *Ms. Magazine,* p. 25.

Scott County District Attorney Kathleen Morris's aggressive handling of the Jordan ritual abuse case thrust her into the spotlight. Her investigation challenges the idea of the typical molester as male — 50% of those she has charged are female. Because of this, and the large scale nature of the case, she does not have uniform support in the community. Some people claim she is only taking advantage of vulnerable children and others even speculate that she brainwashes and drugs them to secure their allegations.

◆ **241**   Oberdorfer, D. (1986, November 24). Sex abuse DA loses in Minnesota. *National Law Journal,* p. 14.

Scott County District Attorney Kathleen Morris, who garnered national attention for her role in the Jordan ritual abuse case, was defeated by a 2–1 margin in her re-election bid.

◆ **242**   Tamarkin, C. (1984, December 24). Kathleen Morris. *People,* pp. 92–94.

Scott County District Attorney Kathleen Morris vows to continue her crusade against child abuse despite being investigated for professional misconduct and sued by those accused in the Jordan ritual abuse case for over $300 million. She is being followed, harassed and has received death threats in the fiercely polarized town, but she admits to no mistakes in her handling of the case.

OFFICIAL INQUIRIES

The Jordan ritual abuse cases prompted two official inquiries, one into the conduct of the District Attorney, the other into the case, itself. In 1985 the Minnesota legislature responded to the latter with a variety of bills aimed at redressing the mistakes in the Jordan ritual abuse case exposed by the inquiry. Bills were passed to minimize long separations of children from their families during abuse investigations and to set visitation rules when they are removed, as well as to expedite the prosecution of abuse cases. The legislature set criteria for oral and taped interviews with abuse victims, and prohibited the mental health treatment of alleged victims until probable cause for abuse is established.

♦ **243**   Commission Established by Executive Order No. 85-10. (1985, October). *Report to Governor Rudy Perpich concerning Kathleen Morris, Scott County attorney.* St. Paul, MN: Author.

The investigation into the conduct of Kathleen Morris, Scott County District Attorney, finds 2 acts of malfeasance: she kept exculpatory evidence from the Bentz defense team about children's stories of murder and mutilation; and she violated a court order to sequester witnesses in the Bentz trial. Five additional charges are supported by clear and convincing evidence but do not reach malfeasance: she dismissed 21 cases that could have been prosecuted; lied to the media by saying the children had not been interviewed on multiple occasions; lied to the presiding judge in the Bentz trial by saying the defense never asked for notes she had already told them did not exist; failed to inform the judge that the children were housed together during the trial; and physically and verbally abused her employees. The commission does not recommend her removal from office.

♦ **244**   Humphrey, H.H. III (1985, February 12). *Report on Scott County investigations.* St. Paul, MN: Office of the Attorney General.

The inquiry into the Jordan ritual abuse case finds: the children's recantation is sufficient reason to doubt the veracity of their allegations; the lack of corroborative evidence of ritual abuse is sufficient reason not to bring charges or reinstate charges against any of the accused; the mistakes made by the police and district attorney destroyed any opportunity to prosecute those who may have sexually abused children; and those same mistakes caused the suffering of those falsely accused. In this case, too many people interviewed the children on too many occasions, created too many opportunities for the children to share stories, and kept too few written notes and records. Criminal charges were filed before comprehensive investigations were conducted and background checks were rarely performed. There is reason to believe that some of the children in this case actually were sexually abused, but there is no evidence to support the charge that sex rings were engaging in ritual abuse. The report can be found at the internet URL: http://www.a-team.org/scottco.html.

Kern County, California

In 1982 a 5 year old, questioned and genitally examined by her step-grandmother for evidence of sexual abuse, said she and her sister were sexually abused in orgies by their parents and others. The girls' parents, Debbie and Alvin McCuan, and their friends, Brenda and Scott Kniffen were arrested.

The Kniffens' two sons, named as victims by the girls, initially denied any abuse but after repeated interviews with state social workers, finally acknowledged it and agreed to testify against their parents. The McCuans and Kniffens were convicted in 1984; each was sentenced to over 200 years. Their convictions were overturned in 1996 on the grounds that the interviews with the children were leading and coercive. Although the McCuan girls never retracted their allegations, the Kniffen boys had years before their parents' release from prison.

The case was not over. By 1985 there were four sex ring trials in Kern County, and four more being investigated. Dozens of children had been named as victims and scores of adults arrested. But it was the allegation of a 5 year old that led investigators to believe that all of the cases were connected to the "Satanic Church" case.

The 5 year old and his two brothers were questioned by their stepmother about whether they had been sexually abused by their mother's new husband, Rick Pitts. They denied they had, but when she beat them and locked them in a room, the 5 year old finally conceded that Pitts had sexually abused all of them. The children's story kept changing during their many interviews with police, state social workers and therapists. The oldest, an 11 year old, finally declared he would tell everything and went on to describe orgies at the Pitts' house with family members and neighbors, and named dozens of children as victims.

All of the adults were arrested. Although none of the children initially disclosed abuse, all eventually did and then went on to add details about pornography production, forced drug ingestion and bondage. The details of the highly publicized McMartin Preschool case prompted investigators, state social workers and therapists, all of whom were conducting individual and group interviews with the children, to question them about ritual abuse. Some of them then began talking about infant sacrifices, forced ingestion of feces, urine and blood in a "Satanic Church." It was this satanic sex ring, allegedly involving 75 adults and 60 children, that investigators believed connected all of the other sex rings in the county.

A task force formed to investigate the "Satanic Church" case was unable to find evidence to corroborate the allegations. Meanwhile the children, most of whom had been placed in foster homes or in the county children's center, also began naming the officials involved in their case as their ritual abusers. Those disclosures, coupled with the skeptical media coverage and community outrage over the arrests, fueled doubt about the veracity of the allegations.

♦ **245**   Givens, R., & Huck, J. (1985, September 16). California: Devilish deeds? *Newsweek*, p. 43.

In Kern County, 10 year old Michael Nokes is one of many children who are telling police and mental health professionals about ritual abuse in a "Satanic Church" by scores of adults, including his own parents. He claims he and other children were forced to throw knives at "Baby Jonathan," dismember him, and then drink his blood.

Investigators throughout California are coming across similar allegations but, like in the Kern County case, are unable to find corroborating evidence.

◆ **246** Newsome, M. (1999, November). My lie sent my father to jail. *Redbook*, pp. 88–90.

The only evidence against Jeffrey Modahl in the Kern County ritual abuse case was the testimony of his 10 year old daughter who had been subjected to intensive interviews. Medicated with Thorazine at the time of her trial testimony, and under the erroneous impression that nothing untoward would happen to her father, the 10 year old told the court about sexual abuse in the context of satanic rituals. Her father was convicted, and although she wrote him a letter admitting she had lied and apologizing for it, his conviction was not overturned until 15 years later. From the age of 10 until 16, she was in 15 different foster homes. Now 25, she is divorced with 2 children. She knows her father forgives her, but she is unable to forgive herself.

◆ **247** Peters, N. (1999, March 8). Frame-up through fantasy. *Justice Denied*, 1. Retrieved 11-February-01 from the World Wide Web: http//www.justicedenied.org/v1issue2.htm.

John Stoll and Grant Self remain in prison after being convicted in the Kern County ritual abuse case. They were named as part of a sex ring that included Margie Grafton and Tim Palomo whose convictions recently were overturned. Their accuser was Stoll's 5 year old son who, upon being questioned by his mother, from whom Stoll was divorced, disclosed his father had abused him and other boys when they came to swim in his pool. Grilled by Deputy Connie Ericcson, the boy went on to give fantastic accounts of ritual abuse that he has since retracted.

◆ **248** Peters, N. (1999, February 8). Conviction without evidence. *Justice Denied*, 1. Retrieved 11-February-01 from the World Wide Web: http//www.justicedenied.org/v1issue1.htm.

Jeffrey Modahl was convicted in 1986 of 6 counts of sexual abuse in the Kern County ritual abuse case. His daughter, 10, testified against him after she was repeatedly questioned by state social worker Velda Murillo and Deputy Connie Ericcson, and given Thorazine, a powerful anti-psychotic drug she was led to believe was administered to treat a gallbladder problem. Modahl was sentenced to 48 years.

◆ **249** Walker, J. (1999, July 8). Waking up from a nightmare. *Justice Denied*, 1. Retrieved 11-February-01 from the World Wide Web: http//www.justicedenied.org/v1issue5.htm.

The California Supreme Court recently ruled that the trial court erred in the Jeffrey Modahl case when it refused to enter into evidence his daughter's medical report that finds no evidence of sexual abuse, and a taped interview with his step-daughter by state social worker Velda Murillo that demonstrates the coercive and leading interview techniques that led to his conviction in the Kern County ritual abuse case. Modahl's conviction was overturned and he was released from prison.

OFFICIAL INQUIRY

In 1985, with dozens of adults already convicted and sentenced to some of the longest prison terms in state history, a grand jury convened to look into the Kern County ritual abuse case. Its report, sharply critical of individuals and systems involved in the case, called for a full inquiry. That $500,000 inquiry was conducted by the state Attorney General. Although it does not deal with the McCuan/Kniffen cases that started the investigation, it finds 23 procedural errors that call into question the credibility of the children's allegations and the security of the subsequent convictions. Although the inquiry provided the basis for the successful appeals of some of those convicted in the Kern County ritual abuse case, 15 years after its publication several remain in prison.

♦ **250** Van de Kamp, J. (1986, September). *Report of the Attorney General on the Kern County child abuse investigation.* Sacramento, CA: Office of the Attorney General.

The Kern County Sheriff's Department had no policies on investigative procedures and no interview protocols. Some deputies had attended a satanic crime seminar but never took the state-mandated training on child sexual abuse. Working without supervision, they deferred to the district attorney and social workers. The 3 agencies involved in the investigation shared no plan and their opposing philosophies about the reliability of children's disclosures hampered their investigation. Interviews were leading, suggestive and reinforcing; only 28 of the 134 interviews were tape-recorded; only half of the written reports of the interviews were signed by a supervisor and many reports paraphrased the interviews incorrectly. Nine searches produced no evidence; no medical tests were conducted on children who claimed they had been drugged and sexually abused. The ritual abuse allegations seriously eroded the credibility of the children and their ability to testify about sexual abuse. Carolyn Heim, the lead therapist working with the children housed in a county shelter, was dismissed from the center but continued to counsel the children on her own. She interviewed them in groups, kept spotty records, and summarized her contacts to avoid discovery motions by the defense.

Ingram Family

In 1988 Paul Ingram, an Olympia, Washington, deputy, was accused by his daughters, 18 and 22, of sexual abuse. He acknowledged he may have sexually abused them, but could not remember for certain. Taken into custody, Ingram was interrogated by his colleagues and after several hours went into a "trance-like state" and confessed to the sexual abuse. He was arrested and charged with 6 counts.

While in jail awaiting trial, Ingram underwent recovered memory sessions with a psychologist who asked him about poker parties during which, according to one daughter, she and her sister would be sexually assaulted. After a time, Ingram began remembering the parties and eventually named two colleagues, Jim Rabie and Ray Risch, as his daughters' abusers. Although also questioned extensively about ritual abuse, Ingram had no memories of it.

Rabie and Risch were questioned. Rabie did not remember abusing the Ingram girls, but admitted he had a "dark side" and could have done it; Risch agreed with investigators that he was guilty but had blocked the abuse from his mind. Both were arrested. Months later, after refusing plea bargains, their charges were dropped for lack of evidence.

Despondent, Ingram asked his pastor to perform an exorcism. As the pastor called out demons, Ingram began remembering people kneeling before a fire and a red-robed Devil excising the heart of a black cat. When questioned about their participation in devil worship, Ingram's daughters then began recovering memories of ritual abuse and infant sacrifice. They named a brother as another of their abusers. During questioning he disclosed that he often heard voices and saw witches flying around his bedroom. Assured these actually were memories of ritual abuse, he then named his father, Rabie and Risch as his abusers. The daughters then went on to accuse their mother who, in prayer sessions with the pastor, began recovering her own memories of ritual abuse.

Ingram was transferred to another jail. No longer interrogated by investigators who had found no evidence to corroborate the various allegations of ritual abuse, he began to question the veracity of his own memories. So did Richard Ofshe, a social psychologist originally hired as a prosecution consultant. He became convinced of Ingram's innocence when, after several hours in thought and prayer, he began recovering memories of a fabricated event Ofshe had suggested to him. The report detailing Ofshe's experiment and his conclusion that Ingram's memories are false can be found at the internet URL: http://members.aol.com/IngramOrg/ofsherp.htm.

Despite his own doubts, Ingram pled guilty to 6 counts of sexual assault and was sentenced to 20 years. His appeals have been denied and he remains in prison. Audio files of his unsuccessful 1996 pardon hearing can be heard at the internet URL: http://members.aol.com/rossingram/loftsq.ra.

The Ingram ritual abuse case is the subject of two 1996 made-for-television movies: *Forgotten Sins*, and *Crimes of the Imagination*.

♦ **251**   Herman, J. (1994). Presuming to know the truth. *Nieman Reports, 48*, 43–44.

To Wright (see citation 259), the Ingram ritual abuse case represents an archetype, a modern equivalent of the Salem witch trials. His sweeping generalizations about an epidemic of false allegations by children would never pass as science, and should not be allowed to pass as journalism. Although trendy, his account of the case rests on unverifiable assumptions: that false allegations are common and increasing; recovered memories are spurious; and quack psychotherapists, religious zealots and survivor groups are fomenting mass hysteria. By privileging Ingram's position in his account and denigrating his daughters', Wright perpetuates the age-old advantage that abusive parents, especially fathers, have over their victimized children.

◆ **252** Ofshe, R.J. (1992). Inadvertent hypnosis during interrogation: False confession due to dissociative state: Misidentified multiple personality and the satanic cult hypothesis. *International Journal of Clinical and Experimental Hypnosis, 40,* 125–156.

After the induction of a dissociative state during interrogation, Ingram developed pseudomemories of ritually abusing his 2 daughters. For 6 months after his confession he was convinced of his guilt, although investigators were unable to find any evidence to corroborate it. An experiment conducted by the author, a social psychologist originally hired as a prosecution consultant, created more pseudomemories and raised questions about the reliability of Ingram's confession. Ingram's confession of ritual abuse is false, as are his daughters' allegations.

◆ **253** Olio, K., & Cornell, W.F. (1998). The façade of scientific documentation: A case study of Richard Ofshe's analysis of the Paul Ingram case. *Psychology, Public Policy, and Law, 4,* 1182–1197.

A review of the original documents and interview transcripts in the Ingram case reveals that Ofshe's conclusions (see citation 252) are based on errors of fact, methodological flaws, and other confounding factors. Therefore, his conclusion that Ingram was inadvertently hypnotized and as a result confessed to ritually abusing his daughters is incorrect. Ofshe's imperfect narrative of this case and his pseudo-scientific conclusions are being uncritically accepted and repeated in the literature, becoming an academic version of an urban legend.

◆ **254** Prettyman, E.B. (1997). False confessions and fundamental fairness. *Boston Public Interest Law Journal, 6,* 719–751.

The Ingram ritual abuse case demonstrates the need for electronic recording of custodial interrogations. Ingram is a quintessential example of a "naïve confessor," that is, someone who is factually innocent but easily swayed by relentless and coercive interrogation techniques, enforced isolation, and attempts to undermine his confidence in his own memory. Because no recording was made of his confession, he would have been defenseless in trial: his attorneys would have had to convince a jury that he was unreliable enough to have signed a false confession, yet reliable enough to give a credible and truthful account of his interrogation.

◆ **255** Rockwell, R.B. (1995). Insidious deception. *Journal of Psychohistory, 22,* 312–327.

After years of attending meetings of the International Society for the Study of Dissociation and Multiple Personality the author, a psychiatrist, has come to believe that ritual abuse is a reality and that it is widespread. He is alarmed at attempts by others to discredit that belief, particularly Wright (see citation 259) in his examination of the Ingram ritual abuse case. Wright relies too much on the opinion of Ofshe (see citation 252) whom the judge did not find a credible witness because he has no expertise in sexual abuse and his experiment in which he created pseudomemories for Ingram was not scientific.

◆ **256** Spadaro, J.A. (1998). An elusive search for the truth. *Connecticut Law Review, 30,* 1147–1198.

The Ingram case illustrates the challenges that recovered memories pose to the court. It is unlikely that all of his recovered memories of ritual abuse are true and equally unlikely that all of them are false. To determine the truth of such memories courts must evaluate their reliability in a pretrial hearing. Employing the criteria set out in the *Daubert* case facilitates that assessment. For recovered memories to be introduced at trial, they must be judged reliable, helpful, and based on scientifically valid reasoning and methodology.

◆ **257** Trott, J. (1992). Satanic panic: The Ingram family and other victims of hysteria in America. *Cornerstone, 20*, pp. 9–10, 12.

In many ways, Ingram is a stereotypical evangelical Christian — he is married, the father of 5, politically conservative, and a pillar of his church — but he confessed not only to sexual abuse, but to ritual abuse as a devotee of a satanic cult. Now in prison serving a 20 year sentence, Ingram no longer believes he is guilty and blames his pastor for persuading him by leading him in prayer and visualization exercises and urging him to confess.

◆ **258** Watters, E. (1991, July/August). The Devil in Mr. Ingram. *Mother Jones*, pp. 30–33, 65–66.

The Ingram case occurred when the idea of ritual abuse seized the minds of many professionals. Undersheriff Neil McClanahan who headed the investigation is convinced there is a satanic conspiracy targeting children, and violated Ingram's due process rights to uncover it. Psychologist Richard Peterson finally persuaded Ingram to confess to ritual abuse by alternating angry diatribes with soothing comfort. Pastor John Bratun met with Ingram repeatedly and took part in his interrogation. In prayer sessions with him, Ingram began visualizing the ritual abuse and satanic activities to which he later confessed. Under his spiritual advice, Ingram fasted, spoke in tongues and had conversations with God. Ingram's daughters' allegations developed after participating in an evangelical Christian youth group and reading *Satan's Underground* (see citation 696). Ingram began hearing God telling him to plead guilty, and he did so.

◆ **259** Wright, L. (1994). *Remembering Satan*. NY: Alfred A. Knopf.

The Ingram case, as fantastical as it is, owes its existence to a number of ideologies that had hold of American consciousness in the late 1980s, including the idea of ritual abuse, the concept of recovered memories, and religious fundamentalism. Every key player in the case, including Ingram, unthinkingly embraced one or more of those ideologies. If there was a miracle in this case, it was that it went no further than it did. If Ingram's recovered memories had not finally become too absurd for even the most credulous investigator to believe, if Rabie and Risch had accepted a plea bargain, and if the Ingram daughters had stuck to a single story, the witch hunt in Olympia would have waged reckless and unchecked. What happened to Ingram, his family, Rabie and Risch, is happening to thousands of others across the United States who are being accused of horrific abuse on the basis of recovered memories. Some of those memories might be true; most of them certainly are not. Whatever the value of repression as a concept and a tool, unquestioning belief in it is as dangerous as belief in witches and demons.

◆ **260** Wright, L. (1993). Remembering Satan, Part 2. *The New Yorker*, pp. 54–66, 68–76.

Ingram is the first person in the United States to confess to ritual abuse and his case is a lightning rod for a national debate about ritual abuse, recovered memories and sex crimes investigations. His memories, recovered during hours of interrogation by police and hours of prayer and visualization exercises guided by his pastor, were shown to be the products of suggestion by Richard Ofshe, a University of California at Berkeley expert on mind control, who originally was hired as a consultant to the prosecutor but became convinced of Ingram's innocence.

♦ **261**   Wright, L. (1993, May 17). Remembering Satan, Part I. *The New Yorker*, pp. 60–66, 68–74, 76–81.

The fragile bonds of the Ingram family unraveled completely in the wake of his confession to the ritual abuse of his 2 daughters, and his wife's and son's recovered memories of ritual abuse. The "cult cops," fundamentalist Christians and psychotherapists whose unflagging belief in ritual abuse and in the veracity of repressed memories not only constructed the ritual abuse panic but destroyed the Ingram family, are unrepentant. To them, the case is reason to believe there is a satanic conspiracy so diabolic that it leaves no evidence or intact memories.

Evansville, Indiana

In 1989 a woman who believed her ex-husband had sexually abused their daughter, went into hiding with her when the court granted her ex-husband supervised visitation. The pair became part of the Children of the Underground program run by Faye Yager of Atlanta, Georgia. Yager, who interviewed the child, determined she had been ritually abused and for the next two years they were hidden under assumed names until they were found by authorities in Oklahoma. While they were hiding, Rick and Pam Doninger, leaders of the Evansville chapter of SLAM (Society's League Against Molestation) acted as couriers, shuttling letters between the woman and her extended family.

At the invitation of SLAM, Yager gave a speech in February 1991 in which she claimed she had learned from the hidden girl that Evansville was a "cesspool populated by satanists in high places." The girl had named several other children as ritual abuse victims and when the police failed to act on the information, the Doningers began interviewing them. Seven children eventually disclosed they were being ritually abused by their own parents, teachers and school officials in a blue house. They talked about being taken from the school to the house in a bus, and being sexually assaulted by robed and hooded adults who sacrificed babies and cut out their hearts.

A two year investigation ensued but found no evidence of ritual abuse and a great deal of evidence to contradict every aspect of the children's allegations and no charges were filed. The Doningers and their supporters insist that police, prosecutors and the accused ritual abusers are all Masons and conspired in a cover-up of the case.

♦ **262**   Degh, L. (1994). Satanic child abuse in a blue house. *Contemporary Legend*, 4, 119–133.

The legend of Satan, so central to Western Judeo-Christian culture, is secularized in the Evansville ritual abuse case, and popularized by the television tabloid news show *A Current Affair* in a 1991 segment titled, "The Devil's Playground." The features of the case — ritual abuse in a blue house, animal sacrifices, satanic symbols — are local redactions of the famous Indiana legend about the "House of Blue Lights" where mysterious deaths take place. The Evansville version of the legend, which had a subterranean existence in rumors and gossip for nearly a decade before any allegations were made public, was reified by interest groups and the media and shows the profound impact folk legends can have on social reality.

Gilmer, Texas

In 1992, Kelly Wilson, 17, failed to return home from work. Despite a year long investigation by Sgt. James Brown, she was not found. Acting on information about ritual abuse they received from attending a seminar, two state social workers once again interviewed the 16 children they had removed from the extended Kerr family in 1990, and questioned them about ritual abuse. After many interviews, some of the children confirmed they had been ritually abused by family members in ceremonies that involved drinking the blood of a sacrificed woman. Convinced the woman was Wilson, the social workers contacted the police.

Assisted by a satanic cult expert, the special prosecutor assigned to the case interviewed the Kerr children; one of them, a 7 year old, confirmed the woman in question was Wilson and went on to name four family members and two friends as her murderers. His disclosure was corroborated by a family member who was in jail awaiting trial.

Sgt. Brown, however, discovered that each of the accused family members had an alibi and when he reported this to the prosecutor, he was accused of trying to derail the investigation. When the prosecutor then questioned the child and the jailed family member as to whether Brown also was present during the ritual abuse and the murder, they eventually disclosed he was.

Despite the fact that the prosecutor was forced to take out ads in the local paper soliciting evidence, Brown, four members of the Kerr family and two of their friends were indicted for murder. Some citizens protested Brown's indictment and wore yellow ribbons in a show of support; the most vocal among them then were named in a new round of indictments. They included the police chief and an animal control officer who was alleged to have procured animals for ritual sacrifices.

The Texas Attorney General took over the case in 1993 and secured a reversal of the indictments against Brown and the others for murder, and dismissed the charges of ritual abuse against the Kerr family. Upon release from jail, the informant retracted her statements and described how she had been coached by the prosecutor into making them.

Before he was returned to his family, Danny Kerr, Jr., was subjected to a "holding session" in which his foster parents pinned him down and rubbed their knuckles across his chest to elicit memories of ritual abuse. He lapsed into an irreversible coma. His foster father then committed suicide, as did his wife two days later. Brown, who has filed a multimillion dollar suit for malicious prosecution, suffered a stroke and is now partially disabled. Kelly Wilson is still missing.

◆ **263**   Wade, R.M. (1999). When Satan came to Texas. *Skeptic, 7,* 40–56.

Gilmer, a bustling east Texas town, has a lumber industry, pottery manufacturers, many churches, the third largest enclave of Latter Day Saints in the state, and an illiteracy rate of 25%. The disappearance of Kelly Wilson and the rumors of satanic conspiracies deeply divided the town and brought out the worst in many of its otherwise stalwart citizens, and the best in a few. Among the worst were state social workers Debbie Minshew and Ann Goar who relentlessly pursued the ritual abuse idea with the Kerr children; prosecutor Scott Lyford who led a pernicious witch hunt that targeted respectable citizens and exploited the vulnerability of a jailed informant with an IQ of 70; and Carl Raschke, University of Denver professor and consultant to Lyford who a year after the indictments were dismissed was urging the Justice for Kelly Wilson Committee to uncover the cabal of public officials and satanists responsible for her death. Among the best were Rev. Richard Spruiell who braved the criticism of his congregation and brought in state officials to stop the witch hunt, and Sgt. James Brown who managed to maintain a semblance of dignity despite being demonized. Even now, some residents say the devil visited Gilmer; others say it was not the devil but a mix of ambition, superstition and ignorance. In the end, Kelly Wilson is still missing, a boy is in a coma, two foster parents are dead by their own hands, and a police officer is disabled and labeled a pariah.

Wenatchee, Washington

In 1992 a 7 year old whose illiterate parents were persuaded by state social workers to sign a voluntary placement agreement was placed in the foster home of Detective Robert Perez who had taken over the sex crimes unit. He was establishing a track record for arresting sexual abusers and securing their confessions.

Two children whose own parents were among those arrested told him about adults who swapped children for sex in a ring known as "The Circle," an account then confirmed by his new foster daughter. Perez drove her around the city where she identified the homes of "The Circle" members; most were near her own, in a poverty stricken section of the city. Perez arrested many of those identified by his foster daughter and interrogated their children who eventually named other perpetrators and victims, leading Perez to conclude several loosely organized sex rings were operating in the city.

Pastor Roby Roberson spoke out against the investigation; weeks later, he and his wife were arrested when a child hospitalized in a psychiatric facility disclosed during recovered memory therapy that children were taken to his church, put into a trance, and ritually raped by him and other adults. The Robersons went on trial in 1995 and were acquitted of all charges.

Carol and Mark Doggett, unaware of the investigation, called state social workers when they discovered their son molested his sister. Although the incident was dismissed as consensual, Perez eventually extracted an allegation from the Doggett children that they were being abused by their parents. They were placed in foster care and their parents were arrested, convicted and sentenced to 11 years. Their conviction later was overturned; the appellate decision can be found at the internet URL: http://www.ags. uci.edu/~dehill/witchhunt/cases/wenatchee.doggett.htm.

Outraged by the investigation, local people organized the Concerned Citizens for Legal Accountability and petitioned the U.S Attorney General to conduct an inquiry into the case. The advocacy organization VOCAL (Victims of Child Abuse Laws) filed suit against state, county and local officials to stop the arrests.

The investigation resulted in the arrests of 43 people on 29,726 charges of sexual abuse against 60 children. Most of the accused pled under an Alford Plea that does not acknowledge guilt, but agrees there is sufficient evidence for a conviction. By January 2001, all 23 of those incarcerated either had served their sentences or had their convictions overturned. The foster daughter who made most of the allegations has since recanted, stating she was pressured by Perez into making them.

Lawsuits now total in the hundreds of millions. In 1996 the City Commission stated it would have to assess property owners $.75/$1,000 of property evaluation until the difference between what the city's insurance carrier would pay and the anticipated settlements and awards is made up.

♦ **264** Amon, E. (1999, August 23). A white knights' tale. *National Law Journal*, p. A1.

The *Seattle Post-Intelligencer's* series "The Power to Harm" (see citations 278–282) prompted the Seattle defense bar to form one of the largest *pro bono* efforts in history. Over 40 attorneys have come together on behalf of 13 indigent defendants convicted in the Wenatchee ritual abuse case. To date, one has been freed from prison and 2 have been granted post-conviction relief hearings.

♦ **265** Armbrister, T. (1996, July). Witch hunt in Wenatchee. *Reader's Digest*, pp. 125–131.

Pastor Roby Roberson and his wife Connie spent $130,000 to defend themselves against charges they ritually abused children, including their own 4 year old daughter, in orgies in the Pentecostal Church of God and House of Prayer. Roberson believes he was targeted because he spoke out against the arrest of parishioners Idella and

Harold Everett on 12,000 counts of rape on their own and other children. The Robersons spent 135 days in jail before their bond was reduced and they were released. At their trial, their daughter denied she had been abused by them, a 15 year old accuser could not identify them, and a 12 year old accuser, the foster daughter of the investigating officer, revealed he had grabbed and twisted her arm to make her testify. The jury deliberated 5 hours and acquitted the Robersons.

◆ **266**　Carlson, M. (1995, November 13). The sex-crime capital. *Time Magazine*, pp. 89–91.

Wenatchee is a town of only 24,000 but scores of adults have been arrested on sexual abuse charges, most of them on the word of the foster daughter of the investigating officer, Robert Perez. Perez has a history of petty crime and domestic problems, and was evaluated by his supervisor as "pompous and arrogant," and "quick to pick out people and target them." His interviews with his foster daughter are unrecorded, as are the interviews with other vulnerable children in the case. One of them, a 10 year old, says Perez pulled her out of school and questioned her for 4 hours about sex orgies. She finally signed a statement that implicated her own mother, Donna Rodriguez, whom Perez then charged with 168 counts of sexual abuse. Unlike most of the Wenatchee accused, she hired a lawyer; 2 days before her trial all charges were dropped.

◆ **267**　Hentoff, N. (1998, April 21). A town possessed by Satan. *Village Voice*, p. 20.

U.S. Attorney General Janet Reno says she may order a thorough investigation of the Wenatchee ritual abuse case after reading the 5-part *Seattle Post Intelligencer* (see citations 278–282) series. The case is the largest sexual abuse investigation in history, and it cast a wide net that snared 43 adults who were charged with a grand total of 29,726 counts of sex abuse involving 60 children. Many of the adults are illiterate and/or developmentally delayed and poor, and were bullied into confessing; if they did not, they were defended in trial by inexperienced and unenthusiastic public defenders.

◆ **268**　Hentoff, N. (1998, April 14). Burning witches all over again. *Village Voice*, p. 22.

Just as in the day care ritual abuse cases, the primary witnesses in the Wenatchee case are children who were browbeaten by investigators into making false and fantastic allegations. Finally, with dozens of adults in prison, it is time to look hard at the record, the inquisitorial role played by Detective Robert Perez, and the credibility of the allegations of children who were removed from their families and schools and some of them medicated, locked in psychiatric facilities or placed in recovered memory therapy, until they told the stories officials wanted to hear.

◆ **269**　Kershner, J. (1996). A witch hunt in Wenatchee? *American Journalism Review*, *18*, 32–35.

The press coverage of the Wenatchee ritual abuse case story is a classic clash between local and national media. The former consistently followed the official line on the case that there were 2 loosely organized and connected sex rings that involved hundreds of perpetrators and victims; the national press and Spokane's KREM-TV, on the other hand, insisted that innocent people were being accused because of improper police techniques and an atmosphere of hysteria. The media's "trial by columnist" appears to have had little effect on the trials, themselves, although the coverage deeply divided the town.

◆ **270**   Lyon, K. (1998). *Witch hunt: A true story of social hysteria and abused justice.* NY: Avon.

The Wenatchee ritual abuse case began with the allegations of a 7 year old and culminated in the arrests of dozens of innocent citizens. It is the most recent and arguably the most horrible of American inquisitions that targeted, for the most part, poor, mentally disabled and otherwise vulnerable adults, some of whom confessed under the pressure of a crusading detective and zealous state social workers, and named others as abusers and more children as victims. Children who failed to agree they had been abused, or who recanted, were threatened with arrest, removed from their families and their familiar surroundings, placed in recovered memory therapy, or locked in psychiatric facilities. The judicial response to the case was equally appalling: inexperienced public defenders urged their clients to confess, prosecutors levied charges hours before trials were to start, and some of the children testified repeatedly.

◆ **271**   Lyon, K. *The Wenatchee report update.* Retrieved 9-February-01 from the World Wide Web: http://user.aol.com/DougHSkept/witchhunt/wen1_report.txt.

Between September and December 1995, charges against some Wenatchee ritual abuse case defendants have been dropped, and the sentences of others have been overturned as the national media bring publicity to the case and advocacy groups are successful in soliciting support for the accused.

◆ **272**   Lyon, K. (1995). *The Wenatchee report.* Retrieved 9-February-01 from the World Wide Web: http://user.aol.com/DougHSkept/witchhunt/wen_report.txt.

By September 1995, 24 people in the Wenatchee ritual abuse case are still in prison and 40 children are still separated from their parents. The community is deeply divided by the course of events that has escalated beyond anyone's imagination and, apparently, beyond everyone's control. The anatomy of the investigation is dissected, from the initial allegations through the trials and guilty pleas.

◆ **273**   Meachum, J. (1995, May 8). Trials and troubles in Happy Valley. *Newsweek*, pp. 58–61.

If prosecutors and Detective Robert Perez are right, Wenatchee is home to dozens of child molesters involved in child-swapping sex and ritual abuse rings. That, coupled with several grisly murders unrelated to the ring, have led people to be frightened and distrustful. What is going on? Part of the answer lies in the city's loosely structured subculture of poverty in which unemployment and crime rates are high, and child abuse common. The poor who are being charged in this case embody the social problems that persist in this otherwise pleasant and affluent city.

◆ **274**   Rabinowitz, D. (1999, September 21). Reckoning in Wenatchee. *Wall Street Journal*, p. A-26.

Most of the Wenatchee residents charged with sexually and ritually abusing children have been named by 2 young girls. One of them accompanied Detective Robert Perez on a drive through town where she pointed out 23 homes in which she and other children were abused, and named passersby as their abusers. That trip that expanded the case came to be known as the "Parade of Homes" by the few local skeptics who spoke out in the early years of the case and braved the city's professional and legal establishments that were enthusiastically supporting this investigation.

◆ **275** Rabinowitz, D. (1995, November 8). Wenatchee, a true story —
III. *Wall Street Journal*, p. A-20.

As their case is about to come trial, Pastor Robie Roberson and his wife Connie are
confident they will be acquitted. The evidence against them is incredibly weak and
their own daughter refuses to testify against them. Despite their confidence, though,
they realize that dozens of others involved in the Wenatchee ritual abuse case have
been convicted on evidence as weak as that against them.

◆ **276** Rabinowitz, D. (1995, October 13). Wenatchee, a true story —
II. *Wall Street Journal*, p. A-14.

The key prosecution witness in the Wenatchee ritual abuse trials is the foster daughter of the detective in charge of the investigation. Without her testimony, there is little, if any, evidence corroborating the allegations against any of the people who have
been charged. And her testimony, such as it is, must be evaluated in the light of the
pressure her foster father is placing on her to tell stories commensurate with his own
biases.

◆ **277** Roberts, P.C. (1996, March 11). The Reno fix on kids, sex and
satanism. *Insight on the News*, pp. 27–29.

U.S. Attorney General Janet Reno's refusal to investigate the Wenatchee ritual abuse
case sends a loud message that no one can be safe from false allegations. The case
revealed itself for the witch hunt it is in December when Pastor Roberson and his wife
were acquitted of ritually abusing children, including their 4 year old daughter. The
only adult witness against the Robersons was a convicted child rapist who agreed to
testify in exchange for having his own 1st degree rape charges reduced to misde-
meanors. The other witness was the foster child of Detective Perez who testified he
had twisted her arm and thrown her to the floor to coerce her to testify. The Wenatchee
ritual abuse case violates every meaning of civil rights, but to the U.S. Justice Department, apparently, race and gender discrimination are the only civil rights violations.

◆ **278** Schneider, A., & Barber, M. (1998, February 27). The power to
harm: Part 5. *Seattle Post-Intelligencer*. Retrieved 9-February-01 from the
World Wide Web: http://www. seattlep-i.nwsource.com.powertoharm

Part 5 of the Bosch Award winning series. By the time of the Wenatchee case, we
should have learned something from the day care ritual abuse cases, the research on
children's suggestibility, and the standards of practice and care for social workers and
mental health professionals, the uses of children as witnesses in courts of law. The case
is so politically compromised that U.S. Attorney General Janet Reno will not investigate; the Wenatchee Report (see citations 271–272) moved no legislator to do anything,
a retired police officer did a one day investigation and exonerated the police of all mis-
doing, and a group of prosecutors demanded that the governor take a hands-off
approach so as not to compromise future prosecutions.

◆ **279** Schneider, A., & Barber, M. (1998, February 26). The power to
harm: Part 4. *Seattle Post-Intelligencer*. Retrieved 9-February-01 from the
World Wide Web: http://www.seattlep-i.nwsource.com.powertoharm

Part 4 of the Bosch Award winning series. The 43 accused are profiled including:
Cherie Lee Town, with an IQ of 70, was charged with 110 counts of sexual abuse, pled
guilty and was sentenced to 10 years; Robert Devereaux, a foster father charged with
670 counts involving 2 of his foster daughters who then recanted, pled guilty to one

count of witness tampering and received a suspended 30 day sentence; Justino Cruz, an orchard worker, was charged with 1660 counts, pled guilty to one count, and was given a suspended sentence. Even officials involved in the case came under suspicion. Among them are child welfare worker Paul Glasser who fled the country with his family when he discovered he had been named in 50 cases; and child welfare supervisor Juana Vasquez who was placed on administrative leave when she questioned the investigation and was later fired.

◆ **280**   Schneider, A., & Barber, M. (1998, February 25). The power to harm: Part 3. *Seattle Post-Intelligencer.* Retrieved 9-February-01 from the World Wide Web: http://www.seattlep-i.nwsource.com.powertoharm

Part 3 of the Bosch Award winning series. In the Wenatchee ritual abuse case, prosecutors filed charges with no evidence, the detective destroyed notes, children and defendants were browbeaten in relentless interrogations, allegations were treated as facts but recantations were dismissed. While prosecutors secured a grant for $140,000 to supplement county costs, underpaid, overworked and inexperienced public defenders took on the unpopular defendants.

◆ **281**   Schneider, A., & Barber, M. (1998, February 24). The power to harm: Part 2. *Seattle Post-Intelligencer.* Retrieved 9-February-01 from the World Wide Web: http://www.seattlep-i.nwsource.com.powertoharm

Part 2 of the Bosch Award winning series. The state has put 17 of the 60 children who are alleged victims in the Wenatchee ritual abuse case up for adoption. Mental health professionals have subjected many of them to intensive recovered memory therapy; 29 of the children were sent to Pine Crest psychiatric facility in Idaho at a cost of $750,000. Children are being hurt by the very systems in place to protect them.

◆ **282**   Schneider, A., & Barber, M. (1998, February 23). The power to harm: Part 1. *Seattle Post-Intelligencer.* Retrieved 9-February-01 from the World Wide Web: http://www.seattlep-i.nwsource.com.powertoharm

Part 1 of the Bosch Award winning series. From the beginning, the Wenatchee ritual abuse case did not add up: in 85% of sexual abuse cases, children disclose to teachers, doctors, relatives or caregivers, but in Wenatchee they disclosed to police and social workers; in 10% of sexual abuse cases, females are perpetrators, but in Wenatchee 51% are. What also does not add up is that the first allegation in this case came from the foster daughter of Detective Robert Perez, yet no one seemed suspicious of that coincidence; the state agency in place to keep families together worked zealously with Perez to tear them apart; and judges on the bench to protect defendants' rights skirted them while organizations like the ACLU turned a blind eye. All of this in the name of justice.

◆ **283**   VanBiema, D. (1995, December 25). The tide turns in Wenatchee, but will justice prevail? *Time Magazine*, p. 136.

Lay pastor Robie Roberson and his wife Connie, acquitted of 14 counts of sexual abuse in the Wenatchee ritual abuse case, finally got their daughter Rebecca back from foster care last week where she has been since their arrest. Roberson intends to file a civil suit against the state, seek the release of those in prison and support a local campaign to get U.S. Attorney General Janet Reno to investigate the handling of the case.

OFFICIAL INQUIRIES

The Wenatchee ritual abuse case prompted calls from the Concerned Citizens for Legal Accountability, the American Civil Liberties Union, the National Association of Defense Attorneys, and the Governor of Washington to the U.S. Attorney General for a federal review of the case. The petitions have been denied twice, each time on the basis that the Wenatchee ritual abuse case demonstrates no prosecutable federal violations. The various requests for a federal review can be found at the internet URL: http://www.ags.uci.edu/~dehill/witchhunt/cases/Wenatchee/action98.htm. The case did prompt two official reports, however, although to date it has eluded a full inquiry.

◆ **284** ACLU of Washington (1997, October). When child protection investigations harm children: The Wenatchee sexual abuse cases. Retrieved 9-February-01 from the World Wide Web: ftp://ftp.calweb.com/users/j/ jmprice/satanic-ritual-abuse/wenatchee-report-aclu-wa

The Wenatchee ritual abuse case reveals 8 ways in which the Washington child protection system harms children: it hospitalized children in an out-of-state psychiatric facility until the allegations were proved; it allowed the lead detective to be an alleged victim's foster parent; it allowed the police to dictate when children's mental health therapy should be terminated; it allowed the records of interviews with the children to be destroyed; it allowed coercive interviews with children; it failed to require that all interviews be well documented; it failed to clarify the proper roles of police and state social workers in the interviews; and it failed to provide a mechanism for quality control and accountability during the investigation.

◆ **285** Wallen, V. (1998). *OFCO 1998 review of the Wenatchee child sexual abuse investigations.* Tukwila, WA: Washington State Office of the Family and Children's Ombudsman.

A review of the procedures used by the State Division of Children and Family Services and local law enforcement officials to investigate allegations of ritual abuse in Wenatchee was prompted by complaints of poorly conducted and improper interviews with the alleged victims and their alleged abusers. An examination of case files, police reports, court transcripts, interviews and media materials in this case finds that: current documentation policies do not adequately facilitate a review of interview techniques to establish their appropriateness and the risk they pose for factual distortion; neither the child protective service workers nor the mental health professionals who conducted interviews in this case were trained in sexual abuse; and child protection services workers also were not trained in how to establish a working relationship with law enforcement agencies. The Ombudsman's Office recommends that both state law and child abuse policies be modified to require proper documentation and adequate training for child protective service workers. The report can be found at the internet URL: http://www.wa.gov/governor/ofco.

4

Canadian, European
and Australasian
Ritual Abuse Cases

Just as day care, family and community-based ritual abuse cases in the United States began slipping into history, the past became prologue. Ritual abuse cases began cropping up again, this time in Canada, Europe and Australasia, each generating its own local controversy while at the same time adding to what has become a vitriolic international debate.

If the ritual abuse controversy can be cast conveniently, for the moment, in the much too simple terms of "believers" at one extreme and "disbelievers" at the other, then the contribution of the international cases to the controversy will be evident. For the "believers," the very appearance of cases in foreign countries, with their disparate social, political, economic, professional and ideological forces, argues for the position that ritual abuse is a social fact, not a social construction. For "disbelievers," their appearance argues the opposite. To them, ritual abuse is an American social construction, exported to other countries, but then uniquely shaped by each country's disparate social, political, economic, professional and ideological forces.

If there is any common ground in this debate, it is a small patch of acknowledgement that American child protectionists and mental health professionals greatly influence international thinking about ritual abuse. Through the media of conferences, invited speeches, and disseminated published and unpublished materials, they reach a wide international audience. For "believers," their influence gives indigenous professionals the knowledge to uncover ritual abuse cases; for "disbelievers," it only persuades them to construct ritual abuse cases. The polemic aside, it is important to also acknowledge that the American influence is not some kind of exercise in cultural colonialism. Rather, as ritual abuse cases begin cropping up in other countries, international professionals reciprocally influence American thinking and activity through participation in conferences and workshops, and the dissemination of their published and unpublished materials.

The eleven cases discussed in this chapter are best considered exemplars of the international ritual abuse cases. Indeed, cases have occurred in Germany, Norway and Sweden but the lack of accessibility to materials on them and to citations in English precludes their inclusion in this chapter. Each of the cases included, however, is introduced by a legalistic precis and, as in previous chapters, is vivified by citations from both scholarly literature and national news sources.

Two Canadian Ritual Abuse Cases

Hamilton, Ontario

In 1985 two half-sisters were placed in temporary foster care when their mother, destitute and distressed, feared she might hurt them. The girls, both under 7, already had a history of involvement with social services for suspected abuse and neglect.

While in foster care, their behavior was sexually inappropriate. Unaware of their background, their foster mother began questioning them and they eventually said they had been sexually abused by their mother, her boyfriend, and the father of the younger girl. While their foster mother took notes, the girls also talked about witnessing the murders of children and consuming their flesh, participating in orgies filmed at a television station in which live birds were inserted into their vaginas, and abuse by a man named "The Blob" whom they later helped kill and bury. They later claimed their parents were planning to kill their foster family and feed the bodies to satanic cannibals. They were then placed in a new foster home.

In 1985 wardship proceedings began in the "Cannibal Case." The girls were not present and did not testify, but over 20 hours of their videotaped play therapy sessions were shown in court. Social workers and child abuse specialists testified there was compelling reason to believe they had been both sexually and ritually abused, although police found no evidence of the latter.

In 1987 the Judge made the girls wards of the Crown and continued their placement in foster care, denying their mother and her estranged husband access to them. Although he found sufficient reason to believe the girls had been sexually abused by them, he refused to rule that their "more florid" allegations of ritual abuse were credible.

Their mother's appeal was denied. The Court stated the ritual abuse allegations were irrelevant to its decision because the evidence that the girls "came from a background of filth, squalor and violence ... and exhibited signs of mental disturbance, neglect and deprivation" was sufficient enough to deny the appeal.

No criminal charges were filed in the case.

◆ **286**   Kendrick, M. (1988). *Anatomy of a nightmare*. Toronto, Canada: Macmillan of Canada.

The Hamilton ritual abuse case serves as a warning about the dangers of the ridiculous belief that allegations of ritual abuse must be believed simply because they are so unbelievable. That belief, sustained by a climate of cultural hysteria, was reified in the $2 million Hamilton case by the uncritical acceptance of the testimony of a foster mother obsessed with satanism, the failure to assess the degree to which the suggestive and repeated interviews by a host of professionals shaped the allegations, the reliance on hearsay evidence, and the failure to hear testimony from less credulous experts. Cases like this always risk infringing on the welfare of children and the rights of adults, and overburdening the social service system and the courts.

◆ **287**   Marron, K. (1988). *Ritual abuse: Canada's most infamous trial on child abuse*. Toronto, Canada: Seal Books.

An account of the Hamilton ritual abuse case by the only reporter who covered the case every day for its 17 month duration. The case stands at the center of a larger debate about the existence of homicidal satanic cults that are ritually abusing children. While the failure to find evidence corroborating the ritual abuse allegations of the girls in the case seems to support the position that their allegations are nothing more than archetypal fantasies, the details of the case argue otherwise. Their allegations persisted despite the disbelief and incompetence of the very system designed to protect them, and the similarity of their allegations to other cases of ritual abuse in the United States lends them all the more credibility.

Sterling Day Care: Saskatchewan

In 1991 a child returned from her unlicensed babysitting service in the home of Ron and Linda Sterling with a reddened perineum and said she was poked by a stranger. The ensuing police investigation intensified when it was discovered that a prior sexual abuse complaint against the Sterlings' 22 year old son, Travis, had been dismissed as unfounded and the investigation file was missing. Suspicious that fellow officers, all friends of Ron Sterling, had covered it up, the investigator began showing their photographs to the other babysitter service enrollees she was interviewing.

Although none disclosed abuse, several later made tentative statements to their parents who questioned them using a sexual abuse indicator list they were given at a meeting at a mental health clinic. In further interviews with the investigator, some of the children then identified officers James Elstad, Daryl Ford and Edward Revesz as their abusers and one child described a blue "Devil Church" where much of the abuse had taken place.

Photographs of the contents of an abandoned blue building were shown to the children in subsequent interviews, and over the next month 30 children, ages 2 through 12, identified the building as the "Devil Church," and named the Sterlings, their young assistant, a minor identified only as "T.S.," the officers and other unidentified adults as their perpetrators. They talked not only about sexual abuse but injections with stupefying drugs, confinement in a cage found in the building, rape with an axe handle discovered there, confinement in a freezer in the basement, suffocation with pillow cases, human sacrifices and eating eyeballs.

By mid–1992, a total of 180 charges were filed against the Sterlings, T.S., the officers, as well as RCMP officer Daryl Sabourin who was a neighbor of the Sterlings, and Saskatoon officer John Popowich.

T.S. was convicted the following year of seven counts and sentenced to two years. All charges against Popowich were stayed three weeks into his trial when none of the three child witnesses was able to identify him in a court line-up. Ron, Linda and Travis Sterling's trial began in September 1993. Seven children testified but retracted most of the details of ritual abuse under cross-examination. Ron and Linda were acquitted of all charges; Travis was convicted of 8 counts and sentenced to 5 years.

All charges against the other defendants then were dismissed. T.S.'s conviction was overturned in 1995; the Appellate decision can be found at the internet URL: http://www.canlii.org/sk/cas/skca/1995/1195skca95057.html. That same year, seven of the counts against Travis were overturned; the remaining charge was based on the complaint that had been dismissed as unfounded by the police years earlier. His appeal on that conviction was denied; the ruling can be found at the internet URL: http://www.canlii.org/sk/cas/skca/1995/1995skca95068.html.

◆ **288**   Bergman, B., & Eisler, D. (1993, July 19). Trials behind closed doors. *Maclean's*, p. 20.

Journalists covering the Martensville ritual abuse trials were severely restricted by court-ordered publication bans in order to protect the identities of the alleged victims and ensure the remaining accused received fair trials. Trials behind closed doors, however, prevent the larger public from assessing the truth.

◆ **289**   Bruck, M. (1998). The trials and tribulations of a novice expert witness. In S.J. Ceci and H. Hembrooke (Eds.), *Expert witnesses in child* *abuse cases* (pp. 85–104). Washington, D.C.: American Psychological Association Press.

The author, an experimental psychologist, served as a defense expert witness in the Little Rascals ritual abuse trial in Edenton, North Carolina and the Sterling Day Care ritual abuse trial in Martensville, Canada. She had not fully anticipated the effects the adversarial trial process has on an expert witness: the attempts to impeach credibility, the attacks on the science of psychology, the barrage of questions on topics unrelated to stated expertise, and the long periods on the witness stand of fear, confusion, boredom and fatigue. Despite all that, experts should make themselves available for testimony in controversial cases such as these. In this era of pseudoscience and antiscience, expert court testimony in ritual abuse cases is urgently needed.

♦ **290**   Came, D. (1994, February 21). End of a sex scandal. *Maclean's*, p. 21.

The Martensville ritual abuse case is prompting discussions among legal experts as to the proper techniques of interviewing children. In the Sterlings' trial, defense expert witnesses convincingly argued the children made false allegations after being subjected to numerous intensive and leading police and mental health interviews.

♦ **291**   Eisler, D. (1997, February 10). A cautionary tale. *Maclean's*, p. 46.

Almost 5 years after their acquittal, Ron and Linda Sterling have yet to put their lives back together. Having lost their home and their savings, both are still unemployed. They are demanding a public airing of their case in an effort to restore their reputations and establish the innocence of their son, Travis. They have sued the police, prosecutors and Saskatchewan government, seeking $11.6 million in damages. Some good has come from the case, however. New interview protocols have been issued to the police, and a children's advocate has been appointed to oversee complex investigations.

♦ **292**   Eisler, D. (1995, November 20). What went wrong? *Maclean's*, p. 66.

The Saskatchewan Court of Appeals overturned 7 of the 8 sexual assault convictions against Travis Sterling, stating that "on the evidence, many of the alleged bizarre acts did not or could not have occurred." Travis, who spent a year in jail and is now in a halfway house, remains bitter that he was convicted on the same evidence that acquitted his parents. The ruling sparks renewed calls for a public inquiry into the case.

♦ **293**   Felton, G. (1993). The thorny dilemma of unpublicized evidence. *Alberta Report/Western Report, 20*, p. 24.

Popowich, whose name has been widely publicized as one of the accused in the Martensville ritual abuse case, now finds the same media that publicized his name are forbidden to identify his accusers or describe any of the children's testimony. The public perception about the quality of the evidence against him and the other Martensville defendants in this controversial case will be severely compromised.

♦ **294**   Fennell, T. (1992, June 22). The Satan factor. *Maclean's*, p. 29.

The Martensville case adds fuel to the growing international controversy over ritual abuse. Several experts insist the allegations must be treated as true because they are similar to those made in other high profile cases in the United States and Europe.

◆ **295**   Harris, F. (1998). *Martensville: Truth or justice?* Toronto, Canada: Dundurn Press.

The trial of the Sterlings for ritually abusing children enrolled in their babysitting service was the culmination of an investigation by Constable Claudia Bryden and Cpl. Rod Moor that proceeded on the credo that children never lie. That same credo was not shared by everyone in Martensville: while some residents sported window signs that read "We Believe the Children!" others flaunted signs that simply read "Star-chamber." In the end, it was the credibility of the children that was put on trial, and the verdicts show the unwillingness of the public to take a stand on this issue.

◆ **296**   Jenish, D.A. (1994, February 14). End of a nightmare. *Maclean's*, pp. 10–13.

The Sterlings' trial was the longest and costliest criminal trial in Saskatchewan history. Their defense rested heavily on attacking the police investigation led by Constable Claudia Bryden and Saskatoon police Cpl. Rod Moor, a child abuse specialist. Defense expert witnesses testified that the poorly trained and overzealous officers used suggestive questions and rewarded the children for giving the desired answer. One of the experts, David Raskin of the University of Utah, testified that this was the most poorly conducted investigation he had ever come across, and was tantamount to a "witch hunt."

◆ **297**   Lees, D. (1995). *Can you remember? The Martensville child abuse investigation.* Toronto, Canada: HarperCollins.

The Sterling family ritual abuse trial at 5 months the longest and at $1 million the most expensive trial in Saskatchewan history. It was the culmination of a relentless investigation led by Constable Claudia Bryden and Cpl. Rod Moor, and supplemented by the recovered memory therapy of Rod Butler of the MacNeill Clinic.

◆ **298**   Lees, D. (1994, May). Martensville. *Saturday Night*, pp. 15–18, 20, 22, 26, 81–83.

The Crown originally brought 60 charges against the Sterlings but dropped 15 during the trial for lack of evidence. Seventeen of those charges were against a single child; although 7 children testified at the trial, he was the oldest and most credible, yet in his summary to the jury, the judge dismissed his accounts of ritual abuse as "stories." What makes no sense about this trial is that the same evidence used to acquit Ron and Linda was used to indict Travis. Either all of them took the children blindfolded and gagged to the "Devil Church" and ritually abused them, or none did. During the 2½ year investigation and trial, everyone has felt free to invent scenarios of abuse; now it seems it was the jury's turn.

◆ **299**   Shafer, P. (1995). Martensville: 180 charges, one conviction. *Alberta Report/Western Report, 22*, pp. 25–27.

Of the 180 charges laid in the Martensville case, a higher court has confirmed just one. That single conviction against Travis Sterling is unrelated to the ritual abuse case and is the result of a voluntary complaint by a young woman who, unlike the babysitter service children, was not interviewed 60 times. The convictions of T.S. were overturned. The Appeals Court ruled the trial judge had erred by relying too heavily on expert medical testimony, failing to appreciate the leading and suggestive interviews of the children by police and mental health professionals, refusing to give proper weight to the children's failure to notice surgical scars on T.S.'s body, failing to consider the lack of evidence corroborating the children's accounts, and misdirecting the jury about the inconsistencies and contradictions in the children's testimony.

♦ **300**   Shafer, P. (1995). Counterattack of the innocents. *Alberta Report/Western Report, 22*, p. 24.

Despite demands that a public inquiry be held into the Martensville ritual abuse case, the Saskatchewan Justice Minister refuses. Yet the accused have uncovered intriguing facts that, they argue in their civil suits, unduly influenced the case. These include a report that alleges Constable Bryden suffered a psychotic episode during her investigation, and information that in his former position the Martensville Police Chief was bent on proving satanic conspiracies.

In Regards to a Community and Its Citizenry

When the Sterling case occurred, the village of Martensville was still reeling from a frightening case of ritual abuse in nearby Saskatoon. The "foster care case," as it was known, involved three siblings who accused their foster parents, the Klassens, of sexually abusing them and other children in devil worship rituals that involved blood-drinking, cannibalism and infant sacrifices. During their intensive interviews with police and mental health professionals, the siblings also named members of the extended Klassen family, their own estranged biological parents, and their mother's boyfriend as their abusers. After a highly publicized 18 month investigation, 60 charges were filed against 16 people.

The siblings' parents and their mother's boyfriend were convicted and sentenced to three to six years, although their convictions later were overturned. The charges against the members of the Klassen family were dismissed in exchange for a guilty plea by the family patriarch. Details of the case and the ongoing and controversial campaign of the Klassen family to restore its reputation can be found at the internet URL: http://www.injusticebusters.com.

Now Martensville, the fastest growing community in Saskatchewan, with its eight straight avenues, two strip malls and strong Mennonite tradition, had its own terrifying case of ritual abuse. The village of 3400 was deeply divided as residents were forced to question their trust in local officials and in each other.

♦ **301**   Howes, J. (1992, June 22). The Martensville scandal. *Maclean's*, pp. 26–28.

The charges filed against the Sterling family and several police officers have shaken the Martensville community's faith in local authorities. The village, established in the 1960s and considered a retreat from urban violence, is deeply disturbed by the case and unsettled by its notoriety. Village officials are planning several town meetings for residents to share their concerns, as well as various events to restore community pride and solidarity. Messages of moral support are pouring into the Mayor's office from all over Canada, and the Social Services Minister visited Martensville to assure the residents that the government will assist them through the crisis.

♦ **302**   Kopvillem, P. (1992, June 15). The agony of Martensville. *Maclean's*, p. 20.

Martensville residents are struggling to cope with the ritual abuse case that is rocking their small town. Some of the parents are publicly expressing relief that their own children are not among the victims, but all are sharing concerns about how to explain the situation to their children and encourage them to trust others when it was village authorities who were named as ritual abusers. Local schools will remain open during the summer to help children and their parents deal with the shock; counseling for the victims and their families will be provided by social service and health departments. The Social Services Minister pledges to provide support to the whole community as needed.

◆ **303** McGovern, C., (1994). The Martensville witch-hunt. *Alberta Report/Western Report, 21*, pp. 48–50.

In Martensville, the fallout from the witch hunt is staggering: good names were smeared, careers and families devastated, children corrupted, and a close-knit community divided. The Crown Prosecution states it is staying the charges against the officers to spare the children the trauma of testimony but Ron Sterling, like some of the residents who support him, charges it with using children as scapegoats for its own incompetence.

◆ **304** Wilson-Smith, A. (1994, February 28). Anger in Martensville. *Maclean's*, p. 18.

Parents of the children involved in the Martensville ritual abuse case believe the justice system betrayed them. Only 2 of the 9 accused were convicted, and the children are frightened that those who went free will come back to harm them.

SEVEN EUROPEAN RITUAL ABUSE CASES

Oude Pekela, The Netherlands

In 1987 a four year old being treated for persistent anal bleeding told his physician that he and his playmates were sexually abused by strangers with "unfamiliar accents." The police were notified and during questioning the boy and his playmates named 25 other village children as victims.

The police were skeptical about the allegations, but the physician and his wife, also a family physician, were not. Their own children revealed they had known for some time about the sexual assaults on their playmates. But it was an anonymous call from someone claiming to be a survivor of a satanic cult that tipped the physician off to ritual abuse. After gathering information from American experts, he began interviewing the children using the ritual abuse materials as a guide.

As the number of alleged victims he interviewed increased to nearly 100 over the next year, so did the horror of their allegations. They described being lured to parties by strangers in clown costumes, given mind-altering drugs, and made to participate in sacrifices of black infants, all while being filmed by their abusers.

The Ministry of Justice labeled the case a "classic case of mass hysteria," but to appease the outraged village it appointed a child psychiatrist to interview the children. After several months of individual and group interviews, he concluded the children's accounts were truthful and speculated that an international satanic pornography cartel was responsible for their ritual abuse.

One year later, no evidence to substantiate the allegations had been found and no arrests made. By this time some of the children had retracted their allegations and many of the parents no longer believed that sexual abuse, let alone ritual abuse, had ever occurred. The case was closed in October 1988.

♦ **305**   Bartlett, N. (1989, December 14). Facing the unbelievable. *Community Care*, pp. 14–16.

Cases of ritual abuse are cropping up throughout Europe. Their disturbingly similar features, as illustrated by a comparison of the Oude Pekela and Broxtowe Estate cases, should warn social workers against a skeptical response to allegations.

♦ **306**   Gedney, N. (1995). A European response to the backlash movement. *Journal of Psychohistory, 22*, 265–271.

Drs. Jonker and Jonker-Bakker, who played a key role in uncovering the ritual abuse case in Oude Pekela, have been socially marginalized by skeptical members of their community, and professionally isolated by their colleagues in a backlash that is spreading across Europe.

♦ **307**   Imminkhuizen, M. (1994). *Satanic ritual abuse*. Utrecht, the Netherlands: University of Utrecht.

As ritual abuse allegations have spread from the United States to the Netherlands, as the Oude Pekela case illustrates, so has the ferocious debate between the so-called "believers" and the "disbelievers." While the former have no evidence to back up their credulity, the latter are generating alternative explanations for the allegations that must be seriously examined.

♦ **308**   Jonker, F., & Jonker-Bakker, I. (1997). Effects of ritual abuse: The results of three surveys in The Netherlands. *Child Abuse & Neglect, 21*, 541–556.

Questionnaires were sent in 1994 to the parents of 87 children ritually abused 7 years ago in Oude Pekela to gather information about the children's behavioral status. The results are compared to the findings of a less extensive survey conducted in 1990. Over the years between surveys, the number of children who have forgotten the incident entirely increased from 20% to 36%; the number of children who frequently relive the ritual abuse increased from 2% to 3%. Most symptoms of ritual abuse, such as nightmares, sexual acting out, aggression and anxiety, decreased over the years. An untested hypothesis in this study is that children who live in warm, supportive families will work through the trauma of ritual abuse better and faster than those who do not.

♦ **309**　Jonker, F., & Jonker-Bakker, I. (1994). Oude Pekela investigation. *Maandblad Geestelijke Volksgezondheid, 49,* 251–276.

The investigation into the Oude Pekela ritual abuse case pitted professionals and parents against the police and the government. The tension between these groups was fueled by the media that took a critical stance on the case, despite the fact that the children involved showed serious symptoms of trauma consistent with severe sexual abuse both during the case and 2½ years later.

♦ **310**　Jonker, F., & Jonker-Bakker, I. (1992). Reactions to Benjamin Rossen's investigation of satanic ritual abuse in Oude Pekela. *Journal of Psychology and Theology, 20,* 260–262.

Rossen's (see citation 316) conclusion that the Oude Pekela case is an example of mass hysteria is specious, especially given the fact that he had no direct contact with the victimized children, their parents or other key players involved in the case. His dubious credentials further weaken the integrity of his conclusion.

♦ **311**　Jonker, F., & Jonker-Bakker, I. (1992). Safe behind the screen of "mass hysteria": A closing rejoinder to Benjamin Rossen. *Journal of Psychology and Theology, 20,* 267–270.

The persistence of the idea that the Oude Pekela ritual abuse case is nothing more than an example of mass hysteria can be traced directly to the allegations of Rossen (see citation 316) who in choosing not to believe the children's disclosures is able to maintain a safe distance from the devastating implications of a ritual abuse case.

♦ **312**　Jonker, F., & Jonker-Bakker, I. (1991). Experiences with ritualistic child sexual abuse: A case study from the Netherlands. *Child Abuse & Neglect, 15,* 191–196.

The parents of 90 of the children ritually abused in the Oude Pekela case were surveyed 6 to 8 weeks after the first disclosures. The survey finds that 87% were certain their children had been ritually abused. The parents indicate that symptoms they noted in their children, such as enuresis, anxiety and sleep disturbance, either began soon after the ritual abuse or increased while it was occurring. The skepticism about whether this is a real case of ritual abuse has been a source of stress for parents. Fathers tend to be angry at first and then deny that ritual abuse occurred, while mothers tend to be consistently concerned about their children's futures.

♦ **313**　Pyck, K. (1995). Mass hysteria in Oude Pekela? *Tijdschrift voor Criminologie, 37,* 219–237.

The belief of so many professionals and parents of the accusing children that the Oude Pekela case is a genuine case of ritual abuse perpetrated by satanists contrasts with the prevailing notion of the Dutch public that this is a classic case of mass hysteria. The public perception was influenced and shaped by the media whose reportage on the case ranged in tone from skeptical to dismissive. The media attention to the Oude Pekela case deflects public attention from common forms of child abuse and, however unintentionally, encourages public skepticism about the credibility of those cases as well.

♦ **314**　Pyck, K. (1994). The backlash in Europe: Real anxiety or mass hysteria in the Netherlands. In J.E.B. Myers (Ed.), *The Backlash* (pp. 70–85). Thousand Oaks, CA: Sage.

The Oude Pekela ritual abuse case has devolved into myth, with most people believing it is a case of mass hysteria. That belief was fueled by the media and a few vocal critics who managed to shape public opinion about the case and about its key players. This interpretation, whether correct or not, only fuels the backlash against all sexual abuse cases that is sweeping over Europe and undermining the best efforts of professionals to deal with the abuse of children.

◆ **315**   Rogers, M.L. (1992). The Oude Pekela incident. *Journal of Psychology and Theology, 20*, 257–259.

Oude Pekela is a village of 8,000 in northeast Netherlands near the German border. The investigation into the ritual abuse allegations lasted 18 months but produced no evidence. A total of 98 children, ranging in age from 4 to 11, were interviewed; approximately half made clear statements of ritual abuse. The conflicts between the various key players in the case, the government and the media, impeded the investigation from the start and made it impossible to come to a firm conclusion about what really happened.

◆ **316**   Rossen, B. (1992). Response to Oude Pekela incident and the accusations of Drs. F. Jonker and I. Jonker. *Journal of Psychology and Theology, 20*, 263–266.

The *ad hominen* attacks of Jonker and Jonker-Bakker (see citation 310) deflect from the real argument about whether the Oude Pekela case is an actual case of ritual abuse or an example of mass hysteria.

◆ **317**   Rossen, B. (1991). *The Oude Pekela story.* Amsterdam: Lisse, Swets and Zeitlinger.

The Oude Pekela ritual abuse case is the result of a moral panic triggered by the allegations of boys who had engaged in sexual exploration with each other, flamed by a local doctor who fancied himself an expert on ritual abuse, and culminated in a search for satanic cultists. A small, economically deprived town rife with labor protests and political conflicts, Oude Pekela was ready for a revitalizing moral panic. As people embraced a narrowing interpretation of what happened, they exaggerated information to support their belief and rejected information that disconfirmed it. With that distortion came an amplification of roles: the abusers became more evil, the children more innocent, the rescuers more heroic. The call to public action turned people against local and national institutions when the ritual abusers could not be found. The moral panic dissipated when emotions were spent and the most vocal proponents were discredited by lack of evidence.

◆ **318**   Rossen, B. (1989). Mass hysteria in Oude Pekela. *Issues in Child Abuse Allegations, 1.* Retrieved 4-March-01 from the World Wide Web: http://www.iptforensics.com/journal/volume1/j1_1_6.htm.

It was a moral panic that seized Oude Pekela, not a ritual abuse case. It arose out of shared beliefs in evil ritual abusers and the fears that belief generated, but it served the function of distracting people from local problems and reaffirming their sense of community and cooperation.

◆ **319**   Sheldon, T. (1994). Dutch investigators find no evidence of ritual child abuse. *British Medical Journal, 308*, 1188.

The report of the Ritual Abuse Workgroup in the Netherlands (see citation 321) finds no compelling evidence to substantiate alleged cases of ritual abuse, such as the Oude Pekela case.

◆ **320** Van der Hart, O., & Boon, S. (1990). Contemporary interest in multiple personality disorder and child abuse in the Netherlands. *Dissociation, 3,* 34–37.

Dutch researchers and clinicians are following the trend set by their American counterparts in locating the origin of multiple personality disorder in severe childhood abuse, including ritual abuse. International cooperation in researching and investigating cases of ritual abuse, such as the Oude Pekela case, and their short- and long-term effects on children, is urgently needed.

◆ **321** Werkgroep Ritueel Misbruik (1994). *Report of the Ritual Abuse Workgroup.* The Hague, Netherlands: Ministerie van Justitie.

The investigation of the Ritual Abuse Workgroup formed after the Oude Pekela case finds no compelling evidence to corroborate alleged cases of ritual abuse in the Netherlands. The Workgroup proposes that more productive lines of inquiry are to examine the role the belief systems of investigators' and clinicians' play in generating and shaping ritual abuse allegations, and to assess the role that American experts play in generating European cases. The English translation of the report can be found at the internet URL: http://www.skepsis.NL/rimi.html.

◆ **322** Wessel, I., & Merkenbach, H. (1994). The Oude Pekela investigation. *Maandblad Geestelijke Volksgezonheid, 49,* 555–558.

The unwavering conclusion of Jonker and Jonker-Bakker (see citation 309) that the Oude Pekela case is a genuine case of ritual abuse does not allow them to consider alternative, albeit less dramatic, explanations for what happened in that case that are more consistent with the evidence.

Broxtowe Estate: Nottingham, England

In 1987, a total of 18 children from related families living on a run-down urban estate were taken into care for abuse. Their families were well known to police and social services, and the joint inquiry that resulted in the arrests of ten family members on 53 counts of incest and cruelty was widely praised. The ten eventually were sentenced to a total of 48 years.

The children were made wards of the court and their foster parents were asked to keep diaries of the children's disclosures to be used as evidence in future wardship hearings. In their conversations with their foster parents, some of the children talked not only of incest but of witch parties and infant sacrifices. In biweekly support group meetings the foster parents shared information about these disclosures and when a consulting expert supplied them with a list of ritual abuse indicators, many more of the children began talking about murders, blood-drinking, animal sacrifices, the forced ingestion of spiders and snakes, and orgies with unidentified adults in mansions, cemeteries and tunnels under the city.

Their allegations were corroborated by three adult family members in interviews with social workers.

An intensive police investigation, labeled Operation Gollom, failed to find evidence supporting the children's allegations and, concerned that the diaries would be available to the defense in the criminal trials of the family members, the police refused to investigate any further. Convinced the children had been ritually abused, social workers were outraged and found some vindication of their belief when in a wardship hearing the judge ruled that the children should stay in care because they were at risk for further abuse, possibly of a ritualistic nature.

An attempt to force closure on the rift between social workers and police took the form of a joint inquiry into the case that was completed in December 1989. The 650 page report concluded that while there was evidence the children in the Broxtowe Estate case had been sadistically abused, there was no evidence of ritual abuse and, in fact, no evidence that the type of ritual abuse the social workers pursued in this case even exists at all.

The summary of the findings of the JET Report, as it is known, can be found at the internet URL: http://samsara.law.cwru.edu/complaw/jetrep.htm. A review of the legal action pursuant to Nottingham Council's attempt to ban the posting of the report can be found at the internet URL: http://insight.cas.mcmaster.ca/org/efc/pages/nottingham/index.html.

◆ **323**   Barwick, S. (1990, March 24). Witch story to believe? *The Spectator*, pp. 20–21.
    The joint inquiry into the Broxtowe Estate ritual abuse case dismisses the allegations of ritual abuse and in doing so dismisses the social workers' belief in it. Their director reluctantly accepted the inquiry's conclusion and forbade them to talk about ritual abuse to the press or the public. The social workers object strenuously to the gag order and are hinting it may be part of an attempt to cover up the case. While it is understandable they are indignant at not being believed, it is legitimate to ask difficult questions and to demand proof of the dubious allegations made in this case. Witchcraft indeed may pose a threat to children, but so do witch hunts.

◆ **324**   Campbell, B. (1990, October 19) Hear no evil. *New Statesman and Society*, pp. 10–11.
    Chief Constable Dan Compton is trying to "kill off for once and for all" claims of ritual abuse in the Broxtowe Estate case. The police already quashed the children's evidence when they began naming adults outside of the family as their perpetrators. The contempt of the police violates a Home Office circular that prescribes the relations between police and social services in cases of child abuse, and the procedures to ensure the safety of the children and the preservation of evidence.

◆ **325**   Campbell, B. (1990, October 5). Children's stories. *New Statesman and Society*, p.15.

The investigation into the Broxtowe Estate ritual abuse case seems to raise questions about the nature of children's evidence, but the real problem is about the difficulty in detection. The police treated the children as credible witnesses to incest, but they refused to do so when they alleged ritual abuse. They stopped the investigation when the children talked about ritual abuse in the posh houses of prominent citizens.

◆ **326**   Dawson, J. (1990, October 5). Vortex of evil. *New Statesman and Society*, pp. 12–14.

The author, the lead social worker in the Broxtowe Estate ritual abuse case, speaks out against ritual abuse after 2 years' enforced silence and defends her colleagues. Contrary to public perception, the children's allegations of ritual abuse were not made in disclosure interviews with social workers but in informal conversations with their foster parents. As the stories began corroborating each other the social workers sought consultation on ritual abuse. The implication that they then closed their minds to other explanations is patently ridiculous. They struggled to work with the police who rejected the ritual abuse explanation, but the real conflict came when the police refused to investigate perpetrators outside of the children's family. Over the last year the social workers have found it necessary to defend themselves and the children, and like the children they know what it is to not be believed.

◆ **327**   Dawson, J., & Johnston, C. (1989, March 30). When the truth hurts. *Community Care*, pp. 11–13.

The authors who headed the social work team in the Broxtowe ritual abuse case experienced a considerable personal toll for their involvement. Not only have they been in constant conflict with the police who refuse to treat the ritual abuse allegations seriously, but they have been pilloried by the media and by skeptics, and silenced by their own supervisor. The truth about ritual abuse is horrifying and unsettling, but it must be faced; the silencing and denying only leave more children at risk.

◆ **328**   Lunn, T. (1991, May 9). Confronting disbelief. *Social Work Today*, pp. 18–19.

Social worker Judith Dawson went through a life-changing experience when she led the team that handled the Broxtowe Estate ritual abuse case. She is now working closely with the Ritual Abuse Information Network and Support group (RAINS).

◆ **329**   Nottinghamshire County Council (1990). *The revised joint enquiry (JET) report*. Nottingham, England: Author.

The summary of the 5 volume Joint Enquiry Report on the Broxtowe Estate ritual abuse case concludes there is no evidence to substantiate the ritual abuse claims in this case, and that the claims were the result of both leading and suggestive questioning and the cross-germination occurring when the children, foster parents and social workers interacted with each other. The inquiry recommends: social workers and police develop a process to effectively manage joint inquiries; social workers immediately end their reliance on information on ritual abuse; therapeutic/disclosure interviews by social workers be rigorously examined for their ability to elicit reliable information; foster parents not be used to gather information on ritual abuse; care be taken in recruiting outside experts and consultants; and caution be exercised in eliciting the services of the media. The summary of the report can be found at the internet URL: http://samsara.law.cwru.edu/complaw/jetrep.htm.

Langley Estate: Rochdale, England

In 1989 a developmentally delayed six year old, hiding in a classroom closet, told his teacher he had seen ghosts and witnessed the sacrifices of babies in a local cemetery, a story he repeated to a child protection social worker. His sister, who also was interviewed, confirmed his story and went on to describe meeting pink ghosts and consuming drinks laced with magic powder, but hastened to add that really had happened in a dream. Nonetheless, the boy, his sister and their two siblings were taken into care in March 1990 where they were interviewed repeatedly by a team of social workers, some of whom had recently attended a seminar where they were warned about a nationwide increase in ritual abuse.

Over the months of interviews the children named other children who lived on the rundown Langley Estate as victims. During the summer, social workers staged dawn raids on the estate, removing 16 children from five additional families and taking them into care, citing ritual abuse as their justification. An injunction prevented the parents from seeking publicity about the case and journalists from investigating it.

Interviewed individually and in groups, the children described terrifying rituals conducted by their parents. An intensive criminal investigation found no evidence of ritual abuse and nothing to tie the parents or any others to the allegations. No criminal charges were filed.

The wardship case was heard in late 1990 when a team of social workers, who now had dropped all references to ritual abuse, proceeded with the charge that the children actually had been physically and emotionally abused and neglected by their parents and therefore should be permanently removed from their care. The judge, however, ruled that the stories of the children were incredible and improbable, giving credence to earlier reports that the six year old actually was describing what he had watched on horror videos. Criticizing the social workers for being "so obsessed with their own belief of what the children were saying that they resolved to remove these children without any appraisal of the material they had gathered," he ordered all but four of the children returned to their parents. The Rochdale Council social service director, admitting his department's mistakes, resigned the next day.

◆ **330** Ackroyd, W. (1990). The Orkney and Rochdale cases. *Family Law, 21*, 207–208.

The revised Children Act, set to go into effect in late 1991, very well might have prevented the debacle of the Orkney Islands and Rochdale Langley Estate ritual abuse cases. The Act, however, is far from perfect. Although it affirms that children must have separate legal representation in all court hearings, the question remains as to how well their views actually will be presented by counsel in court; and although courts are mandated to look to the future to determine what actions will be in their best interest, it is very likely that children still will be removed from their families.

♦ **331**   Green, M. (1991, March). Rochdale — The lessons. *Solicitors Journal*, p. 317.

After a 47 day hearing, Justice Brown sharply criticized social workers in the Langley Estate ritual abuse case for failing to videotape the first disclosure interview, properly record further interviews, and take detailed notes of interview questions and answers. He further criticized them for their "reckless" use of anatomically correct dolls that encouraged sexual play by the children; their mistaking the children's descriptions of dreams as reality; and their swearing out inaccurate affidavits that led judges to authorize the removal of the children from their families.

♦ **332**   Jenkins, C.A. (1992). Sociological argument applied to a historical example of deviance: A response to Professor Victor. *Journal of Psychology and Theology, 20*, 254–256.

Victor (see citation 336) fails to consider alternative theoretical paradigms to explain collective behavior, and to link ideology and action. His examination of the Langley Estate case, then, falls short of explaining why a collective response welled up around the allegations of ritual abuse and how that response was sustained over time.

♦ **333**   Jervis, M. (1991, March 21). Judge and fury. *Social Work Today*, pp. 24–25.

The Langley Estate ritual abuse case reveals how social workers can lose their bearings when confronted with complex and bizarre cases. The kind of "disclosure interviews" used in this and other British ritual abuse cases are fraught with problems and increase the danger of misdiagnosis.

♦ **334**   Ogden, J. (1990, November 15). Post-Rochdale study planned. *Social Work Today*, p. 13.

The Social Service Inspectors examined the handling of 30 cases of abuse by Rochdale social services following the public outcry about the Langley Estate ritual abuse case. The report makes 42 recommendations for change, including involving both parents and children in case conferences, and obtaining parents' permission for medical evaluations of their children.

♦ **335**   Rickford, F. (1991, March 21). On record. *Social Work Today*, p. 26.

Justice Brown of the Children's Division of the High Court of Manchester criticized Rochdale social workers for their interviewing techniques with the children in the Langley Estate ritual abuse case, saying that in some cases the videotape was not started until the child began to disclose, and in others the social workers did not even know how to use the equipment. Videotaping interviews has both pros and cons that must be considered by social workers.

♦ **336**   Victor, J.S. (1992). Ritual abuse and the moral crusade against satanism. *Journal of Psychology and Theology, 20*, 248–253.

Allegations of ritual abuse are products of the social construction of an imaginary form of deviance that is being promoted by a moral crusade against satanism. This crusade is exemplified by the Langley Estate case in which the vague allegations of a child were worked into a case of ritual abuse by social workers who found it more entrancing to chase imaginary satanists than deal with real world problems.

♦ **337**   Victor, J.S. (1991). The satanic cult scare and allegations of ritual abuse. *Issues in Child Abuse Accusations, 3*. Retrieved 4-March-01 from the World Wide Web: http://www.ipt-forensics.com/journal/volume3/j3_3_1.htm.

The international ritual abuse moral panic is a product of collective behavior, and the emotions associated with it — fear, outrage and vindictiveness — are legitimated by interest groups and in conferences. The ritual abuse scare persists because it resonates with cultural and professional belief systems, as the Langley Estate case in Rochdale, England illustrates.

Orkney Islands, Scotland

In 1990 a 16 year old whose father was in prison for sexually abusing her and her 14 siblings revealed she and her sister were being sexually abused by their older brothers. Social workers and police launched a joint investigation that, over the vehement protests of their mother, her friends and Rev. Morris McKenzie, eventually resulted in the 16 year old and her seven younger siblings being taken into care. Their subsequent medical examinations revealed signs of chronic, penetrative sexual abuse.

Although forbidden contact, their mother and her friends deluged the children's foster families with letters that soon were being screened for coded messages that warned against disclosure. The suspicion that multiple abusers were involved grew when the 16 year old told her foster parents she was "sexually involved" with Rev. McKenzie.

Social workers and police continued to interview the younger children. One of them eventually disclosed that Rev. McKenzie took children to a quarry where they were made to dance naked in a circle around him. Dressed in a black robe and mask and calling himself "The Master," he would grab them with a crook and sexually assault them. The child identified the singing and chanting adults who also participated in the abuse as the family friends who had protested their removal.

In February 1991, teams of social workers and police descended in dawn raids on four families and removed the nine children named as victims. Rev. McKenzie's home was searched and a black cloak used in funeral services, animal masks and a broken cross were confiscated. He, his wife and the children's parents were interrogated, then released without charge.

Although the medical exams for these children were negative for sexual abuse, they were placed in separate foster homes and denied physical contact with their parents. They were interviewed repeatedly and a few of them confirmed the "circle" account of ritual abuse and added details about blood-drinking and confinement in caskets.

The Children's Panel upheld their removal, but the parents contested its finding that there was sufficient reason to believe the children had been sexually abused and exposed to "moral danger." The children were not present at either of the subsequent Panel hearings at which warrants for their continued placement were issued. The contested finding was referred to the Sheriff (Judge) for proof.

In April 1991 the Sheriff, who heard no evidence, found the Children's Panel proceedings incompetent and ordered the return of the children. Social workers, stung by local criticism of their actions, appealed the decision, although they had no intention of pursuing the case further. The Sheriff's decision was overturned, but not before the children were returned to their families in April 1991.

Two of the children from the initial family adjusted poorly and returned to foster care; both later were adopted by their foster parents.

◆ **338** Black, R.D.T. (1993). *Orkney: A place for safety?* Edinburgh, Scotland: Canongate Press.

From the start of the investigation through adjudication the Orkney Islands ritual abuse case shows the inadequacies in the practice of child protection and the weakness of child protection law in Scotland.

◆ **339** Bruce, A.J. (1991). Orkney — A practitioner's view. *Solicitors Journal, 135,* 432.

The horrific allegations made in the Orkney Islands ritual abuse case, its multiple victims, multiple perpetrators, and the intense media scrutiny of it quickly overwhelmed the resources of a local firm of solicitors, to which the author belongs, and necessitated forging an alliance with other firms on the Islands.

◆ **340** Carlisle, D. (1992, December 9). Storm over Orkney. *Nursing Times,* pp. 14–15.

Four district nurses and health visitors share their concerns about the Orkney Islands ritual abuse case. None was consulted before the children were taken away in dawn raids, and none believes the allegations are true. They provided support to the families of the children and to the small, close-knit community in the wake of the removal of the children, and endured the criticism of island officials for speaking out on behalf of the parents.

◆ **341** Cohen, P. (1992, November 26). Lines of defense. *Social Work Today,* p. 10.

Val Howarth, director of ChildLine, explains in an interview that the greatest lesson social workers can learn from the Orkney Islands ritual abuse case is to exercise strategic thinking and careful planning before acting on their well conditioned instinct to respond to children they suspect are being abused.

◆ **342** Cousin, J., Cousin, G., McGrath, S., & Fine, R. (1991). System abuse of children: The Orkney case. *Probation Journal, 38,* 121–126.

The removal of child from their families in dawn raids in the Orkney Islands ritual abuse case shows how a poorly thought-out policy is a form of system abuse. The children were isolated from their families and each other and stripped of their identities. Requests for culturally relevant fostering for the Quaker and the Jewish children taken in the raids were denied, known dietary requirements neglected, and letters from the children to their parents unsent. In addition, they were subjected to hours of "disclosure interviews" that in their relentless search for details of ritual abuse took the form of interrogations. The Children Act of 1989 is designed to prevent such system abuse, and social workers must be thoroughly trained in its provisions.

♦ **343**   DeCruz, P. (1993). The Orkney affair: Another cautionary tale. *Practitioners Child Law Bulletin, 6*, pp. 7–8.

It is not only the complexity of the Orkney Islands ritual abuse case that poses challenges to lawyers and to the legal system, but the intense media scrutiny and public criticism of the case.

♦ **344**   Ellis, B., Bennett, G., & Hobbs, S. (1993). *The Orkney Islands SRA case: A checklist of British newspaper reports*. St. John's, Newfoundland, Canada: The International Society for Contemporary Legend Research.

The headlines about the Orkney Islands ritual abuse case from Scottish and English newspapers covering the breaking of the case in March 1991 through the official findings of the Clyde Report (see citation 357) made public in December 1992 illustrate the changing focus of reportage on the case, from credulity, to skepticism, to criticism.

♦ **345**   Fager, C. (1991, May). The Orkney case: Quakers caught in a modern satanic witch hunt. *A Friendly Letter,* no. 121. Retrieved 18-February-01 from the World Wide Web: http://www.afriendlyletter.com/afl121.html.

In February 1991, the children of William and Sandra McEwan were taken by social workers in a dawn raid on their Orkney Islands home. The children, ages 11 and 15, were trundled into a waiting van, placed in foster care, interrogated daily about ritual abuse and denied contact with their parents. The McEwans, devout Quakers originally from England, believe they were targeted by social workers because of their defense of a woman whose youngest children were removed for suspected sexual abuse by their older brothers. The British Friends Society sent thousands of letters to the children and in support of the parents; its protest of the case may have had an impact on the recent decision to conduct a formal inquiry.

♦ **346**   Kitzinger, J. (2000). Media templates: Patterns of association and the (re)construction of meaning over time. *Media, Culture and Society, 22*, 61–84.

Some high-profile events become media templates that function as rhetorical shorthand, helping journalists and lay audiences make sense of fresh news stories. The 1987 Cleveland child abuse scandal in which over 100 children were taken into care in northern England for alleged sexual abuse serves as a media template for the Orkney Islands ritual abuse case. As such, it encourages a simplified understanding of the Orkney Islands case that focuses on innocent families torn apart by incompetent social workers.

♦ **347**   Kitzinger, J., & Skidmore, P. (1995). Playing safe: Media coverage of child sexual abuse prevention strategies. *Child Abuse Review, 4*, 47–56.

An analysis of media coverage of child sexual abuse prevention efforts over a year period finds that the majority of the coverage was case-based, much of it focusing on the Orkney Islands ritual abuse case, and generally avoided broader discussions about the abuse of children, both inside and outside of the family, the socioeconomic factors that contribute to it, and the ways it can be prevented.

♦ **348** Lockyear, A. (1994). Interests and advocacy: Identifying the role of safeguarders in the Scottish Children's Hearings. *Children and Society, 8*, 55–68.

The role of the safeguarders, persons appointed to protect the interests of children in Scottish court proceedings, was called into question after the Orkney Islands ritual abuse case. The case shows the need for safeguarders to more actively advocate for the interests and the views of the children they represent.

♦ **349** Reid, D.H.S. (1993). *Suffer the little children: The Orkney child abuse scandal.* St. Andrews, Scotland: The Medical Institute for Research into Child Cruelty.

The Orkney Islands ritual abuse case lays bare the ways in which the Scottish system of child protection fails to protect children and their families. Not only were the allegations in this case extracted by social workers through suggestive and even coercive interviewing, but the children's rights were violated by their exclusion from hearings held by the Children's Panel. To compound the injustice, the Sheriff ordered the return of the children without considering the evidence in the case or giving the Children's Panel Reporter an opportunity to be heard.

♦ **350** Rickford, F. (1992, July 9). Hot seat on the islands. *Social Work Today*, pp. 12–14.

Paul Lee, director of social work on the Orkney Islands, defends the decision to take children from their families in dawn raids in the controversial ritual abuse case. The department acted in good faith and according to statutory guidelines. Although the action to remove the children was a joint operation with the police, the media target the social workers for blame and in doing so play on the public's latent distrust of the profession.

♦ **351** Sutherland, E.E. (1992). The Orkney case. *Juridical Review, 12*, 93–108.

The challenges the Orkney Islands ritual abuse case pose to the system of Children's Panels in Scotland are considerable. The case raises questions about the duties of local authority, the standard of proof for removing children from their homes, the need for preliminary meetings prior to official hearings, the civil rights implications of not allowing children to be present at hearings, and the right of the Sheriff to examine potential evidence prior to a hearing and to dismiss a case without hearing evidence.

♦ **352** Thomson, J. (1993). Children's hearings — A legal perspective after Orkney. In L. Waterhouse (Ed.), *Child abuse and child abusers: Protection and prevention* (pp. 166–177). London: Jessica Kingsley Publishers.

The legal framework in which children's hearings operate in Scotland was shaken by the Orkney Islands ritual abuse case. The case prompts questions about whether the hearing system is able to maintain an acceptable balance between the state's powers and family autonomy, and reveals that the legal framework, itself, rests solely on the professionalism and integrity of the social workers, judiciary and hearing panel members.

◆ **353**   Winter, K. (1992). *The day they took our children away: Ritualistic abuse, social work, and the press.* Norwich, England: Social Work Monographs.

The Orkney Islands ritual abuse case brought out the worst in the social work profession. The sensationalistic media coverage of the case probably deterred the social workers from even more egregious action but it also turned social workers into new folk devils to be vilified by the public.

OFFICIAL INQUIRY AND ITS AFTERMATH

In 1991, the Secretary of State for Scotland appointed James J. Clyde to conduct a full inquiry into the Orkney Islands ritual abuse case. After hearing seven months of testimony from 75 witnesses, Clyde determined that the return of the children was justified, although precipitate, and set out 194 recommendations for improving child protection in Scotland.

◆ **354**   Asquith, S. (Ed.) (1993). *Protecting children. Cleveland to Orkney: More lessons to learn?* Edinburgh, Scotland: HMSO.

One of the unresolved questions emerging from the Clyde Report (see citation 357) is how to establish legal guidelines for the urgent removal of children for their own protection while at the same time recognizing parental rights, particularly the right to challenge the removal of the children. The edited proceedings of a 1992 conference sponsored by Children in Scotland and the National Children's Bureau deal with the tenuous relationship between children's best interests, parental rights and state intervention.

◆ **355**   Black, A. (1993). The Orkney inquiry: A summary of some key comments and recommendations. *Child Abuse Review, 2,* 47–50.

The key recommendations put forth in the Clyde Report (see citation 357) on the Orkney Islands ritual abuse case include: pre-investigative strategy sessions between social workers and police in complex cases; issuance of child protection orders when there is compelling evidence of vulnerability to continued harm in the family; advanced and joint training for social workers and police in interviewing techniques; formation of a pool of skilled consultants; and establishment of better relationships with the media.

◆ **356**   Clyde, J.J. (1993). Orkney revisited: The process of inquiry. *Juridical Review, 13,* 229–246.

The procedural rules for setting up an "investigative inquiry" such as the one the author (see citation 357) conducted in the matter of the Orkney Islands ritual abuse case must take into consideration whether the inquiry should be conducted in a public or private venue, which counsel should be appointed, what terms of remit are to be drawn up, who the parties to the inquiry will be, and how evidence should be presented.

◆ **357**   Clyde, J.J. (1992). *The report of the inquiry into the removal of children from Orkney in February 1991.* Edinburgh, Scotland: HMSO.

The £6 million inquiry into the Orkney Islands ritual abuse case details the chronology of the case and sets out 194 recommendations for improving child protection in

Scotland, social work intervention in complicated and controversial cases, foster care involvement, and reform of the Children's Panels.

◆ **358**   King, M. (1995). Law's healing of children's hearings: The paradox moves north. *Journal of Social Policy, 24*, 315–340.

The Clyde Report (see citation 357) on the Orkney Islands ritual abuse case exposes the paradox at the heart of Children's Panels: social workers are charged with the task of protecting children but sometimes are not given the legal authority to act by the panels. That same paradox was resolved in England by reconstructing child protection into legal terms, and although that is now occurring in Scotland, ambiguities in the Children's Panel system continue to perpetuate the paradox. Systems theory provides a framework for analyzing both the paradox and the evolution in Scottish Children's Panels.

◆ **359**   MacLean, L. (1992, November 19). Secrets and silence. *Social Work Today*, p. 19.

The author, a social worker for the Royal Scottish Society for the Prevention of Child Abuse, interviewed the children after the dawn raids in the Orkney Islands ritual abuse case and believes the Clyde Report (see citation 357) is based on an ignorance of the dynamics of sexual abuse. Her interviews respected and safeguarded the well-being of the children in the case; the kind of interviews the Report recommends as an alternative ignores the real difficulties children have in disclosing and talking about abuse.

◆ **360**   Sutherland, E.E. (1993). Clyde and beyond: The report of the inquiry into the removal of children from Orkney in February 1991. *Juridical Review, 13*, 178–184.

The Clyde Report (see citation 357) into the Orkney Islands ritual abuse case uncovers flaws in the Scottish system of child protection, but the major problems with this case have more to do with the inadequate training of social workers and the paucity of resources available to them. The Clyde Report should be treated as an invitation to Parliament and the Treasury to provide more funding and resources to social workers, and to take a leadership role in implementing the recommendations of the Report.

◆ **361**   Wilson, M. (1992, November 5). Orkney report. *Social Work Today*, p. 14.

The Clyde Report (see citation 357) on the Orkney Islands ritual abuse case is a stinging indictment of social workers, but also sets an agenda for social work practice.

Ayshire, Scotland

In 1990 a child complained his father had slipped into his bed and tickled him. His mother, suspicious that her husband was sexually abusing their sons, had them medically examined but no conclusive evidence of sexual abuse was found. She and the three boys sought refuge in a community shelter where she told social workers that her mother-in-law, the matriarch of a Traveller family that moved around the country to work in fairs, was drugging the children so they could be sexually abused by an "evil ring" of family members.

For protection, she and her sons were sent to live in eastern Scotland where they continued to be interviewed by social workers. Although the children initially disclosed little, when later asked about specific acts of ritual abuse, such as the ingestion of feces and blood, and confinement in cages, they answered in the affirmative, and named family members as perpetrators and cousins as victims.

The three boys and four of their cousins, ranging in age from 10 months to 11 years, were removed from their families by social workers using place of safety orders. They were interviewed repeatedly in individual and group sessions where they talked about the forced extraction of teeth, orgies in graveyards, and a "wise man" who directed the rituals by consulting a "secret book." They named another cousin as a victim. Taken into care, that 10 year old denied any abuse and her medical exam, like that of her cousins, was negative. At the initial hearing of the case, the Sheriff found the children had been sexually abused and that there was evidence of "sinister elements of sadism, ritualism and torture." He referred the case to the Children's Panel and the children were taken into care.

Every petition by the parents for the children's return was denied, although the investigation found no evidence to corroborate the accounts of ritual abuse. In a rare legal move in 1993, the parents persuaded the Court of Session to order a rehearing of the case. That private inquiry, conducted by Sheriff Colin Brown Miller, concluded there was not enough compelling medical evidence to support the allegations of sexual abuse, and no corroborating evidence of ritual abuse. He ordered the return of the children. In 1995, after 5 years in care, seven of the children were returned to their parents; one chose to remain in care.

An external inquiry ordered by the regional council concluded that the social workers in the case were "naïve and gullible" in their belief in ritual abuse, had used "flawed" interviewing techniques, and were "singularly unprepared" for Court testimony, but that they had acted "honestly and in good faith."

◆ **362**   Kelly, A. (1996). *Introduction to the Scottish children's panel.* Winchester, United Kingdom: Waterside Press.

In each Scottish local authority council area, a Children's Panel composed of 3 citizens and a Reporter (Attorney), oversees cases of child maltreatment. The Panel considers the advice of social workers, mental health professionals and educators before deciding what is in the best interest of the children before them. The removal of children from their families on specious evidence in the Ayrshire and the Orkney Islands ritual abuse cases seriously damaged the credibility of Children's Panels and forced them to be more sensitive to the rights of children. Radical reforms still are needed. The Panels should be replaced by a children's court, presided over by a judge with the assistance of panelists, in which children's rights are protected by counsel. Reforms like this will bring Scotland into conformity with international standards set by the United Nations Convention on the Rights of the Child.

◆ **363**   Miller, C.B. (1994). *In the Sheriffdom of South Strathclyde, Dumfries and Ayr: Report*. South Strathclyde, Scotland: Author.

The inquiry ordered into the Ayrshire ritual abuse case by the Court of Session took 152 days to complete and heard testimony from 103 witnesses. The 450 page report of the inquiry sets out a chronology of the case and discusses the legal grounds for referring it to the Children's Panel, the findings in fact, the evidence presented by the child witnesses, their social workers and the expert witnesses. It indicts the social workers for conducting leading and suggestive interviews with the children, and for pursuing single-mindedly the ritual abuse idea. The inquiry concludes that the evidence in this case was so ineptly collected and so contaminated that it is impossible to decide whether any of it is credible; on balance, the case had not been proven. The inquiry concludes that the children should be returned to their families.

Epping Forest, England

In 1990 two sisters, wards of the court and living with their grandparents, disclosed incidents of sexual abuse by their parents. A subsequent medical exam was positive for sexual abuse. Over the next several months the girls, ages 9 and 13, were interviewed by social workers who had just been trained in ritual abuse dynamics by an American expert, Pamela Klein, as well as by Klein, herself. During the interviews they began talking about sexual abuse during rituals near the Gypsy Monument in Epping Forest that included blood-drinking, infant sacrifices and cannibalism. They named their parents, a friend of the family, and their godparents, Rosemary Ridewood and George Gibbard as their ritual abusers. The five were arrested and charged with a total of 20 counts of rape and indecent assault.

Their trial began in 1991. The younger of the girls was the first to testify. Sitting behind a screen and clutching a doll, she acknowledged under cross-examination that while she could remember the sexual abuse, she may have imagined the infant sacrifices and the acts of cannibalism. With nothing more to be entered into evidence, the Judge directed the jury to acquit the defendants on the basis that the case was "uncertain, inconsistent and improbable." In late 1991, just four days into the "Black Magic" trial, the defendants were acquitted of all charges.

The case prompted widespread criticism that the 1991 Criminal Justice Bill that allows children to testify and be cross-examined via live video link-up insufficiently protects them from the trauma of court testimony.

◆ **364**   Anning, V. (1991, November 29). Court out? *New Statesman and Society*, pp. 14–15.

Gibbard and Ridewood, 2 of the defendants in the Epping Forest ritual abuse case, are taking their claims for compensation to the European Court of Human Rights in Strasbourg, France. The charges against the two, both devout Christians, were dismissed 4 days into their trial when one of the accusing girls, 10 years old, stated she imagined her account of infant sacrifice, animal dismemberment and blood-drinking at the site of the memorial to the Gypsy Evangelist in Epping Forest. The collapse of the case raises serious questions about the legal system that brought it to trial in the first place.

Bishop Auckland, England

In 1993 a 14 year old boy was charged with sexually assaulting 6 children. As interviews with social workers and police continued with the children they began making allegations of ritual abuse including orgies, animal sacrifices, voodoo rituals, vaginal and rectal insertions of fish hooks, and devil worship, and also named four neighborhood couples as their ritual abusers: Brian and Pauline Marsh, Robert and Vivienne Crosby, John and Patricia Staines, and David and Victoria Thomas.

During the 17 month investigation police found no corroborating evidence but the four couples and the 14 year old were criminally charged. Their trial began in January 1995 but the prosecution offered no evidence and declared the children were making "palpably false" allegations against the couples because they were afraid of identifying the unknown people who really had abused them. All charges against the couples and the 14 year old then were dismissed.

For an independent report, Dr. Bill Thompson of Reading University assessed hundreds of hours of videotaped interviews and concluded that interviewers ignored information pointing to the innocence of the accused, asked leading questions, and ignored the extent to which the parents of the alleged victims influenced their accounts when meetings between the parents resulted in fresh claims. A Durham County Area Child Protection Committee report, however, defended social workers and police as acting in accordance with "a high standard of practice," and also set out 29 recommendations for improved practice. The Health Secretary rejected calls for a public inquiry into the case.

♦ **365**   Jervis, M. (1995, January 20). Panic over satanic abuse strikes again. *New Statesman and Society*, p. 11.

The collapse of the Bishop Auckland case in which 4 married couples and a 14 year old boy were accused of ritually abusing children as a part of a satanic pornography ring exposes how much of a hold the American-inspired satanic panic still has on the British child welfare and criminal justice systems. The highly touted joint training sessions proposed to prevent cases like this seem only to provide a vehicle to introduce police to social workers' fallacious beliefs about ritual abuse.

Various Studies, United Kingdom

◆ **366**   Bennett, G. (1991). Sex and cannibalism in the service of Satan: A checklist of articles about satanic abuse in the British quality press, February 1989 to October 1990. *Dear Mr. Thoms, 20*, 36–44.

To folklorists, allegations of ritual abuse are contemporary examples of centuries old libel myths that demonize minority groups. The folkloric nature of these allegations is evident in a list of headlines from the British quality press on the subject.

◆ **367**   Bibby, P. (1991, Oct. 3). Breaking the web. *Social Work Today*, pp. 17–19.

The characteristics that differentiate ritual abuse from more prosaic forms of family abuse include its systematic nature, the severity of the abuse itself, and the attending rituals that confuse and terrorize the victims. The spread of ritual abuse cases around the United Kingdom cannot be ignored, and social workers must become aware of its dynamics, and better organized to respond to cases of it.

◆ **368**   Boyd, A. (1991). *Blasphemous rumours: Is satanic ritual abuse fact or fantasy?* London: Fount.

The key to understanding ritual abuse in the United Kingdom is to listen to the children's allegations; they are consistent with allegations made against satanists around the world for a millennium. While some of the details will vary according to place and time, the common threads in these allegations are descriptions of costumes, chants and the invocation of deities, sexual abuse, ritual sacrifices of infants and fetuses, cannibalism, hypnosis and the forced ingestion of drugs. The satanic cults responsible for ritual abuse are well organized and funded, count respectable and influential people as members, and are international in scope.

◆ **369**   Clapton, G. (1993). *The satanic abuse controversy: Social workers and the social work press.* London: University of North London Press.

Between 1989 and 1992, 149 children from 11 British cities were taken from their families by social workers and put into foster care or made wards of the court because of allegations of ritual abuse. The themes that emerge from an analysis of the reporting on these cases by the social work press include: an emphasis on women as ritual abusers; the rise of a new social work orthodoxy that children never lie; and the intrusion of the irrational into social work practice and reporting. The socioeconomic, ideological and professional forces that give rise to the idea of ritual abuse must be taken into account, and the consequences of involvement in ritual abuse cases for the beleaguered social work profession must be considered.

◆ **370**   Core, D. (1991). *Chasing Satan.* London: Gunther Press.

The author, the director of Childwatch, documents her personal crusade to alert a skeptical British society about the nature and extent of ritual abuse. Her investigation reveals that ritual abuse is an exigent threat, affecting tens of thousands of children across the country. The author has lectured widely and consulted on several sensational British ritual abuse cases.

◆ **371**   Dyer, O. (1994). Ritual abuse dismissed as mythical in Britain. *British Medical Journal, 308*, 1527–1528.

The LaFontaine report (see citation 379) finds no evidence corroborating the ritual abuse allegations that have captured so much attention in Great Britain.

◆ **372**   Eaton, L. (1991, September 26). Ritual abuse: Fantasy or reality? *Social Work Today*, pp. 8–11.

There is no doubt that controversial ritual abuse cases in the United Kingdom have confused and divided the public, the press and the social work profession. Despite the lack of a clear definition of ritual abuse, social workers are taking sides on the issue; the believers argue that the extreme emotional distress of survivors is evidence enough of their claims of ritual abuse, while the skeptics counter that in the absence of material evidence the claims should not be believed.

◆ **373**   Harper, J. (1991, December 12). What about the wounded? *Social Work Today*, 99, 20–21.

Social workers working beyond the boundaries of their knowledge in ritual abuse cases throughout the United Kingdom are experiencing a great deal of stress that adversely affects their health, well-being, work, relationships and world view. Organizations must engage in preventive work and damage limitation by supporting their staff and structuring opportunities for them to talk about their experiences and feelings.

◆ **374**   Hayward, J. (1997). Ritual abuse: Trial and error. *Criminologist*, 21, 3–25.

Those who believe in ritual abuse often refer to at least 9 criminal prosecutions in the United Kingdom for the sexual and/or physical abuse of children as conclusive evidence of ritual abuse. The cases, however, are far from conclusive and show the difficulty in defining ritual abuse, especially given the fact that magic and the supernatural have been employed as strategies in acts of abuse that are neither satanic nor ritualistic. The same problems attend to other cases of alleged organized satanic abuse such as the Langley Estate and the Broxtowe Estate cases where it was alleged organized satanic cults were responsible for the abuse. The investigations into these and other British cases, all unproven, have cost the tax payers £25 million.

◆ **375**   Hopkins, J. (1991, October 17). Trial and error. *Social Work Today*, p. 21.

There are 5 ways for social workers to make evidence more credible in ritual abuse cases in the United Kingdom: allow the evidence of ritual abuse to speak for itself; explain how the bizarre features of the case are outside of stated experience; demonstrate open-mindedness and the search for alternative explanations; show adherence to good practice guidelines; and keep meticulous records.

◆ **376**   Jenkins, P. (1992). *Intimate enemies: Moral panics in contemporary Great Britain*. Hawthorne, NY: Aldine deGuyter.

The changing socioeconomic, political and ideological climate of Great Britain during the 1980s generated beliefs that children were being ritually abused. The moral panic that belief generated culminated in several infamous ritual abuse cases in England and Scotland. Far from an isolated event, the British ritual abuse moral panic is discursively and ideologically linked to recent moral panics about pedophile rings, bogus social workers, and serial killers.

◆ **377**   LaFontaine, J.S. (1998). *Speak of the devil: Tales of satanic abuse in contemporary England*. Cambridge, England: Cambridge University Press.

Despite the fact that no corroborating evidence has been found, the belief persists that diabolical satanists pose an exigent threat to English children. There are disturbing parallels between the present day social movement to uncover ritual abuse and historic and contemporary witch hunts around the world and in different cultures. The roots of the current concern about ritual abuse are found in the unsettling socioeconomic and ideological changes in English culture, but the themes of ritual abuse — devil worship, sexual violation, cannibalism, infant sacrifice — are deeply historic and universal.

◆ **378**   LaFontaine, J.S. (1998). Ritual and satanic abuse in England. In N. Scheper-Hughes & Sargent, C. (Eds.), *Small wars: The cultural politics of childhood* (pp. 277–294). Berkeley, CA: University of California Press.

A survey of 116 social service departments and 43 police forces in England finds 84 cases of alleged ritual and satanic abuse between 1988 and 1991, most of them involving young children who variously disclosed sexual abuse by robed and hooded adults, the production of pornography, and animal and human sacrifices. The influence of adult interviewers on the children's accounts cannot be overlooked, but the allegations are best understood as representations of cultural images of evil, and therefore are analogous to historical accusations of witchcraft and blood libel.

◆ **379**   LaFontaine, J.S. (1994). *Extent and nature of organised and ritual abuse: Research findings.* London, England: HMSO.

A survey of police and social service agencies, commissioned by the Department of Health, finds 967 cases of organized abuse in England and Wales over a 4 year period; 85 of those involve allegations of ritual abuse. While substantiated cases of organized abuse comprise only a small percentage of all cases of child abuse, the ritual abuse cases garner the most attention and concern. This is especially problematic because no evidence corroborating these allegations has ever been discovered, and a review of the case files of children made wards of the court shows that their ritual abuse disclosures were influenced and shaped by their adult interrogators. The roles that British evangelical Christians and American experts play in spreading the ritual abuse myth across Great Britain are considered, and the types of cultural axioms the myth resonates with are discussed.

◆ **380**   Pithers, D. (1990, Oct. 4). Stranger than fiction. *Social Work Today*, pp. 20–21.

In the wake of controversial ritual abuse cases in the United Kingdom, training for social workers in child development and in critical thinking skills is urgently needed. Social work management must be radically revised so that it can provide guidance and direction to line staff in complicated and controversial ritual abuse cases.

◆ **381**   Sinason, V. (Ed.) (1994). *Treating survivors of satanist abuse.* London: Routledge.

The 34 short chapters of this edited text cover all aspects of ritual abuse from a British perspective, including its nature and dynamics, its effects on children and adults with childhood histories of it, and the strategies of mental health professionals who treat it and of foster families that provide support.

◆ **382**   Tate, T. (1991). *Children for the Devil.* London: Metheun Press.

The allegations British children are making about ritual abuse in ceremonies including torture, cannibalism and infant sacrifice are consistent with satanic practices documented over 500 years. These children not only must be believed but must be provided with intensive long-term therapy to deal with potentially devastating seque-lae.

◆ **383**   Tate, T. (1991, August 28). Beyond belief. *Nursing Times*, pp. 16–17.

The shift in priority from securing the child's welfare in abuse cases to prosecut-ing the abuser is not without consequence when the abuse is ritualistic, as recent con-troversial court cases attest. Yet, there were at least 6 successful prosecutions for ritual abuse in the United Kingdom over the last decade, demonstrating that judges and juries do understand and accept the notion of ritual abuse. It is imperative. then, that any nurse or health visitor report suspected cases using established child abuse pro-tocols.

◆ **384**   Wilkinson, L.E. (1994). *Burn witch, burn: Media hype and the new inquisition*. Driffield, England: Wyrd Press.

Following several sensational court cases and legal hearings in the United King-dom, the dramatic claims of religious fundamentalists and other passionate experts, and the media hype, the reality of ritual abuse remains unproved. Ritual abuse is a dangerous chimera because it deflects energy and resources from cases of more com-mon forms of abuse, and the inquisition the belief in it has generated is ruining lives and reputations.

◆ **385**   Wood, H. (1990, November 15). Exposing the secret. *Social Work Today*, pp. 18–19.

British social workers must acknowledge and recognize the reality of ritual abuse and support each other as they deal with these controversial cases.

Two Australasian Ritual Abuse Cases

Mr. Bubbles: Sydney, Australia

In 1988 a woman, suspicious that her daughter had been sexually abused, contacted other parents with children enrolled at the private Seabeach Kindergarten and asked them to question their children. She and two other sets of parents who shared her suspicion then informed Sydney, Australia police that Tony Deren, the husband of the center's owner, had sexually abused their children.

The police surveillance of the center provided no information, so parents continued to question their children. One of the children dis-closed that Deren, dressed in a clown costume, took children to a motel across the street, coaxed them into a bath and sexually assaulted them while unidentified adults filmed the abuse. The motel manager agreed that Dawn Deren may have been the woman walking with children through the motel several weeks before. The Derens were then charged with mul-tiple counts of abduction and sexual assault.

A news radio show identified the center and spawned sensational news coverage that prompted other parents of enrollees to demand that their children be interviewed and medically examined. A probationary constable assigned to interview the children quickly became overwhelmed, so the Chief of Detectives developed a pro forma set of questions for parents to ask their children. As the children made more disclosures, two of the center's teachers, Louise Bugg and Rima Muir, also were arrested.

Angry with the pace of the "Operation Bubbles" investigation, the parents of the 17 children identified as victims formed the action group Parents Against Child Abuse. They met frequently and discussed the details of the case, including the allegations of ritual abuse that were emerging in the interviews of the children with a consulting psychiatrist. In those interviews, the children were talking about devil worship, blood-drinking, forced ingestion of drugs, cannibalism as well as animal sacrifices.

In 1989 a preliminary hearing was held to determine the competency of the children to testify as witnesses in the trial. Testifying for the defense, Ralph Underwager stated that young children are unreliable witnesses and the poorly conducted police interviews further compromised the integrity of their accounts. The Magistrate agreed. Ruling that the children's evidence was inadmissible because of excessive interference by the police and the parents, he directed the prosecutor to withdraw the 54 charges against the four defendants.

In the wake of the dismissal, the controversy burgeoned. In a television interview Deren admitted that he had previously pled guilty to sexually assaulting two young girls, was fined and ordered to receive psychiatric treatment. A fundamentalist Christian, Deren also claimed that Satan had entered his body and pitched him in a battle between good and evil. Expert witness Ralph Underwager was unflatteringly portrayed in a 1990 *Australia 60 Minutes* segment as a hired gun with dubious credentials. A transcript of that segment can be found at the internet URL: http://www.nostatusquo.com/ACLU/NudistHallofShame/MrBubbles.html. Underwager responded with a flurry of defamation lawsuits. In testimony before the Wood Royal Commission that reviewed the case, psychiatrist Ann Schlebaum admitted she had misrepresented some of the children's ritual abuse allegations to their parents who received $A500,000 from the Accident Compensation Board for a case that the Commission described as "a debacle."

♦ **386**   Cooke, J. (1998, February 21). $950,000 damages for couple in Mr. Bubbles case. *ABIX: Australasian Business Intelligence*, p. 22.

The Supreme Court upheld the $A948,558 in damages awarded to Tony and Dawn Deren in their defamation suit against the New South Wales Police Service. The Derens sued the police for issuing details about the Mr. Bubbles ritual abuse case that allowed them to be publicly identified and that asserted their guilt before trial.

◆ **387**   Hatty, S.E. (1991). Of nightmares and sexual monsters: Struggles around child abuse in Australia. *International Journal of Law and Psychiatry*, *14*, 255–267.

Data from various studies conducted in welfare and hospital settings in New South Wales, Australia, reveal the persistence of the ideology that women are responsible not only for the welfare of their families, but the abusive behaviors of their husbands or male partners, and that women who abuse their children are mentally disturbed. That ideology also is evident in the media accounts of the Mr. Bubbles case where the mother who was the first to report abuse was depicted as psychotic, allowing the media to proceed with the assumption that the case was nothing more than the mass hysteria that grew up around the bizarre allegations of an unbalanced mother. The persistence of this ideology in welfare and medical settings as well as in the media renders men's abusive behavior invisible and makes appropriate solutions to child abuse elusive.

◆ **388**   Schmertz, J.R., & Meier, M. (1996, January). In case of first impressions, Ninth Circuit holds in defamation case brought by public figure. *International Law Update*, p. 1.

Two American attorneys allegedly defamed psychologist Ralph Underwager on an *Australia 60 Minutes* segment on the Mr. Bubbles ritual abuse case. Australian physician Kim Oates, who examined the children in that case, showed the segment at a California conference. Underwager unsuccessfully sued, and then appealed the ruling, arguing that 1st Amendment protections do not apply to Oates because he is not an American citizen. The court ruled in Oates' favor, finding that free speech protections apply to Australian citizens legally present in the United States.

◆ **389**   Wood, J.R.T. (1996). *Royal Commission into the New South Wales Police Service*. Sydney, Australia: Royal Commissioner.

This 6 volume inquiry examines police corruption and pedophilia investigations in New South Wales, Australia. Chapter 5 of volume 4 discusses the difficulties posed by ritual abuse allegations. Chapter 7 of volume 4 discusses the Mr. Bubbles case. The report concludes that the case was "a debacle," due to the lack of training of investigating officers, the use of a probationary constable as an interviewer, the multiple interviews conducted with the children, the use of parents as interviewers, the unauthorized use of hypnosis in an interview with a 3 year old, inattention to the discrepancies in the children's accounts, and the failure to assess the role the consulting psychiatrist played in generating the ritual abuse details. The Commission makes no finding of guilt or innocence in the Mr. Bubbles case, concluding that "the trail is too old, the evidence of the children too contaminated, and there was nothing the Commission could find to independently corroborate or disprove the matters raised." The report can be found at the internet URL: http://www.premiers.nws.gov.au/pubs.htm.

Civic Creche: Christchurch, New Zealand

In 1991 a parent reported her son had been sexually abused by Peter Ellis, a provider at the Civic Creche. The boy did not repeat the allegation to the police so no criminal charges were filed. As rumors spread,

Creche officials recommended that parents have their children evaluated by a psychologist.

Some did, but none of their children disclosed anything initially. At a follow-up interview, however, one of them revealed she, too, had been molested by Ellis. The re-opened investigation still could find no evidence, but many of the parents became adamant that it continue when the media reported that the police suspected as many as 200 children were victims. When frantic parents met with the police, they were urged to question their own children and then take them to social welfare workers for further disclosure interviews.

Inundated with referrals, social welfare workers began identifying many more victims, leading to the arrest of Ellis on 30 counts of sexual abuse. Charges also were filed against Creche supervisor Gaye Davidson, and providers Jan Buckingham, Debbie Gillespie and Marie Keys who were named as perpetrators by some of the children; these charges later were dropped for lack of evidence. The Creche was closed and the 13 remaining providers were dismissed from employment.

As the interviews continued, some of the 80 children identified as victims began talking about ritual abuse. They described the consumption of urine and feces, confinement in cages, the sacrifice of a child named Andrew, abuse in tunnels, cemeteries and Masonic lodges. They described the "circle incident" in which they were taken to a private home and made to stand naked and kick each other in the genitals while adults danced around them.

Ellis's trial began in 1993. He was convicted of 16 charges and acquitted of 9; 3 charges were dismissed during the trial. He was sentenced to 10 years. Three of the charges involving a child who later recanted were overturned, but in a second review of the case the Court of Appeals upheld the remaining charges. That decision can be found at the internet URL: http://www.austlii.edu.au/nz/cases/NZCA/1999/226.html. Ellis was released from prison in February 2000. An inquiry into the case is in progress.

◆ **390**   Bander, J. (1997). *A mother's story: The Civic Creche child sex trial.* Auckland, New Zealand: Howling at the Moon.

An account by the pseudonymous mother of a 6 year old who was one of the key witnesses in the Civic Creche ritual abuse trial. She tells about how her son began to unfold a story of ritual abuse, including torture, confinement and human sacrifice, his experiences at the trial, and both his and her own dissatisfaction with the 10 year sentence imposed on Peter Ellis.

◆ **391**   Barnett, J., & Hill, M. (1993). When the Devil came to Christchurch. *Australian Religion Studies Review*, 6, 25–30.

Allegations of ritual abuse in the Civic Creche case can be analyzed from a sociological perspective. That perspective shows that childhood has become a symbolic focus of stress caused by female participation in the work force, and gender role changes in the home. That stress, combined with representations of satanic evil promulgated by religious fundamentalists and social workers and mental health professionals who unthinkingly accept it, created the new threat of ritual abuse.

◆ **392**   Goodyear-Smith, F. (1993). Civic Creche case, Christchurch. *Issues in Child Abuse Accusations, 5*. Retrieved 4-March-01 from the World Wide Web: http://www.ipt-forensics.com/journal/volume5/j5_4_3.htm

The Civic Creche ritual abuse case follows the pattern set by the American day care ritual abuse cases: a concerned parent interprets the child's symptoms or behaviors as indicative of sexual abuse and activates an investigation by authorities; repeated interrogations of the child eventually lead to allegations of ritual abuse and the naming of other children as victims and other adults as perpetrators; the absence of evidence does not impede the momentum of the investigation that foments public outrage and results in a criminal trial. The Civic Creche case was expensive: it cost $A1 million to bring to trial; over $A500,000 was paid to parents by the Accident Compensation Board; $A200,000 was paid as redundancy compensation for the providers who lost their jobs and who are now suing for additional $A3 million.

◆ **393**   Hill, M. (1998). Satan's excellent adventure in the Antipodes. *Issues in Child Abuse Accusations, 10*. Retrieved 4-March-01 from the World Wide Web: http://www.ipt-forensics.com/journal/volume10/j10_9.htm.

The importation of the ritual abuse scare to New Zealand is due to American "experts" whose conference presentations and published materials influenced Australasian professionals to start a witch hunt. Notable among them are Kee MacFarlane, of McMartin Preschool fame, and Roland Summit, a psychiatrist who consulted on many of the American day care cases; both gave papers on ritual abuse at the International Conference on Child Abuse and Neglect in Sydney, Australia in 1986. Pamela Klein, an American who was instrumental in starting the ritual abuse panic in England, spoke at a conference in New Zealand. In response to these presentations, the Ritual Abuse Action Network was formed. It was a workshop presented by that group in a Christchurch child abuse conference that fomented the hysteria that led to the Civic Creche case.

◆ **394**   McLoughlin, D. (1996, Aug.). Second thoughts on the Christchurch Civic Creche case: Has justice failed Peter Ellis? *North and South*, pp. 54–59, 61–63, 65–66, 68–69.

The uncorroborated evidence of young children should have made the prosecutors and the judge in the Peter Ellis trial more cautious. Had the jury been allowed to hear testimony about the intensity of the parental hysteria over ritual abuse that created many of the allegations, and the tapes that demonstrate how seriously flawed interview techniques elicited the grisly tales of ritual abuse from the children, it never would have found Ellis guilty beyond a reasonable doubt.

Various Studies, Australia

◆ **395**   Guilliatt, R. (1996). *Talk of the Devil*. Melbourne, Australia: Text Publishing Co.

The hysteria over ritual abuse and repressed memories began sweeping across Australia in the late 1980s. Court records, media accounts and investigative documents, the responses of psychotherapists, social workers, police, lawyers and juries to these claims are testimony not only to the controversy they have caused, but the complicated belief structure that supports them. While ritual abuse is being debated in Australia, lives are being ruined: people are being falsely accused, patients are having their biographies gerrymandered by overzealous therapists, and the credibility of the professions of mental health and social work is being undermined.

5

Clinical Features of Ritual Abuse: Children

Sexual abuse was "discovered" in the 1970s when feminists and others turned the hot light of public scrutiny on the dirty little secrets of family life. Once discovered, sexual abuse colonized Western consciousness—it was talked about, revealed to others, debated, assessed, analyzed, represented, portrayed, punished and treated. And out of that cacophonous discourse and nearly frenetic activity emerged some simple yet dearly held truths: children never lie about sexual abuse and, if they are too young or too frightened or too confused, their symptoms will tell their stories—the worse they are, the more horrible was the sexual abuse.

Even simple truths like this are disputed, of course, but they became the stuff of controversy a decade later when it was ritual abuse that children began disclosing. To Western culture, so accustomed by this time to the mundane horror of sexual abuse and all of its consequences, the Gothic horror of ritual abuse called for another look at those simple truths that had become the bedrock of clinical assessment and public intervention.

The citations from the clinical literature that follow debate those simple truths. Do children lie after all, and if they do, do they lie about something as ghastly as ritual abuse? If they do lie, are they really just honest lies, formed in response to what they perceive as the expectations of their older and wiser confidantes? If the simple truth holds that the worst symptoms are produced by the worst abuse, then what kind of sequeale can be expected for children who have been ritually abused? And, if there was no abuse after all, are the symptoms, just like the allegations, nothing more than responses to those who believe them to be true?

DISCLOSURE AND THE SPECTER
OF FALSE ALLEGATIONS

Children rarely, if ever, spontaneously disclose ritual abuse. The case studies and the citations in the chapters on the American day care, family and community-based cases, as well as on the international cases are illustrative of that point. In those chapters the word "eventually" serves as a kind of semiotic semaphore to signal the passage of weeks, months and, in a few cases, even years before the children in the cited cases revealed the details of ritual abuse. And that begs the question: how should the delay in disclosure be understood? Does disclosure occur only after children slowly have peeled away layers of fear, confusion and secrecy that surround ritual abuse or, perhaps, only after they have been convinced by their confidantes that it was indeed ritual abuse they had experienced?

♦ **396**   Bitz, M. (1990). The impact of ritualistic abuse for sexually abused children and their adoptive families. In J. McNamara & B.H. McNamara (Eds.), *Adoption and the sexually abused child* (pp. 119–130). Portland, ME: University of Southern Maine.

Ritually abused children present with fear, anxiety, grief and shame that often interfere with their ability to disclose promptly and completely. Adoptive parents can facilitate disclosure of the details of ritual abuse by providing constant reassurance and support to the children.

♦ **397**   Bradway, B. (1993). Ritual sexual abuse. *School Intervention Report, 7,* 1–10.

Ritual abuse occurs in a variety of settings including families and day care centers; although it has devastating psychological sequelae for children, including eating disorders, homicidal urges and substance abuse, it is the most difficult type of child abuse for mental health professionals and educators to detect. Children fear the consequences of disclosure, and the larger institutional and cultural contexts of skepticism about the authenticity of ritual abuse only enhance that fear.

♦ **398**   Bravos, Z. (1993). Iatrogenically induced personality disorder and ritual abuse memories in a 10-year-old child. *Issues in Child Abuse Accusations, 5.* Retrieved 4-March-01 from the World Wide Web: http://www.ipt-forensics.com/journal/volume5/j5_4_5.htm.

During an attempted exorcism of a 10 year old by her mother, who was recovering her own memories of ritual abuse, the child disclosed that she, too, had been ritually abused. She was then hospitalized and during recovered memory therapy began demonstrating alter personalities that led to the diagnosis of multiple personality disorder. She also disclosed that her father was a member of the cult that ritually abused her. The court ordered the parents to have no contact with their daughter during the ensuing investigation. Segments of the *in camera* hearing that took place when her father filed for visitation rights illustrate the devastating effects of iatrogenically induced memories and multiple personality disorder, as well as of false allegations.

♦ **399**   Garven, S., Wood, J.M., & Malpass, R.S. (2000). Allegations of wrongdoing: The effects of reinforcement on children's mundane and fantastic claims. *Journal of Applied Psychology, 85,* 38–50.

Reinforcement, a specific component of the McMartin Preschool ritual abuse case interviews, is examined with a sample of 120 children between the ages of 5 and 7. Reinforcement elicits 3 times more false allegations against a classroom visitor than simple questions alone, and 10 times more agreement that a fantastic event occurred, in this case being taken from the school in a helicopter, than simple questions alone. The findings indicate that reinforcement can swiftly induce children to make persistent false allegations as it did in the McMartin Preschool ritual abuse case.

♦ **400**   Garven, S., Wood, J.M., Malpass, R.S., & Shaw, J.S. (1998). More than suggestion: The effect of interviewing techniques from the McMartin Preschool case. *Journal of Applied Psychology, 83,* 347–359.

Child interviewing techniques derived from the interview transcripts of the children in the McMartin Preschool case elicit almost 4 times more false allegations from preschool children about a classroom visitor than simple suggestive questions alone. The SIRR model is set out to explain how false statements are elicited through suggestive questions, social influence, reinforcement and removal from direct experience.

♦ **401**   Gonzalez, L.S., Waterman, J., Kelly, R.J., McCord, J., & Oliveri, M.K. (1993). Children's patterns of disclosures and recantations of sexual and ritualistic abuse allegations in psychotherapy. *Child Abuse & Neglect, 17,* 281–289.

A sample of 63 ritually or sexually abused children, all currently in therapy, reveals the processes of disclosure and recantation. The majority (76%) of the sexually abused children disclosed within the first month of therapy, but it took an average of 5 months for the ritually abused children to disclose. Although 17 (27%) of the ritually abused children recanted their disclosures, most later redisclosed and in doing so revealed even more horrific types of abuse. Recantation appears to be a reaction to the children's negative experiences with the legal system.

♦ **402**   McFarland, R.B., & Lockerbie, G. (1994). Difficulties in treating ritually abused children. *Journal of Psychohistory, 21,* 429–434.

The cases of 4 children illustrate the challenges mental health professionals face in dealing with ritual abuse, especially in the climate of cultural and professional skepticism that it exists. Two of the children are siblings who were referred after having been sexually abused by their older siblings. In therapy the older of them spontaneously recalled ritual abuse by black-robed adults in a church basement; these memories then were confirmed by his sister. A 9 year old spontaneously recalled black-robed relatives who sacrificed an infant. She was so hysterical upon disclosure that she had to be hospitalized. A 10 year old also spontaneously recalled ritual abuse by relatives. All of the cases were difficult to treat; they also demonstrate that in a credulous and supportive therapeutic climate, children will disclose ritual abuse.

ASSESSMENT AND THE SPECTER OF MISDIAGNOSIS

The controversy over the veracity of ritual abuse disclosures by children has consistently stymied efforts to introduce a new diagnosis, such as the much discussed "cult and ritual abuse trauma disorder," into standard psychiatric nosologies like the *Diagnostic and Statistical Manual of Mental Disorders (DSM)*. A diagnosis requires both a reliable concept and diagnostic criteria that are robust and sensitive enough to identify all true cases and to distinguish them from other similar cases. Ritual abuse provides none of that. Therefore, the process of assessing alleged cases of it is not only complicated but controversial, if only for the specter of misdiagnosis that surrounds it.

♦ **403**   Bernet, W., & Chang, D.K., (1997). The differential diagnosis of ritual abuse allegations. *Journal of Forensic Sciences, 42,* 32–3.

A review of 60 articles, chapters and books reveals behaviors that represent, or can be mistaken for, ritual abuse: pseudo-rituals, satanic abuse, repetitive psychopathological abuse, sexual abuse by pedophiles, child pornography, adolescent behavior simulating ritual abuse, distorted memory, false memory, pseudologia phantastica, deliberate lying, false reports due to mental illness, hoaxes, and mass hysteria.

♦ **404**   Cozolino, L. (1990). Ritualistic child abuse, psychopathology and evil. *Journal of Psychology and Theology, 18,* 218–237.

Ritual abuse is an extreme form of child maltreatment conducted by cultists in the context of satanic ceremonies. It produces complex psychological, emotional, cognitive and spiritual sequelae that challenge treatment. The challenge to assessment, however, is that the very ideal of ritual abuse requires mental health professionals to accommodate within their world views the disturbing link between the familiar psychological concepts of psychopathology and what is likely to be the unfamiliar theological notion of evil.

♦ **405**   Goodman, G.S., Quas, J.A., Bottoms, B.L., Qin, J., Shaver, P.R., Orcutt, H., & Shapiro, C. (1997). Children's religious knowledge: Implications for understanding satanic ritual abuse allegations. *Child Abuse & Neglect, 21,* 1111–1130.

A sample of 48 children, evenly distributed between age groups 3–4, 7–8, 11–12, and 15–16 years, participated in structured interviews designed to assess their knowledge of religion and religious worship, religion-related symbols and pictures, and movies, music and television shows with religious and horror themes. Although few of the children have direct knowledge of ritual abuse, many have general knowledge about satanism and satanic worship. Increased exposure to nonsatanic horror media is associated with more nonreligious knowledge that can be considered a precursor to satanic knowledge. Increased exposure to satanic media is associated with more knowledge about satanism. The findings suggest that children do not generally have sufficient knowledge of satanic ritual abuse to independently fabricate convincing allegations of it, but many have just enough knowledge about satanism and satanic worship to confound the assessment process.

♦ **406**   Johnson, C.F. (1990). Inflicted injury versus accidental injury. *Pediatric Clinics of North America, 37*, 791–814.

Medical personnel often find it difficult to differentiate inflicted from accidental injuries in children. Physicians must improve their skills in assessing factors that put children at risk for injury, including the systematic assaults and acts of torture they experience during ritual abuse.

♦ **407**   Kelley, S.J., Brant, R., & Waterman, J. (1993). Sexual abuse of children in day care centers. *Child Abuse & Neglect, 17*, 71–89.

Allegations of sexual abuse in day care pose unique challenges to mental health professionals because they typically allege multiple victims, multiple perpetrators, bizarre ritualistic acts and severe threats to prevent disclosure. Ritually abused children experience more and more severe symptoms than do sexually abused children, and their parents experience more stress than do parents of sexually abused children. Ritually abused children also are more reluctant to disclose the details of their abuse and often do not have the kind of language and memory development necessary for full and convincing disclosure. The implications of all of this for clinical intervention with ritually abused children and their families are considerable.

♦ **408**   Kinscherff, R., & Barnum, R. (1992). Child forensic evaluation and claims of ritual abuse or satanic activity: A critical analysis. In D.K. Sakheim & S.E. Devine (Eds.), *Out of darkness: Exploring satanism and ritual abuse* (pp. 73–107). NY: Lexington.

The forensic evaluation of children who are alleged ritual abuse victims can generate information that eventually will lead to legal action on behalf of the child or against an alleged perpetrator. The evaluation process begins with a sophisticated and rigorous assessment and analysis of the information about the case obtained from various sources, including law enforcement. Evaluators must be familiar with the general literature on ritual abuse as well as on the dynamics of cults. Interviews with the children must be conducted in ways that avoid the problems often found in ritual abuse cases of leading and suggestion. Evaluators should be aware that empirical studies on ritual abuse sequelae are rare, but that frequently reported sequelae include post-traumatic stress disorder. There is a great deal of uncertainty in the assessment process, and evaluators must avoid the temptation to over-interpret ambiguous data and get lost in the relentless pursuit of details about the alleged ritual abuse.

♦ **409**   Mandell, H.E., Schiff, M. (1993). Schizophrenia or terrifying reality? A supervisor's dilemma. *Clinical Supervisor, 11*, 127–133.

The case of a 16 year old male demonstrates how careful supervision can work through a diagnostic dilemma. Initially diagnosed as schizophrenic on the basis of projective test findings, the clinical supervisor later discovered that he had a previously undisclosed history of ritual abuse. Test results then were reinterpreted and the diagnosis of schizophrenia was reconsidered.

♦ **410**   Nurcombe, B., & Unutzer, J. (1991). The ritual abuse of children: Clinical features and diagnostic reasoning. *Journal of the American Academy of Child and Adolescent Psychiatry, 30*, 272–275.

A 5 year old girl, ritually abused by her parents and currently in foster care, exhibits attacks of rage, over-familiarity with strangers, inability to concentrate, and delays in language and conceptual development. Her parents deny the ritual abuse but confirm her sexual abuse by a neighbor; they ascribe the ritualistic elements of her disclosure to emotional instability and exposure to horror videos. From an assessment point of view, however, she can be confidently evaluated as having been ritually abused as part of her parents' satanic belief system, because she disclosed spontaneously, shows indicators of both sexual abuse and ritual abuse, and is not delusional.

♦ **411**   Valente, S.M. (2000). Controversies and challenges of ritual abuse. *Journal of Psychosocial Nursing and Mental Health Services, 38*, 8–17.

Ritually abused children endure extreme sexual, physical and psychological trauma that forces them to cope through denial, self-hypnosis, dissociation and self-mutilation. What differentiates ritual abuse from other types of child abuse is its context. Occurring within a community of abusers that may include parents and family members, victimized children learn early to trust no one and to see their world as hostile and threatening. Unlikely to disclose the ritual abuse, they must be carefully assessed. Because of their frequent contacts with hospitalized children, nurses can play an important role in case-finding and assessment.

♦ **412**   Valente, S.M. (1992). The challenge of ritualistic child abuse. *Journal of Child and Adolescent Psychiatric and Mental Health Nursing, 5*, 37–46.

Children cope with the trauma of ritual abuse through denial, self-hypnosis, dissociation and in extreme cases through multiple personality disorder and/or self-mutilation. Because their trauma is often confounded by forced ingestion of mind-altering drugs, children often find it difficult to talk about their experiences. Nurses, then, have to assess the subtle cues in their behavior and in the content of their flashbacks, and must monitor their own attitudes about ritual abuse and guard against countertransference.

♦ **413**   Wakefield, H., & Underwager, R. (1992). Assessing credibility of children's allegations in ritual sexual abuse allegations. *Issues in Child Abuse Accusations, 4*. Retrieved 2-February-01 from the World Wide Web: http://www.ipt-forensics.com/journal/volume4/j4_1_6.htm.

In determining the veracity of children's allegations of ritual abuse, it is critical to assess the degree of adult influence on their disclosures. When adults believe ritual abuse is a real possibility, and repeatedly interview children in such a way as to confirm that belief, they shape and reinforce children's stories.

♦ **414**   Weir, I.K., & Wheatcroft, M.S. (1995). Allegations of children's involvement in ritual sexual abuse: Clinical experience of 20 cases. *Child Abuse & Neglect, 19*, 491–505.

Using a standard format for assessing the validity of sexual abuse allegations, 20 cases of alleged ritual abuse are analyzed. The standard format assesses the nature of the allegation, the presence of sexualization, the presence of risk factors for sexual abuse, nonspecific signs and symptoms, forensic and medical evidence, and the presence of risk factors for false allegations. On the basis of that format, 15 of the 20 ritual abuse allegations are assessed as false. The very notion of ritual abuse is so compelling that many professionals abandon well established procedures for evaluation and assessment when they suspect it, leading to false positive identifications.

THE RITUAL ABUSE SEQUELAE CONTROVERSY

Much of the "stuff" that passes as research on ritual abuse, and that continues to this day to circulate through the labyrinthine communication and conference networks that link professionals of various stripes and advocates around the world, is comprised of so-called "symptom lists." These catalogues of horror that purport to be inventories of the sequelae of ritual abuse certainly have contributed to the problem of misdiagnosis, if only because of their powerful confirmatory effect: all of the symptoms listed appear to have equal weight, so that any one, or any combination, can be taken as an indicator of ritual abuse.

Over the last twenty years, a dozen or more of these lists have appeared, none exactly like any other. While the differences between them are curious, the even greater disparity between any of them and the findings of thorough case studies and empirical studies is remarkable as the following citations, a somewhat eclectic mix of lists, cases and research, illustrate.

◆ **415**   Ben-Meir, S.L. (1989). Emotional functioning in children alleging ritualistic sexual abuse in preschool. *Dissertation Abstracts International, 50* (12-B), 5873. (University Microfilms No. AAG90-05174)

The emotional sequelae of ritual abuse in preschool were assessed for 55 children between the ages of 6 and 11; their responses to a battery of psychological tests were compared to a matched group of 28 non-abused children. The ritually abused children show significantly more emotional problems, including pervasive anxiety and fearfulness, aggressive acting out, depression, extreme defensiveness and avoidant coping.

◆ **416**   Burgess, A.W., Hartman, C.R., & Baker, T. (1995). Memory presentations of childhood sexual abuse. *Journal of Psychosocial Nursing, 33,* 9–16.

In this case study, the memories of abuse of 10 children ritually abused in day care are compared to those of 13 sexually abused in a family run day care and 11 sexually abused by unrelated day care providers. Four different types of memory are noted for each group over time: somatic, behavioral, verbal and visual.

◆ **417**   Caradonna, M. (1992). Ritual child abuse. *Dissertation Abstracts International, 52* (10-B), 5519. (University Microfilms No. AAD92-09147)

An in-depth survey eliciting descriptive data on ritually abused children was administered to 12 mental health professionals identified by their peers as experts on sexual abuse. A clinical profile of ritually abused children is revealed: they have more severe signs and symptoms of post-traumatic stress disorder and dissociation, disclose more severe and bizarre features of abuse, and have more disturbed free play than do other traumatized children. The surveyed mental health professionals use a broad range of therapeutic media to interact with ritually abused children and find traditional modes of child therapy inadequate to the task.

◆ **418**   Cozolino, L.J. (1989). The ritual abuse of children: Implications for clinical practice and research. *Journal of Sex Research, 26*, 131–138.

Ritually abused children, according to case studies, exhibit a wide range of seque-lae, including fears and phobias, eating disorders, obsessions, aggression, hyperactiv-ity, multiple personalities, and a variety of behavior problems. Clinicians and researchers are encouraged to become more aware of ritual abuse so that a sophisti-cated and tested classification system of symptoms can be developed and prognostic outcomes can be assessed.

◆ **419**   Edwards, L.M. (1990). Differentiating between ritual assault and sexual abuse. *Journal of Child and Youth Care, 6*, 67–89.

Ritual abuse can be differentiated from sexual abuse through the presentation of symptoms. These symptoms often are related to menstrual periods and include dis-tress at the sight of blood, fear of confined spaces and the dark, fear of being killed, and preoccupations with phases of the moon.

◆ **420**   Ehresaft, D. (1992). Preschool child sex abuse: The aftermath of the Presidio case. *American Journal of Orthopsychiatry, 62*, 234–244.

Using process notes and evaluation records from the assessment and treatment of 2 young girls victimized at the Presidio Child Development Center, the sequelae of ritual abuse for the children, their parents and the family systems are examined. Both of the children present with sleep disturbances, sexually inappropriate behaviors, tem-per outbursts, magical thinking and sudden mood shifts. The reactions of their par-ents diverge along gender role lines: their mothers report reactive depression and pervasive feelings of failure in their maternal role; the fathers report rage and feelings of emasculation for failing to protect their daughters. The sense of betrayal by the mil-itary is pervasive both in family systems and the larger community.

◆ **421**   Fewster, G. (Ed.) (1990). *In the shadow of Satan. The ritual abuse of children.* Calgary, Alberta, Canada: University of Calgary Press.

This compilation of articles from a special issue of the *Journal of Child and Youth Care* examines the nature and dynamics of ritual abuse, its medical and psychologi-cal sequelae, and strategies for its successful treatment.

◆ **422**   Gould, C. (1992). Diagnosis and treatment of ritually abused children. In D.K. Sakheim & S.E. Devine (Eds.), *Out of darkness: Explor-ing satanism and ritual abuse* (pp. 207–248). NY: Lexington.

The major impediment to diagnosing ritual abuse is that children rarely sponta-neously disclose it. Mental health professionals, therefore, must be aware of the wide array of signs and symptoms of ritual abuse that can be categorized under the head-ings of: sexual behaviors and beliefs; toilet and bathroom problems; supernatural, occult and religious beliefs; fears of small spaces and of being tied up; obsessions with death; fears about medical examinations; preoccupations with certain colors; eating problems; emotional problems including sleep, speech and learning problems; difficul-ties in maintaining family relationships; difficulties in play and peer relations; gener-alized fears and strange beliefs. The treatment of choice for ritually abused children is play therapy which addresses the nature of the ritual abuse, the sensations it cre-ates, its emotional impact, and the indoctrinated cult-related messages. Successful treatment strategies have as their goal the resolution of trauma as well as the identi-fication and healing of the dissociative system that cult indoctrination produces in rit-ually abused children.

♦ **423**   Hudson, P.S. (1991). *Ritual child abuse: Discovery, diagnosis and treatment*. Saratoga, CA: R&E Publishers.

A telephone survey of parents whose children were ritually abused in day care facilities in 5 states finds that the children report similar experiences, including sexual abuse, death threats, forced drug ingestion, confinement in coffins, animal sacrifices, mock marriages to the devil, and infant sacrifices. According to the parents' reports, all of the children experienced post-traumatic stress disorder, with severe separation anxiety, phobias, hyperaggression, somatic symptoms and eating disorders.

♦ **424**   Hudson, P.S. (1990). Ritual child abuse: A survey of symptoms and allegations. *Journal of Child and Youth Care, 6*, 27–53.

A telephone survey of parents whose children were ritually abused in day care facilities in 5 states reveals that all 11 of the children in the sample present with post-traumatic stress disorder and experience severe separation anxiety, refusal to sleep alone, and fear of the dark. Another cluster of symptoms includes extreme fear of the bathroom, bathing and/or the rain, hyperaggression and eating disorders. Vomiting and somatic symptoms occur for 8 of the 11 children. Most of the children report having witnessed the torture of children, the mutilation of animals and the sacrifices of infants in the ritual abuse ceremonies.

♦ **425**   Hunt, P., & Baird, M. (1990). Children of sex rings. *Child Welfare, 69*, 195–207.

A sex ring is a group of adults, males and/or females, who gather for the express purpose of sexually exploiting children. Ten children, ranging in age from 3 to 5 years, who were victimized in either a day care or family-based ring are the subjects of this case study. All report a wide range of sexual abuse, pornography, bondage, bestiality, death threats, "snuff" films, animal mutilation and infant sacrifices. They differ from sexually abused children in terms of gender confusion, inconsistency in reporting, and leakage of trauma material into daily life. All of the children in this study require long-term therapy to reestablish trust, negate the effects of mind control or brainwashing, and reestablish a sense of self. Parents also need help in maintaining normalcy in their relations with their children.

♦ **426**   Kelley, S.J. (1996). Ritualistic abuse of children. In J. Briere & L. Berliner (Eds.), *The APSAC handbook on child maltreatment* (pp. 90–99). Thousand Oaks, CA: Sage.

Research indicates that allegations of ritual abuse from children around the country share many of the same features and characteristics, including forced sexual activity, physical abuse or torture, the ingestion of blood, urine, semen or feces, death threats, animal mutilations, and human sacrifices. The sequelae of ritual abuse, as evidenced by case studies, are similar as well and include anxiety, excessive fearfulness, behavioral disturbances, sexual acting out and sleep disorders.

♦ **427**   Kelley, S.J. (1994). Abuse of children in day care centres: Characteristics and consequences. *Child Abuse Review, 3*, 15–25.

The characteristics of abuse in day care settings merit special attention because of their ritualistic nature, the extreme abuse they describe, and the large number of victims and perpetrators alleged. The sequelae of ritual abuse in day care include anxiety, excessive fearfulness, behavioral disturbances, sexual acting out and sleep disorders. The parents of the children also experience psychological distress that often meets the diagnostic standards of post-traumatic stress disorder.

♦ **428**   Kelley, S.J. (1989). Stress responses of children to sexual abuse and ritualistic abuse in day care centers. *Journal of Interpersonal Violence, 4,* 505–513.

The results of the Parent-Child Behavior Checklist for 35 children ritually abused in day care centers are compared to those for 32 children sexually abused in day care centers, as well as to those of 67 non-abused children. Ritually abused children score significantly higher in behavior problems than either sexually abused or non-abused children; they also have higher scores for social withdrawal, depression, somatic complaints and sex problems than either sexually abused or non-abused children.

♦ **429**   Kelley, S.J. (1988). Ritualistic abuse of children: Dynamics and impact. *Cultic Studies Journal, 5,* 228–236.

Ritualistic abuse may occur in families or outside of them, as they have in the American day care cases. In both settings, the dynamics are similar: children are physically, emotionally and sexually abused in ceremonies that involve such rituals as blood-drinking and animal sacrifice. The sequelae of ritual abuse include fear, anxiety and dissociation.

♦ **430**   Kelley, S.J. (1988). Responses of children and parents to sexual abuse and satanic ritualistic abuse in day care centers. *Dissertation Abstracts International, 49* (12-B), 5521. (University Microfilm No. AAG89-04202)

A sample of 67 children, 35 of whom had been ritually abused in the Fells Acres day care center and 32 who had been sexually abused in other day care centers, was compared to 67 nonabused children. The findings indicate that both children and parents are severely traumatized by sexual abuse in day care settings. The ritually abused children have significantly more behavior problems than the sexually abused and the nonabused children, and the parents of ritually abused children score significantly higher on measures of stress than do the parents of the sexually abused and nonabused children.

♦ **431**   King, G.F., & Yorker, B. (1996). Case studies of children presenting with a history of ritualistic abuse. *Journal of Child and Adolescent Psychiatric Nursing, 9,* 18–26.

A review of the hospital records of children with a history of ritual abuse shows they had a variety of medical/somatic symptoms, a distortion of self-concept and of world view, and a variety of emotional disturbances.

♦ **432**   Snow, B., & Sorensen, T. (1990). Ritualistic child abuse in a neighborhood setting. *Journal of Interpersonal Violence, 5,* 474–487.

A sample of 39 ritually abused children referred for therapy was analyzed to determine the common characteristics of ritual abuse and its predictable sequelae. Most of the children describe multiple perpetrators and victims, death threats, sexual abuse, filming of sex acts, forced ingestion of feces and urine, animal killings or mutilations, and ingestion of drugs. While most of the children seemed to be functioning normally when referred for therapy, and all initially denied ritual abuse, a closer examination reveals they are all symptomatic, with reports of night terrors, somatic problems and sexual acting out most common.

♦ **433**   Stafford L.L. (1993). Dissociation and multiple personality disorder: A challenge for psychosocial nurses. *Journal of Psychosocial Nursing and Mental Health Services, 31,* 15–20.

Most multiple personality disorder patients report childhood histories of severe trauma, particularly ritual abuse. Although not usually diagnosed until adulthood, patients experience their first dissociative episodes during early childhood. Nurses must be apprised of the diagnostic significance of dissociation for finding cases of ritual abuse.

♦ **434**   Valente, S.M. (1999). Ritual abuse. In R. Gottesman (Ed.), *Encyclopedia of violence* (pp. 222–223). NY: Scribners Prentice Hall.

Children's accounts of ritual abuse often are difficult to hear and believe, yet research indicates that ritual abuse does occur in day care, family and community settings. Because ritual abuse involves sexual, physical and psychological abuse, children are profoundly traumatized. Their pathological coping mechanisms, such as self-hypnosis, self-mutilation and dissociation, coupled with psychological sequelae, including flashbacks and sexual preoccupations, make working with them difficult and challenging.

♦ **435**   Waterman, J., Kelly, R.J., Oliveri, M.K., & McCord, J. (1993). *Behind the playground walls.* NY: Guilford Press.

The short- and long-term effects of reported ritual abuse on the children in the McMartin Preschool case are examined and compared to those for children sexually abused in a day care center, and children with no history of abuse. At initial assessment, the ritually abused children show significantly higher scores on all levels of distress, more school problems, more symptoms of post-traumatic stress disorder, less social competency, and more body image dissatisfaction than do the sexually abused and non-abused children. Symptoms tend to dissipate over time, with 17% of the children exhibiting clinically significant symptoms after 5 years. The parents of ritually abused children report significant stress, with mothers more likely to blame themselves, and to experience depression. At the peak of their involvement with the ritually abused children, 78% of their psychotherapists met the diagnostic criteria for post-traumatic stress disorder.

RITUAL ABUSE AND THE FAMILY SYSTEM

The family system enters into the ritual abuse controversy as the most immediate and intimate context in which the simple truths that children never lie and that their symptoms tell their stories can be reexamined. Parents and family members have more than a little vested interest in uncovering every detail of the ritual abuse their children disclose, and experience more than a little distress in hearing it. And herein lies the controversy: could the children's disclosures and details be formed in conversational partnership with their anxious parents, and is it possible that their symptoms actually are responses to their parents' distress and the disruptive effects the disclosures have on their families?

♦ **436**   Burgess, A.W., Hartman, C.R., Kelley, S.J., Grant, C.A., & Gray, E.B. (1990). Parental response to child sexual abuse trials involving day care settings. *Journal of Traumatic Stress, 3*, 395–405.

Parents' stress responses to the decision as to whether their children should testify in a day care ritual abuse trial are examined. The results of the Symptom Checklist-90-R and the Impact of Event Scale were compared for the parents of 17 testifying children and the parents of 50 non-testifying children. The parents of the testifying children present greater symptoms of psychological distress; the reported stress is higher for fathers than mothers. These parents also report more stressful life events after their children's disclosures of ritual abuse, including loss of income, marital problems, and periods of separation. The motives underlying the parents' decision to permit their children to testify are analyzed, and the need for trauma-specific interventions for parents in cases like this is emphasized.

◆ **437** Hartman, C.R., Burgess, A.G., Burgess, A.W., & Kelley, S.J. (1992). Extrafamilial child sexual abuse: Family-focused intervention. In A.W. Burgess (Ed.), *Child trauma I: Issues and research* (pp. 307–333). NY: Garland.

The parents of 41 children either ritually or sexually abused in day care submitted to a battery of psychological tests to measure their level of stress. Parents of ritually abused children experience significantly more stress than the parents of sexually abused children, with fathers exhibiting more stress than mothers. A strong interaction between the stress of the parents and the symptomatic reaction to the abuse of the children in both groups is noted. A family-focused intervention program is needed.

◆ **438** MacDonald, V.M. (1992). Reported ritualistic sexual abuse in preschools: Impact on family processes. *Dissertation Abstracts International, 53* (03-B), 1612. (University Microfilms No. AAG92-13647)

To explore how families are affected by ritual abuse and how they mediate children's subsequent adjustment, 62 families of 78 children ritually abused in day care were compared to 29 families of 37 children with no known or suspected history of sexual abuse. Parents of ritually abused children report significantly more intrafamily strain and conflict and more total family stress and change for the year prior to assessment. These family processes, in turn, are significantly related to adjustment problems for ritually abused children. The importance of clinical interventions with families of these children must not be underestimated.

◆ **439** Stone, L., & Stone, D. (1992). Ritual abuse: The experiences of five families. In D.K. Sakheim & S.E. Devine (Eds.), *Out of darkness: Exploring satanism and ritual abuse* (pp. 175–183). NY: Lexington.

The mothers of 5 children who were ritually abused by their fathers, report they experience depression and emotional distress for not having protected their children, and frustration and outrage at the child protection system for also failing to protect them once the ritual abuse was made known. The child protection mandate to keep families together at all cost must be reconsidered in suspected cases of ritual abuse.

THERAPEUTIC INTERVENTIONS

On the subject of therapeutic intervention with ritually abused children, the literature is deafeningly quiet. After two decades of allegations, controversial cases and dire prognoses, there have been no real treatment innovations, and no specialized approaches to therapeutically intervening with this most horrific of childhood traumas.

◆ **440**   Boat, B.W. (1991). Caregivers as surrogate therapists in treatment of a ritualistically abused child. In W.N. Friedrich (Ed.), *Casebook of sexual abuse treatment* (pp. 1–26). NY: W.W. Norton.

The case of a 3 year old ritually abused girl illustrates the use of foster parents as surrogate therapists in treatment. Foster parents can encourage memory retrieval and mastery through discussion and play, manage behavioral and psychological sequelae, and advocate for children with the various systems of intervention and control.

◆ **441**   Clifford, M.W. (1994). Social work treatment with children, adolescents, and families exposed to religious and satanic cults. *Social Work in Health Care, 20,* 35–59.

The role of the social worker in treating ritual abuse victims focuses on four areas: education, practice, legal and research. The case of a 3 year old victim illustrates how each of these areas complicates therapeutic intervention with ritual abuse cases.

◆ **442**   Gould, C., & Graham-Costain, V. (1994). Play therapy with ritually abused children, part II. *Treating Abuse Today, 4,* 14–19.

Abreactive play therapy is the treatment of choice for ritually abused children. It allows children to symbolize their victimization in ways that cannot be approximated by traditional talk therapy. A wide range of toys, such as knives and guns, cages and coffins, medical kits, animals, chalices, crucifixes, witches and devils should be used. The better the toy represents some feature of ritual abuse, the better able children are to represent and act out their abuse in play.

◆ **443**   Gould, C., & Graham-Costain, V. (1994). Play therapy with ritually abused children, part I. *Treating Abuse Today, 4,* 4–10.

The recommended 3-part model for therapy with ritually abused children involves treating the children's post-traumatic stress disorder, identifying and working with their dissociative personality systems, and assisting them to distinguish and work through cult-indoctrinated messages. Abreactive play therapy is the treatment of choice for ritually abused children.

◆ **444**   Harvey, S. (1993). Ann: Dynamic play therapy with ritual abuse. In T. Kottman & C. Schaefer (Eds.), *Play therapy in action: A casebook for practitioners* (pp. 371–415). Northvale, NJ: Jason Aronson Inc.

Dynamic play therapy is helpful in the treatment of ritually abused children. Their family members can participate in adjunct expressive therapies such as art, movement, drama and music therapy. Mental health professionals then can help families to understand and interpret their reactions to, and interactions with, their ritually abused children. The case of Ann, ritually abused by her father, illustrates the uses of dynamic therapy.

◆ **445**   Hoier, T.S. (1991). The course of treatment of a sexually abused child: A single-case study. *Behavioral Assessment, 13,* 385–398.

The assessment of an 8 year old boy, a victim of long-term ritual abuse, necessitated the use of various modalities to assess his functioning and mental health needs. In complex cases such as his, therapy must proceed in stages, beginning with establishing safety and boundaries, and must be refined as the child discloses more details and memories of the ritual abuse.

◆ **446**   McShane, C. (1993). Satanic sexual abuse: A paradigm. *Affilia,*
8, 200–212.

A domination-legitimation-resistance paradigm is helpful in understanding ritually abused girls and their treatment needs. As victims they are dominated by satanists
who recruit them into the cult as young children through coercion and seduction, and
then torture them to secure their compliance as servants to the cult. The cults adhere
to satanic teachings that assert that females exist only for the pleasure of males; eventually, victims internalize their role as oppressed sex objects and submit to the ritual
abuse. Since resistance in any form is punished, girls oppose their domination either
by rising in the ranks of the cult from victim to perpetrator, or by leaving the cult
when they are old enough and resourceful enough to do so.

◆ **447**   Uherek, A.M. (1991). Treatment of a ritually abused preschooler.
In W.N. Friedrich (Ed.), *Casebook of sexual abuse treatment* (pp. 70–92).
NY: W.W. Norton.

The case of a 4½ year old ritually abused boy illustrates the challenges posed to mental health professionals in assessing ritual abuse cases, determining and carrying out
effective treatment strategies, and interacting with the many other agencies and organizations, such as the police and child protective services, that are likely to be involved
in the cases.

6

Clinical Features of Ritual Abuse: Adults

During the most recent epoch of interest in childhood trauma, mental health patients were encouraged to reclaim their long-silenced voices by talking about their personal histories of abuse and its legacy in the emotional, cognitive, interpersonal and sexual spheres of their lives. Those who did, finally and with relief, gave voice to uninterrupted memories, but by the mid–1980s during the first crest of the wave of ritual abuse allegations by children, an increasing number of often floridly symptomatic adult patients with no known history of abuse began recovering memories of it in psychotherapy. And often those recovered memories are of ritual abuse.

THE RITUAL ABUSE SEQUELAE CONTROVERSY

Ritual abuse certainly is not the kind of lamentably common type of abuse that occurs during childhood. Recovered memories of it are testimony to that assertion. Adults who reclaim long-repressed memories of childhood ritual abuse remember not only acts of violent sexual assault, but of torture, mind-numbing ceremonies, and ghastly rituals. The logic of the predominate model of childhood trauma is that horrific acts have horrific consequences, therefore much attention is being paid in the clinical literature to differentiating the type and the severity of the sequelae of ritual abuse from those of the more recurrent, albeit prosaic, types of childhood abuse.

The findings are not without controversy if only because they are without consistency. To date, no constellation of symptoms, no ritual abuse syndrome for lack of a better term, has emerged from these investigations, and nothing convincingly has been shown to differentiate the sequelae of this most horrific form of abuse from any other type of abuse or, arguably, from any other type of childhood trauma.

◆ **448**   Bensinger, T.T. (1990). Long-term effects on adult women who report sexual and ritual abuse in their childhoods. *Dissertation Abstracts International, 51* (01-B), 0420. (University Microfilms No. AAG90-18317)

Findings from interviews and psychological tests of 53 women with childhood histories of ritual abuse were compared to findings for 49 women with childhood histories of sexual abuse. Although both groups were traumatized by their experiences, ritually abused women report more severe symptomatology and more severe types of abuse experiences than do sexually abused women. They score significantly higher on measures indicating post-traumatic stress disorder, dissociation and self-attribution of blame, and report more environmental triggers that set off repetitions of traumatic responses than do sexually abused women.

◆ **449**   Charles, P.G. (1996). An exploration of experiences of extreme abuse. *Dissertation Abstracts International, 58* (09-A), 3722. (University Microfilms No. AAGNQ-21926)

As a means of triangulating the subject's experience, the life history of a person who was ritually abused as a child is compared to the life histories of 2 others who report childhood histories of ritual abuse. The analysis of the experiences contributes to the development of a theoretical perspective on the process of healing from ritual abuse.

◆ **450**   Coleman, J. (1994). Presenting features in adult victims of satanist ritual abuse. *Child Abuse Review, 3,* 83–92.

Five adult psychiatric patients with childhood histories of ritual abuse present with low self-esteem, feelings of guilt and worthlessness, sleep and eating disorders, mood swings, sexual dysfunction, somatic symptoms, behavior disorders, phobias, religious conflicts, dissociation and auditory and/or visual hallucinations. Each patient disclosed sexual abuse first and then over the next few months ritual abuse. Their disclosures reveal that ritual abuse includes a wide range of physical, psychological, spiritual, emotional and sexual abuse acts, the primary purpose of which is to gain total control of the children and indoctrinate them into becoming adult perpetrators.

◆ **451**   Cook, C. (1991). Understanding ritual abuse: A study of thirty-three ritual abuse survivors. *Treating Abuse Today, 1,* 14–19.

Thirty-three adults reporting childhood histories of ritual abuse report similar types of experiences, present with similar psychological and emotional sequelae, and are faced with similar questions about the veracity and credibility of their accounts.

◆ **452**   Hill, S., & Goodwin, J.R. (1993). Demonic possession as a consequence of childhood trauma. *Journal of Psychohistory, 20,* 399–411.

A 17th century case of demon possession and exorcism studied by Freud has parallels to a contemporary case of a 42 year old woman whose demonic possession was the result of childhood ritual abuse by a satanic cult. Freud posited that on a symbolic level, the demons represent internalized abusers. The analysis of the contemporary case extends that understanding by suggesting that the demons also represent keepers of the secret of abuse, protectors of the patient, and substitutes for memory.

◆ **453**   Ireland, S.J., & Ireland, M.J. (1994). A case history of family and cult abuse. *Journal of Psychohistory, 21,* 417–428.

A 35 year old woman entered therapy for depression, anxiety, substance abuse and unresolved grief. Over 5 years of psychotherapy she recovered memories of physical and sexual abuse, and ritual torture. The first memories recovered were of bizarre rituals conducted by her mother to help her communicate with ghosts and spirits; these were followed by memories of sexual abuse by her mother. Although she initially remembered her father in positive terms, she eventually recalled he was physically and sexually abusive. Later, after an intense recurrence of her symptoms, she recovered memories of ritual abuse by a cult that forced her to participate in the sacrifices of children.

◆ **454**   Juhasz, S. (1995). Coping skills of ritual abuse survivors: An exploratory study. *Smith College Studies in Social Work, 65,* 255–269.

Data were gathered for this qualitative study from 14 mental health professionals who specialize in treating ritual abuse patients and 3 adult patients to explore their coping skills at the time of the ritual abuse and later in adulthood as they recovered memories of it. Dissociation is the primary coping mechanism at both times, although coping skills and psychological defense mechanisms changed over the life course to defend against memories of ritual abuse and later to process those memories.

◆ **455**   Kay, J.A. (1995). Semper fidelis: The experience of healing from ritual abuse. *Dissertation Abstracts International, 55* (7-B), 3016. (University Microfilms No. AAM94-29772)

Semi-structured interviews were conducted with 9 adult psychotherapy patients who remembered childhood histories of ritual abuse as to their experiences of healing from the abuse. Analysis shows a trajectory of healing, beginning with the expression of grief for those who were tortured and murdered by satanic cults as a foundation for developing love for the living; the creation of a spiritual orientation to contain the psychic pain; and the generation of connections with other ritual abuse victims.

◆ **456**   Kent, C.C. (1991). Ritual abuse. In R.T. Ammerman & M. Hersen (Eds.), *Case studies in family violence* (pp. 187–207). NY: Plenum Press.

Three cases studies illustrate the effects of ritual abuse, its medical and legal issues, and social and family factors. The psychological assessment of ritual abuse victims must take into account their often unusual symptoms, including preoccupation with urine and feces and a fear of foreign objects inside their bodies, as well as their confusion about values, deep mistrust of authority figures and social institutions, and concerns about being different and unacceptable. The goal of psychotherapy must be to help these patients establish a positive sense of their identity and an optimism about their future.

◆ **457**   Lawrence, K.J., Cozolino, L., & Foy, D.W. (1995). Psychological sequelae in adult females reporting childhood ritualistic abuse. *Child Abuse & Neglect, 19,* 975–984.

The results of a battery of psychological tests were compared for a group of women outpatients reporting childhood histories of ritual abuse and a group of women patients reporting childhood histories of sexual abuse. The ritual abuse group was more likely to report abuse over a longer duration, a greater number of perpetrators, penile penetration and severe physical abuse than was the sexual abuse group. No significant differences were found between the two groups for post-traumatic disorder diagnostic status, severity of post-traumatic disorder, or dissociative experiences. While these findings cannot attest to the validity of ritual abuse accounts, they do suggest the need for treating those accounts as indicators of severe childhood abuse and its predictable sequelae.

◆ **458**   Leavitt, F. (1998). Measuring the impact of media exposure and hospital treatment on patients alleging satanic ritual abuse. *Treating Abuse Today, 8*, 7–13.

Critics of ritual abuse reports allege that exposure to media accounts of ritual abuse, and/or exposure to other psychiatric hospital inpatients plays a central role in generating memories of ritual abuse. The Word Association Test (WAT) was used to determine the impact of these variables for 43 hospital inpatients who report memories of ritual abuse. Neither of the exposure variables is a significant predictor of satanic associations on the test; paradoxically, less media exposure is associated with significantly higher rates of satanic word associations on the test. While media and hospital exposure may allow patients to respond conversationally about ritual abuse, these variables do not account for unique satanic word association knowledge found among patients reporting memories of ritual abuse.

◆ **459**   Leavitt, F. (1994). Clinical correlates of alleged satanic abuse and less controversial sexual molestation. *Child Abuse and Neglect, 18*, 387–392.

A sample of 87 female patients admitted to a dissociative disorders unit was divided into two groups based on the reporting of childhood ritual abuse by satanists. Although both groups show high levels of psychological distress as measured by the Minnesota Multiphasic Personality Inventory (MMPI), the ritual abuse group exhibits significantly more disturbance on the Paranoia scale (Pa). That group also shows significantly higher levels of overall psychological disorganization on the Dissociative Experiences Scale, as well as on the 3 dissociative subscales. Although it is unlikely the ritual abuse accounts are fabricated, these findings should not be used to assess their authenticity.

◆ **460**   Leavitt, F., & Labott, S.M. (2000). The role of the media and hospital exposure on Rorschach response patterns by patients reporting satanic ritual abuse. *American Journal of Forensic Psychology, 18*, 35–55.

The Rorschach content of 131 female inpatients reporting a childhood history of ritual abuse was compared to the content of 92 female inpatients reporting a childhood history of sexual abuse, and 92 female inpatients reporting no childhood history of either. The mean number of satanic content for each group was 6.74, 1.71 and .88, respectively. The significant degree of shared satanic content by the ritual abuse group then was examined as an artifact of both media exposure and exposure to the hospital milieu. The unexpected findings indicate that less media exposure and less hospital milieu exposure actually are related to the highest satanic content for the ritual abuse group. The best predictors of satanic content in Rorschach responses, therefore, are low media exposure and the patient's report of ritual abuse.

◆ **461**   Leavitt, F., & Labott, S.M. (1998). Revision of the Word Association Test for assessing the associations of patients reporting satanic ritual abuse in childhood. *Journal of Clinical Psychology, 54*, 933–943.

The Word Association Test (WAT) was modified to assess patients' experiences with ritual abuse, producing two domains: normative and satanic. The responses to the revised WAT by female inpatients reporting a childhood history of ritual abuse were compared to patients reporting a childhood history of sexual abuse, and patients reporting no history of sexual abuse. The ritual abuse patients give more total associations, significantly fewer normative associations and significantly more satanic associations than the other two groups. The findings suggest that ritual abuse patients shared an experience, giving credence to arguments that ritual abuse reports are veridical.

◆ **462** Mangen, R. (1992). Psychological testing and ritual abuse. In D.K. Sakheim & S.E. Devine (Eds.), *Out of darkness: Exploring satanism and ritual abuse* (pp. 147–173). NY: Lexington.

Clinicians conducting psychological testing with patients reporting a childhood history of ritual abuse must be aware that the language of the inventory-style tests, and the physical stimuli of the projective tests, can trigger specific memories of ritual abuse. While administering psychological tests, the clinician should be particularly attentive to the patient's affect organization, defensive functioning, intellectual functioning, formal thought processes, and experiences of self and others.

◆ **463** Narron, G. (1991). The effects of intrafamilial ritualistic abuse on an adult survivor: A systemic perspective on recovery. *Dissertation Abstracts International, 52* (04-A), 1535. (University Microfilms No. AAG91-23743)

An in-depth interview with an adult woman who reports a childhood history of ritual abuse by family members reveals the impact of the abuse on the performance of her various roles of wife, mother, friend, and church member. While ritual abuse deleteriously affected each of those roles, she was able to recover her role performance through therapy that integrated her own unique expression of creativity with standard therapy techniques.

◆ **464** Noblitt, J.R. (1995). Psychometric measures of trauma among psychiatric patients reporting ritual abuse. *Psychological Reports, 77*, 743–747.

The Minnesota Multiphasic Personality Inventory's PK and PS scales measuring trauma were compared for psychiatric patients reporting a childhood history of ritual abuse and those reporting no childhood abuse. Mean trauma scores are significantly higher for patients reporting ritual abuse than for those who did not; in addition, 91% of the ritual abuse patients had clinically elevated scores on at least one of the two scales.

◆ **465** Sachs, R.G. (1990). The role of sex and pregnancy in Satanic cults. *Pre- and Peri-Natal Psychology Journal, 5*, 105–113.

The sexual practices and abuses during pregnancy that take place in satanic cult rituals are intended to cause dissociative disorders in victims by selectively breeding for high dissociative ability and repeated trauma which force the continual exercise of dissociative defenses in order to survive. Those who do survive have been indoctrinated since childhood to keep cult practices secret, and this may lead health professionals to miss or overlook the signs and symptoms of past and present ritual abuse, as well as prevent the victims from receiving needed treatment.

♦ **466**   Shaffer, R.E. (1991). Reports of childhood ritualistic abuse in adult outpatients. *Dissertation Abstracts International, 52* (09-B), 4986. (University Microfilms No. AAG92-04123)

Twenty adult outpatients were interviewed to assess their experiences of childhood ritual abuse and any long-term psychological sequelae they produced. Although the patients originally came from different parts of the country, they describe similar abuse experiences. They also have similar impairments in functioning, including unusual fears, substance abuse, post-traumatic stress symptoms and dissociation.

♦ **467**   Shaffer, R.E., & Cozolino, L.J. (1992). Adults who report childhood ritualistic abuse. *Journal of Psychology and Theology, 20,* 188–193.

A sample of 19 women and one man in outpatient therapy illustrates the process and effects of recovering memories of childhood ritual abuse. They entered therapy for such problems as depression, anxiety and dissociation, but during recovered memory therapy retrieved memories first of sexual abuse and then of ritual abuse that included such acts as cannibalism and human sacrifices. The recovery of these memories brought on panic, depression and/or suicidal ideation that necessitated the hospitalization of 11 of the patients. Once memories were recovered, the patients agreed that ritual abuse had severely impacted all aspects of their lives, including sexual functioning, physical health, and spirituality. The prognosis for ritual abuse patients is good if therapy focuses on memory retrieval and the reassociation of dissociated experiences and feelings.

♦ **468**   Stroh, G.M. (1995). Ritual abuse: Traumas and treatments. In M. Hunter (Ed.), *Child survivors and perpetrators of sexual abuse: Treatment innovations* (pp. 50–76). Newbury Park, CA: Sage.

The traumatic effects of ritual abuse are severe, but mental health professionals must pay special attention to dissociation, the primary psychological coping mechanism of children and adults with histories of ritual abuse. Other therapeutic issues of concern include repetition compulsion of abuse patterns, distorted and false memories, and countertransference.

♦ **469**   Waites, E.A. (1993). Ritualization and abuse. In E.A. Waites (Ed.), *Trauma and survival: Post-traumatic and dissociative disorders in women* (pp. 202–210). NY: Norton.

Ritual abuse produces post-traumatic and dissociative sequelae that profoundly disrupt healthy functioning in all aspects of life. Its dynamics pose significant challenges to mental health professionals whose work is being carried out in a cultural context of denial and skepticism.

♦ **470**   Wallace, H. (1991). Ritualistic child abuse. In H. Wallace (Ed.), *Family violence: Legal, medical and social perspectives* (pp. 111–131). Boston, MA: Allyn and Bacon.

Ritual abuse within satanic cults may be sexual, physical, and/or emotional in nature and often also involves torture, forced drug ingestion and sleep deprivation. Sequelae include obsession with death, fear of enclosed places, and sexual acting out.

♦ **471**   Wong, B., & McKeen, J. (1990). A case of multiple life-threatening illnesses related to early ritual abuse. *Journal of Child and Youth Care, 6,* 1–26.

The case of a 25 year old woman with a life-threatening lymphoma who reports childhood ritual abuse is presented. In group and individual counseling, she worked through the meanings of her medical symptoms and overcame numerous episodes of unrelated cancers. She believes the cancers protected her from memories and from the cult killing her when she refused to come back. She also feels that the cancers permitted her to express her will in a way that is distinct from how she was indoctrinated by cult.

◆ 472   Young, W.C. (1993). Sadistic ritual abuse: An overview in detection and management. In B.A. Elliott, K.C. Halverson, & M.K. Hendricks-Matthews (Eds.), *Primary care. Clinics in office practice: Family violence and abusive relationships* (pp. 447–458). Philadelphia, PA: W.B. Saunders.

Reports of ritual abuse may be authentic or may be metaphors for other traumas; regardless of their origin, however, they are experienced as real by patients. The indicators of ritual abuse, including multiple personality disorder, deviant behavior and dissociation, are illustrated by 5 case studies that also are instructive about how medical examinations should be performed, and what kinds of medications should be prescribed to ameliorate symptoms.

◆ 473   Young, W.C. (1992). Recognition and treatment of survivors reporting ritual abuse. In D.K. Sakheim & S.E. Devine (Eds.), *Out of darkness: Exploring satanism and ritual abuse* (pp. 249–278). NY: Lexington.

Patients with a childhood history of ritual abuse often present with elaborate dissociative defenses that block access to memories. These memories are so severe that when they are recovered they often activate abreactions in which the patients recall the ritual abuse with such vivid intensity that they may become suicidal or dangerous. Other sequelae include multiple personality disorder, post-traumatic stress disorder, survivor guilt, indoctrinated beliefs, unusual fears, sexualization of sadistic impulses, bizarre self-abuse and substance abuse. Successful treatment strategies will focus on developing a therapeutic alliance, clarifying the system of alters in cases of multiple personality, recovering memories and dissolving dissociative barriers, countering indoctrinated beliefs, desensitizing cult triggers and cues, and coming to terms with the past and finding new meaning and purpose in life.

◆ 474   Young, W.C., Sachs, R.G., Braun, B.G. & Watkins, R.T. (1991). Patients reporting ritual abuse in childhood: A clinical syndrome. Report of 37 cases. *Child Abuse & Neglect, 15*, 181–189.

Thirty-seven adult inpatients originally referred for the treatment of dissociative disorders were evaluated after they recovered memories of ritual abuse. The memories occurred spontaneously in the contexts of working through memories of familial abuse, abreactions, dreams, and/or hypnosis. All remember sexual abuse and torture, animal mutilations or sacrifices, and death threats. Most also remember forced drug ingestion, human sacrifices, cannibalism, marriage to the devil ceremonies, and forced impregnations with sacrifices of the infants. The clinical syndrome presented by the patients is characterized by severe post-traumatic stress disorder, dissociative states with satanic overtones, survivor guilt, indoctrinated beliefs, unusual fears, sexualization of sadistic impulses, bizarre self-abuse and substance abuse.

RITUAL ABUSE AND THE
RECOVERED MEMORY CONTROVERSY

The transformation of childhood abuse from silent memory to spoken testimonial prompted furious controversy over the veracity of recovered memories of ritual abuse. On one side of the debate are those for whom recovered memories are long repressed but nevertheless authentic images of otherwise unspeakable acts of childhood ritual abuse; on the other are those for whom recovered memories are nothing but imaginative fictions.

♦ **475**   Calof, D.L. (1991). Regarding the credibility of ritual abuse reports. *Treating Abuse Today, 1*, 35–39.

Ritual abuse is a profoundly traumatizing experience, and clinicians should expect disclosures of it to be confusing, bewildering and evocative. These accounts should not be summarily dismissed, however. Completely credible and historically accurate narratives of ritualistic abuse will emerge over time if mental health professionals remain patient and objective.

♦ **476**   Coons, P.M. (1994). Factitious disorder (Munchausen type) involving allegations of ritual satanic abuse: A case report. *Dissociation, 3*, 177–178.

The case of a 25 year old hospitalized female who recovered memories of a childhood history of ritual abuse is presented. A careful evaluation which includes clinical observation, thorough history-taking, psychological testing and evaluation of collateral material fails to corroborate her account. A diagnosis of Factitious Disorder (Munchausen type) is considered appropriate.

♦ **477**   Driscoll, L.N., & Wright, C. (1991). Survivors of childhood ritual abuse: Multi-generational satanic cult involvement. *Treating Abuse Today, 1*, 5–13.

Psychotherapy patients who completed a questionnaire regarding the childhood ritual abuse they remembered report remarkably similar details, including the characteristics of the abuse, ritual locations and symbols, and the role identities of perpetrators. They also experience similar sequelae of the abuse. These similarities suggest their reports are credible and should be believed.

♦ **478**   Goldstein, E. (1997). False memory syndrome: Why would they believe such terrible things if they weren't true. *American Journal of Family Therapy, 25*, 307–313.

Over the last decade, tens of thousands of adults in therapy have recovered memories of ritual abuse and sexual abuse that have destroyed the lives of the people they have accused. The role that therapeutic techniques, such as hypnosis and guided imagery may play in creating and encouraging these false memories must be considered.

♦ **479**   Golston, J.C. (1992). Ritual abuse: Raising hell in psychotherapy, part two: Comparative abuse: Shedding light on ritual abuse through the study of torture methods in political repression, sexual sadism and genocide. *Treating Abuse Today*, *2*, 5–16.

The comparative study of torture provides a basis for the external validation of recovered memories of ritual abuse, as well as a framework for understanding those allegations.

◆ **480**   Goodwin, J.M. (1994). Credibility problems in sadistic abuse. *Journal of Psychohistory*, *21*, 479–496.

The primary credibility problem that obscures the study and understanding of ritual and other types of sadistic abuse is the simple unwillingness to believe it occurs despite evidence that it has throughout history. One strategy for overcoming this problem is to collect data on the epidemiology of ritual and sadistic abuse; another is to listen to the allegations of children and adult survivors, realizing that the very experience of ritual abuse — fragmenting, terrorizing and disorienting as it is — will interfere with their ability to give a full, consistent and credible account. History reveals that only a thin line separates "normal" people from sadistic perpetrators, as the cases of Gilles de Rais and the Marquis de Sade illustrate. Only when that final hurdle is cleared will the denial of ritual and sadistic abuse finally be overcome.

◆ **481**   Goodyear-Smith, F.A. (1998). Parents and other relatives accused of sexual abuse on the basis of recovered memories: A New Zealand survey. *New Zealand Medical Journal*, *111*, 225–228.

A survey completed by 73 New Zealanders with a family member who recovered memories of sexual abuse shows that most of the accusers are white, highly educated women from large families who recovered memories during the course of therapy. Most of the memories recovered were not just of sexual abuse and incest, but of ritual abuse. Because those latter memories are improbable, it is important that mental health professionals treat these memories as patients' narrative, rather than historical, truth.

◆ **482**   Goodyear-Smith, F.A., Laidlaw, T.M., & Large, R.G. (1997). Surveying families accused of childhood sexual abuse: A Comparison of British and New Zealand results. *Applied Cognitive Psychology*, *11*, 31–34.

Surveys of parents accused of sexual abuse by adult children conducted in Great Britain and New Zealand show similar results: most of the accusers are white, well-off women who recovered memories of childhood abuse and ritual abuse during therapy. Although the survey results suggest similar experiences that would seem to validate the memories of ritual abuse, mental health professionals must be cautious and seek objective data to validate the memories before taking them as truth.

◆ **483**   Gow, K.M. (1999). Recovered memories of abuse: Real, fabricated, or both? *Australian Journal of Clinical and Experimental Hypnosis*, *27*, 81–97.

The literature on recovered memories of ritual abuse and of sexual abuse suggests that recovered memories may by true in some cases, true but inaccurate in all details in others, and partially or completely false in still others. No standard for differentiating between these possibilities can be gleaned from a review of the literature.

◆ **484**   Gow, K.M. (1998). The complex issues in researching false memory syndrome. *Australasian Journal of Disaster and Trauma Studies*, *3*.

Retrieved 2-February-01 from the World Wide Web: http://www.massey.ac.nz/~trauma/issues/1998-3/gow1.htm

False memories, including those of ritual abuse, are the products of complex inter-actions between socioperceptual conditioning, secondary gain, family dynamics, media induction, and mental health professionals' beliefs and treatment approaches.

◆ **485**   Hill, S., & Goodwin, J.R. (1989). Satanism: Similarities between patient accounts and pre–Inquisition historical sources. *Dissociation, 2,* 39–44.

Primary historical sources reveal 11 practices of 4th century satanic cults that are consistent with recovered memories of ritual abuse: orgiastic sex, nocturnal feasts, imitations and reversals of the Christian mass, ritual use of semen and blood, sacrifices of fetuses and infants, cannibalism, ritual uses of candles and torches, chanting, drug ingestion, dancing backward in circles, and dismemberment of corpses. The histori-cal similarities give credence to the position that these recovered memories are accu-rate and should be believed.

◆ **486**   McCulley, D. (1994). Satanic ritual abuse: A question of mem-ory. *Journal of Psychology and Theology, 22,* 167–172.

The findings of prominent memory researchers dispute the argument that recov-ered memories of ritual abuse are always false and are iatrogenically created. The nature of traumatic memory formation and retrieval precisely matches the patterns of memory recovery by ritual abuse patients, lending considerable credence to the veracity of their memories.

◆ **487**   Ofshe, R.J. (1992). Inadvertent hypnosis during interrogation: False memory confession due to dissociative state; misidentified multiple personality and the satanic cult hypothesis. *International Journal of Clin-ical And Experimental Hypnosis, 11,* 125–156.

After the induction of a dissociative state during interrogation, Paul Ingram devel-oped pseudomemories of ritually abusing his 2 daughters. For 6 months after his con-fession he was convinced of his guilt, although investigators were unable to find any evidence to corroborate it. An experiment conducted by the author, a social psychol-ogist originally hired as a prosecution consultant, created more pseudomemories and raised questions about the reliability of Ingram's confession. Ingram's confession of ritual abuse is false, as are his daughters' allegations.

◆ **488**   Olio, K., & Cornell, W.F. (1998). The façade of scientific docu-mentation: A case study of Richard Ofshe's analysis of the Paul Ingram case. *Psychology, Public Policy, and Law, 4,* 1182–1197.

A review of the original documents and interview transcripts in the Ingram case reveals that Ofshe's conclusions (see citation 487) are based on errors of fact, method-ological flaws, and other confounding factors. Therefore, his conclusion that Ingram was inadvertently hypnotized and as a result confessed to ritually abusing his daugh-ters is incorrect. Examples are given of how Ofshe's imperfect narrative of this case and his pseudoscientific conclusions are being uncritically accepted and repeated in the literature, becoming an academic version of an urban legend.

◆ **489**   Palermo, G.B., & Del Re, M. (1999). Children in satanic rituals. In G.B. Palermo & M. Del Re (Eds.), *Satanism: Psychiatric and legal views* (pp. 68–85). Springfield, IL: Charles C. Thomas.

Satanic rituals are so terrorizing that memories of being victimized in them usually are repressed by children and have to be recovered years later in psychotherapy. While hypnosis can facilitate memory recovery, it also may result in false memories of childhood ritual abuse. In the cultural climate of debate about false memories, any allegations of ritual abuse should be thoroughly investigated before admission in court.

♦ **490**   Paley, J. (1997). Satanist abuse and alien abduction: A comparative analysis theorizing temporal lobe activity as a possible connection between anomalous memories. *British Journal of Social Work, 27,* 43–70.

There are interesting parallels between the reports of alleged ritual abuse survivors and alleged alien abductees: both are fantastic in nature, retrieved over a period of time, contain inconsistencies and contradictions, allege multiple perpetrators of sexual violence and threats and warnings against disclosure, and result in a range of intense fears and anxieties. The parallels may have a neurophysiological basis. Partial complex or temporal lobe epilepsy can produce sensations of levitation, anxiety, sexual pleasure, out-of-body experiences, amnesia and lost time as well as a variety of visual, auditory and tactile hallucinations that are all consistent with ritual abuse and alien abduction reports.

♦ **491**   Paley, J. (1995). Memories of satanist abuse. *Health and Social Care in the Community, 3,* 125–128.

The parallels between reports of ritual abuse and of alien abduction are impressive and include a disproportionate number of women victims; repetitive experiences over time; multiple perpetrators, many of them female; and recovered memories after long periods of amnesia or repression.

♦ **492**   Qin, J., Goodman, G.S., Bottoms, B.L., & Shaver, P.R. (1998). Repressed memories of ritualistic and religion-related child abuse. In S.J. Lynn & K.M. McConkey (Eds.), *Truth in memory* (pp. 260–283). NY: Guilford Press.

A survey of 720 mental health professionals who treated at least one case of alleged ritual or religion-related abuse reveals that most of the patients presented with symptoms of depression and that approximately 10% of them had repressed all memories of the abuse. Slightly more than 66% of those who repressed the memories are diagnosed with multiple personality disorder. Despite the absence of corroborating evidence, most of the clinicians indicate they believe their patients' disclosures. A second survey of a sample of clinicians from the initial study as well as clinicians who have not treated an alleged case of ritual or religion-related abuse finds that those who believe in the veracity of repressed memories also believe allegations of ritual abuse.

♦ **493**   Smith, B.J. (1993). Believing heals. *Survivor Times, 1,* 5–7.

Recovered memories of ritual abuse are real and must be believed before survivors can process, work through and heal from their childhood trauma. Authentic memories match the depth and severity of symptoms, which include dissociation, memory blanks, and unexplained fears, attractions and/or avoidances.

♦ **494**   Smith, B.K. (1994). Ritual abuse and recovered memories. *Conscious Choice: The Journal of Ecology and Natural Living, 7,* 28–29.

The controversy regarding the veracity of recovered memories of childhood ritual abuse is having a divisive impact on health and mental health professionals, and as yet remains unresolved by scientific studies.

♦ **495**   Spanos, N.P., Burgess, C.A., & Burgess, M.F. (1994). Past-life identities, UFO abductions, and satanic ritual abuse: The social construction of memories. *International Journal of Clinical and Experimental Hypnosis, 42,* 433–446.

The research on memories of ritual abuse, past life experiences, and alien abductions reveals that the memories frequently are recalled through hypnotic procedures or structured interviews with strong demand characteristics. The research supports the hypothesis that recall is reconstructive and is organized in terms of current beliefs and expectations. The article can be found at the internet URL: http://www.psychwww.com/asc/hyp/memories.html.

♦ **496**   Stroup, K.L. (1996). The rediscovery of evil: An analysis of the satanic ritual abuse phenomenon. *Dissertation Abstracts International, 57* (4-A), 1668. (University Microfilms No. AAM96-26297)

Objective evidence fails to corroborate the memories of ritual abuse recovered by patients across the United States, yet many mental health professionals and other advocates insist the memories should be taken literally. Object Relations Theory provides an alternative to this position. It hypothesizes that the memories are unconscious, metaphoric representations of actual childhood incest that draw on cultural symbols of evil and death. When shared with clinicians whose beliefs resonate with these cultural themes, the memories often are treated as reliable and truthful.

♦ **497**   Yeager, C.A., & Lewis, D.O. (1997). False memories of cult abuse. *American Journal of Psychiatry, 154,* 435.

The case of a 39 year old female patient, diagnosed with dissociative identity disorder, who recovered memories of ritual abuse by a satanic cult and sexually abuse by her parents after attending a survivor support group, demonstrates the necessity of exploring the context of memory recovery before believing patients were ritually and/or sexually abused and then treating them for it.

RITUAL ABUSE AND THE MULTIPLE PERSONALITY CONTROVERSY

The most recent revival of cultural sensitivity to child abuse also renewed interest in a disorder that has intrigued since it first was "discovered" well over a century ago. Dissociative Identity Disorder, or Multiple Personality Disorder as it was previously and much more descriptively termed, was always interpreted as a reaction to childhood trauma. Trauma, the argument goes, makes such demands on coping for children that some of them dissociate and split into separate personalities that take on different roles and functions to ensure the physical and psychological survival of children. Always contestable, the very idea of multiplicity and the theoretical assumptions that underlie it became the subjects of volatile debate when so many adults diagnosed with the disorder began remembering that the childhood trauma that fractured them into separate personalities was actually ritual abuse.

♦ **498**   Aldridge, M.R. (1994). A skeptical reflection on the diagnosis of multiple personality disorder. *Irish Journal of Psychological Medicine, 11,* 126–129.

Despite increasing prevalence, questions should be raised as to whether multiple personality disorder is a naturally occurring diagnostic entity. Several reasons for skepticism must be noted, especially the role that ritual abuse, itself a controversial and contested issue, allegedly plays in its etiology.

♦ **499**   Cook, K., & "A" Team. (1995/1996). Survivors and supporters: Working on ritual abuse. *Trouble and Strife, 32,* 46–52.

Many women diagnosed with multiple personality disorder report childhood histories of ritual abuse. Mental health professionals must support them as they recover and work through the memories and recognize that once connection and cooperation between the fragmented personalities is achieved, it is possible for these women to live normal lives.

♦ **500**   Fraser, G.A. (1990). Satanic ritual abuse: A cause of multiple personality disorder. *Journal of Child and Youth Care, 6,* 55–65.

Two cases illustrate the etiological role of ritual abuse in the formation of multiple personality disorder. Ritual abuse is a thoroughly traumatizing experience that can only be coped with through dissociation and splitting into alter personalities.

♦ **501**   Friesen, J.G. (1992). Ego-dystonic or ego-alien: Alternate personality or evil spirit? *Journal of Psychology and Theology, 20,* 197–200.

Multiple personality disorder is a predictable consequence of childhood ritual abuse. Treatment must focus on the integration of alters and the expulsion of the evil spirits which may mask as personality fragments. A new diagnostic category called "Oppressive Supernatural States Disorder" is recommended, with the following diagnostic criteria: experience of the oppressive states as ego-alien, absence of schizophrenia, marked revulsion to Christian symbols and/or the name of Jesus, evidence of supernatural occurrences, and the perception of an "evil presence" by someone other than the patient.

♦ **502**   Gelb, J.L. (1993). Multiple personality disorder and satanic ritual abuse. *Australian and New Zealand Journal of Psychiatry, 27,* 701–708.

The popularity of ritual abuse and multiple personality disorder as diagnoses does not reflect any scientific validation of either disorder. Mental health professionals must refrain from therapy techniques that perpetuate and amplify the symptomatology and dysfunction of patients previously diagnosed with, or suspected of having, either of these disorders.

♦ **503**   Gould, C., & Cozolino, L. (1992). Ritual abuse, multiplicity, and mind-control. *Journal of Psychology and Theology, 20,* 194–196.

Through the psychologically intolerable experience of ritual abuse, satanic cults deliberately create multiple personalities in their victims. Some of these created alters are programmed to stay in regular contact with the cult, others to self-injure or to attempt suicide, and others still to disrupt any therapeutic intervention. Successful treatment of ritual abuse patients necessitates the creation of a therapeutic alliance, a plan to explore their alter personalities and determine the function of each, an understanding of the cult triggers that access alters, and the recovery of memories of the ritual abuse.

◆ **504**   Kelly, B.L.F. (1993). Multiple personality disorder — satanic ritual abuse: An issue with God? *Dissertation Abstracts International, 54* (11-B), 5973. (University Microfilms No. AAG94-12600)

Previously diagnosed with multiple personality disorder, 10 adult women who report childhood histories of ritual abuse were surveyed as to their spirituality and relationship with God. The women score high on spirituality measures and report positive relations with God. They report that faith assists their ability to cope with daily problems and plays a fundamental role in their healing. The findings suggest that psychotherapeutic intervention with patients who report a history of ritual abuse should be sensitive to, and work with, the spirituality of the patient.

◆ **505**   Lockwood, C. (1993). *Other altars: Roots and realities of cultic and satanic ritual abuse and multiple personality disorder.* Minneapolis, MN: CompCare.

In addition to sexual abuse, ritual abuse involves such horrific acts as human sacrifices, cannibalism, blood-drinking and torture. The cumulative experience of ritual abuse is a significant etiological factor in the development of multiple personality disorder.

◆ **506**   Mayer, R.S. (1991). *Satan's children.* New York: Avon.

Five patients, all diagnosed with multiple personality disorder, recover memories of ritual abuse in satanic cults during the course of therapy. All were successfully treated and integrated by the author, a psychologist, who examines his own growing awareness of ritual abuse acquired through extensive reading of psychological and popular literature and consultations with colleagues. These patients challenged everything he knew about treating multiple personalities, forced him to expand his world view to accommodate a specific vision of evil, and made him fear for his own and his family's safety. Although the author still is not convinced there is a national satanic conspiracy targeting children, as his patients believe, he finds it impossible to reject the notion of ritual abuse altogether, especially in the face of his patients' profoundly fractured personalities.

◆ **507**   McCarty, M. (1991). Multiple personality disorder: Fact or fiction? *Journal of Christian Healing, 13,* 29–32.

Most patients with multiple personalities were ritually abused as children. The successful integration of their alters can only be accomplished if their treating psychotherapists reprogram their satanic beliefs, encourage them to accept Jesus Christ, and cast out their demonic spirits.

◆ **508**   Middleton, W. (1994). Further comments on multiple personality disorder. *Australian and New Zealand Journal of Psychiatry, 28,* 154–156.

Gelb (see citation 502) overlooks the clinically documented association between childhood abuse, especially ritual abuse, and multiple personality disorder.

◆ **509**   Mulhern, S.A. (1994). Satanism, ritual abuse, and multiple personality disorder: A sociohistorical perspective. *International Journal of Clinical and Experimental Hypnosis, 42,* 265–288.

The historical and social underpinnings of the epidemic of patients in treatment for multiple personality disorder who have recovered memories of ritual abuse must be taken into account. The received clinical wisdom that ritual abuse is the cause of multiple personality disorder is logically coherent with the new trauma/dissociation model of psychopathology, but it has led to a conspiracy theory that collapses when it is examined from a social psychological perspective.

♦ **510**   Neswald, D.W., & Gould, C. (1992). Basic treatment and program neutralization strategies for adult MPD survivors of satanic ritual abuse. *Treating Abuse Today, 2,* 5–10.

The most significant challenge posed to the treatment of patients with multiple personality disorder who report a childhood history of ritual abuse is neutralizing the cult-induced mind control program. Strategies for overcoming the barrier include re-associating, counter-conditioning, matching enactment with reversal triggers, implementing an alter personality "buddy system," helping alters share abilities among themselves, using assertive vertical approaches to personality system exploration, recruiting cult-loyal alters, identifying internal programmers, and disputing the idea that multiple personality disorder is untreatable.

♦ **511**   Paley, K.S. (1992). Dream wars: A case study of a woman with multiple personality disorder. *Dissociation, 5,* 111–116.

By engaging in dream work with multiple personality disorder patients, clinicians can break down barriers to the memory of childhood abuse, identify alter personalities, control malevolent alters and reduce conflicts between alters. The case of dream work therapy with a 28 year old female with multiple personality disorder and a childhood history of ritual abuse illustrates the benefits of a clinical focus on dreams.

♦ **512**   Ross, C.A. (1995). *Satanic ritual abuse: Principles of treatment.* Toronto, Canada: University of Toronto Press.

Patients with multiple personality disorder who also report a childhood history of ritual abuse often have hypercomplex personality systems that pose real challenges to treating clinicians. The effective treatment of these patients involves managing counter-transference responses, mapping the personality system, forming a treatment alliance with persecutory alters, staying alert to suicidal ideation and self-injury, increasing communication and cooperation between alters, reducing post-traumatic hyper-arousal, and limiting trauma memory recovery to specific memories driving suicidal ideation. A problem-oriented treatment approach is most efficacious. Satanic cults have a long history, as does society's denial of ritual abuse; both of those factors complicate therapeutic intervention.

♦ **513**   Scott, S. (1999). Fragmented selves in late modernity: Making sociological sense of multiple personalities. *Sociological Review, 47,* 432–460.

Drawing on life history interviews with women who report childhood histories of ritual abuse and who define themselves as multiple personalities, it is apparent that an adequate sociological account of multiple personality disorder must combine an analysis of clinical and popular discourses about dissociation and multiplicity with an understanding of their relationship to individual autobiographies. The very production of such an autobiography requires an active engagement with previously denied and silenced experiences as well as with dominant cultural discourses that encourage the episodic denial of those experiences. Because the diagnosis of multiple personality disorder is more often given to women than men, questions must be raised about the impact of the adoption of multiple identities on the integrity and autonomy of women.

◆ **514** VanBenschoten, S.C. (1990). Multiple personality disorder and satanic ritual abuse: The issue of credibility. *Dissociation, 3,* 22–30.

Because there are more differences than similarities between the accounts of ritually abused children and the memories of childhood histories of ritual abuse by adults diagnosed with multiple personality disorder, inevitable questions arise about the validity and accuracy of the reports. Mental health professionals must exercise critical judgment before deciding whether the memories are true or false.

◆ **515** Wycoff, D. (1996). Now everything makes sense: Complicating the contemporary legend picture. In G. Bennett & P. Smith, *Contemporary Legend: A Reader* (pp. 363–380). NY: Garland Press.

Multiple personality disorder is discussed as an idiom of distress through which people express their sense that the social order is as fragmented as they feel they are personally. In locating the cause of this disorder in a history of childhood ritual abuse, they exorcise this pervasive anxiety by projecting on demonized family members or on the larger culture's current folk devils.

THERAPEUTIC INTERVENTIONS

The trauma model of therapy that experienced a revival in this most recent period of cultural sensitivity to childhood trauma rests on the assumption that the disempowering and dislocating experiences of abuse cause the mind to dissociate, that is, to separate the memory of the trauma from everyday consciousness. Held at abeyance behind an amnestic barrier, or within an alter personality, the repressed memory occasionally manages to slip into consciousness in the form of disturbing and uninvited flashbacks, or bewildering arrays of emotional and physical symptoms. The goal of therapy, then, is to use any number of eclectic interventions to break down the barrier, expose the traumatic memory in all its grisly detail, and work through it from a position of increasing mastery.

◆ **516** Feldman, G.C. (1993). *Lessons in evil, lessons from the light: A true story of satanic abuse and spiritual healing.* NY: Crown.

The successful therapy of the pseudonymous patient Barbara Maddox is presented. She entered therapy for sexual dysfunction and unwarranted anger at her daughter, and through hypnosis recovered memories of ritual abuse by her mother, grandparents and other satanic cultists. The author, her treating psychologist, examines her own journey from skepticism to belief in her patient's memories. Once the author had expanded her own world view to accept the reality of evil, she became so preoccupied with understanding evil that her already difficult marriage became even more troubled, and she became fearful about the safety of her own children. In an attempt to discover her own encounters with violence, she participated in past life therapy and recovered memories of being an 18th century Indian girl struggling to free herself from a patriarchal culture. She maintains a friendship with Maddox, whom she considers an inspiration.

♦ **517**   Fraser, G.A. (Ed.) (1997). *The dilemma of ritual abuse: Cautions and guides for therapists.* Washington, D.C.: American Psychiatric Association Press.

An 11 chapter edited text covering the clinical recognition, assessment and treatment of ritual abuse.

♦ **518**   Goodwin, J.M, Hill, S., & Attias, R. (1990). Historical and folk techniques of exorcism: Applications to the treatment of dissociative disorders. *Dissociation, 3,* 94–101.

Christian and Jewish exorcism practices have elements common to the treatment of dissociative patients with a childhood history of ritual abuse, including the uses of special diagnostic techniques, incantations, music and ritual objects; physical interventions; and verbal confrontations with the possessing spirit.

♦ **519**   Hill, S., & Goodwin, J.M. (1993). Freud's notes on a 17th century case of demonic possession: Understanding the uses of exorcism. In J.M. Goodwin (Ed.), *Rediscovering childhood trauma: Historical casebook and clinical applications* (pp. 45–63). Washington, D.C.: American Psychiatric Press.

A 17th century case of demon possession and exorcism studied by Freud has parallels to a contemporary case of a 42 year old woman whose demonic possession was the result of childhood ritual abuse by a satanic cult. Freud posited that on a symbolic level, the demons represent internalized abusers. The analysis of the contemporary case extends that understanding by suggesting that the demons also represent keepers of the secret of abuse, protectors of the patient, and substitutes for memory.

♦ **520**   Hruby, K. (1995). Two cases of ritual abuse. *Small Remedies and Interesting Cases: Professional Case Conferences, 7,* 188–254.

Two cases of adult women with childhood histories of ritual abuse illustrate the challenges posed to the homeopathic treatment of patients with post-traumatic stress disorder and/or dissociative disorders.

♦ **521**   McCann, L., & Pearlman, L.A. (1992). Constructivist self-development theory: A theoretical model of psychological adaptation to severe trauma. In D.K. Sakheim & S.E. Devine (Eds.), *Out of darkness: Exploring satanism and ritual abuse* (pp. 185–206). NY: Lexington.

Constructivist self-development theory of trauma and adaptation can be used to understand the sequelae of childhood ritual abuse for adult patients. The theory takes into account identity formation, world view, frame-of-reference schemas, and the assimilation of traumatic memories. The theory posits that all individuals have psychological needs for safety, trust/dependency, esteem, independence, power and intimacy, and that personal thoughts, feelings and behaviors are associated with each. Any or all of these needs also can remain unfulfilled by the traumatic experience of ritual abuse. A major goal of therapy is to understand, acknowledge and explore the significance of these unfulfilled needs for patients reporting a childhood history of ritual abuse.

♦ **522**   Peach, P.H. (1997). The experience of spirituality in the healing process of ritual abuse survivors. *Dissertation Abstracts International, 58* (02-B), 0987. (University Microfilms No. AAG97-20723)

The spirituality of 5 adults with childhood histories of ritual abuse, and the relationship it has to psychotherapy, theology and mysticism are explored. The findings show that spirituality has a significant impact on every stage of the healing process.

◆ **523**   Ryder, D. (1992). *Breaking the circle of satanic ritual abuse*. Minneapolis, MN: CompCare.

The author, a counselor who recovered his own memories of ritual abuse, now treats others who have recovered memories through a 12-Step Program in which they share their stories of ritual abuse, acknowledge their helplessness over its effects, turn their healing over to a higher power, take moral inventory of themselves and admit their shortcomings, make amends to people they have offended, and carry the message of healing to others. Triggers in the group experience that set off memories of ritual abuse or cue alter personalities to disrupt or block therapy must be assessed, and mental health professionals must be aware of satanic symbols, roles and rituals.

◆ **524**   Schacter, C.L., Stalker, C.A., & Teram, E. (1999). Toward sensitive practice: Issues for physical therapists working with survivors of childhood sexual abuse. *Physical Therapy, 79,* 248–262.

Interviews conducted with 27 women with childhood histories of ritual abuse as to their experiences with physical therapy reveal that their crucial concern is the assurance and protection of their physical safety during physical therapy. The implications for physical therapists of working with patients whose physical and emotional boundaries are strongly defended are discussed.

◆ **525**   Smith, M. (1993). *Ritual abuse: What it is, why it happens, and how to help*. San Francisco, CA: Harper Collins.

The author, who has memories of childhood ritual abuse, surveyed 52 adults with similar memories to gather information about their experience of ritual abuse and recovery. Their experiences illustrate how cults operate, how they brainwash their victims, and how that programming interferes with recovery.

◆ **526**   Williams, M.B. (1994). Establishing safety in survivors of severe sexual abuse. In J.F. Sommer (Ed.), *Handbook of post-traumatic therapy* (pp. 162–178). Westport, CT: Greenwood.

The creation of a safe therapeutic environment for patients reporting a childhood history of ritual abuse is paramount in therapy. Techniques for doing so include establishing clear boundaries, assuring confidentiality, and guarding against self-injury.

◆ **527**   Woodsum, G.M. (1998). *The ultimate challenge: A revolutionary, sane and sensible response to ritualistic and cult-related abuse*. Laramie, WY: Action Resources International.

A framework for recovery from ritual abuse involves breaking the cycle of indoctrination, engaging in regression work to recover memories, and assessing safety. Traditional therapeutic strategies, such as hypnosis, group work, medication administration and hospitalization are not proving successful with ritual abuse patients.

◆ **528**   Young, W.C. (1992). Recognition and treatment of survivors reporting ritual abuse. In D.K. Sakheim & S.E. Devine (Eds.), *Out of darkness: Exploring satanism and ritual abuse* (pp. 249–278). NY: Lexington.

The treatment of adults with a childhood history of ritual abuse involves developing alliances, evaluating and assessing, uncovering and reconstructing repressed memories, dissolving dissociative barriers, desensitizing triggers and cues, counter-ing indoctrinated beliefs, and coming to terms with the past and the future. Expres-sive strategies, such as journaling, art work and sandtray approaches, are particularly helpful adjuncts to more traditional therapy.

RITUAL ABUSE AND THE
IATROGENESIS CONTROVERSY

In dealing with memories of childhood abuse, mental health profes-sionals confront both vulnerability and evil. As a corrective to the silence that greeted memories of trauma during those long periods of cultural insensitivity to abuse, the contemporary trauma model exhorts them to ally with their patients as they recover their memories. The shift in the therapeutic role from neutral observer to active partner in the retrieval and report of memories is central to the iatrogenesis controversy. Critics charge that in acting as allies with their patients, mental health profes-sionals actually create and shape recovered memories of ritual abuse, and therefore collude in the creation of false memories.

◆ **529**   Baumeister, R.F., & Sommer, K.L. (1997). Patterns in the bizarre: Common themes in satanic ritual abuse, sexual masochism, UFO abduc-tions, factitious illness, and extreme love. *Journal of Social and Clinical Psy-chology, 16*, 213–223.
    Ritual abuse, sexual masochism, alien abduction, factitious disorders and extreme love have features in common. In each, the person embraces a victim role with atten-dant feelings of humiliation, rage and helplessness. This new role transcends and transforms the person's identity and cultivates a compelling relationship with power-ful others, most particularly mental health professionals who encourage the role-tak-ing. This relationship, in turn, has the secondary gain of boosting the person's self-esteem.

◆ **530**   Coons, P.M. (1994). Reports of satanic ritual abuse: Further implications about pseudo-memories. *Perceptual and Motor Skills, 78*, 1376–1378.
    To assess the possibility that memories of childhood ritual abuse are specious, the charts of 29 patients in a dissociative disorders clinic were reviewed. In each case, the memories can be accounted for, at least in part, by the provocative and suggestive hyp-notic and regressive therapies in which the patient participated.

◆ **531**   Ganaway, G.K. (1992). Some additional questions: A response to Shaffer and Cozolino, to Gould and Cozolino, and to Friesen. *Journal of Psychology and Theology, 20*, 201–205.
    Shaffer and Cozolino (see citation 467), Gould and Cozolino (see citation 503), and Friesen (see citation 501) draw *a priori* conclusions about satanic cults and ritual abuse in the absence of any corroborating evidence. Their approach is more a leap of faith than a scientific inquiry, and their articles would be rejected for publication by any

reputable peer-reviewed scientific journal. While it is important to be sensitive to the needs of trauma patients, the suspension of clinical judgment on the part of mental health professionals, which they advocate, has deleterious effects and is one of the most significant contributing factors to the growing cottage industry in ritual abuse assessment and treatment.

◆ **532**   Karlin, R.A., & Orne, M.T. (1996). Commentary on *Borawick v. Shay:* Hypnosis, social influence, incestuous child abuse, and satanic ritual abuse: The iatrogenic creation of horrific memories for the remote past. *Cultic Studies Journal, 13,* 42–94.

The *Borawick v. Shay* case involved hypnotically recovered memories of ritual abuse and incest. A statistical analysis of this and other similar legal cases suggests that at least 70% of all diagnoses of ritual abuse and incest that are based on recovered memories are false. The greatest contributor to iatrogenesis is the mental health profession's adherence to the trauma/dissociation model, and the use of therapeutic techniques such as hypnosis that are consistent with that model.

◆ **533**   Mulhern, S.A. (1991). Patients reporting ritual abuse in childhood: A clinical response. *Child Abuse & Neglect, 15,* 609–611.

Young *et al.* (see citation 474) fail to consider that their own beliefs in ritual abuse and the introspective therapeutic techniques they employed with their sample patients could be the major factor that contributes to the similar stories of ritual abuse by the patients.

◆ **534**   Scheflin, A.W. (1996). Commentary on *Borawick v. Shay:* The fate of hypnotically retrieved memories. *Cultic Studies Journal, 13,* 26–41.

The U.S. Federal Court of Appeals for the 2nd Circuit correctly applied the "totality of the circumstances" test in the admissibility of hypnotically refreshed memories of ritual abuse in *Borawick.* The court was incorrect, however, in denying the plaintiff her day in court to prove her allegations. Research clearly shows that, when properly used, hypnosis does not contaminate or alter memory, and does assist in the recovery of true memories.

CONTROVERSIAL NARRATIVES OF RITUAL ABUSE

The private and confidential therapeutic setting is not the only one in which memories of childhood ritual abuse are being heard. Some adults who identify themselves as survivors choose much more public arenas for sharing their stories, thereby positioning themselves in the center of the cultural debate over ritual abuse.

◆ **535**   deYoung, M. (1996). Breeders for Satan: Toward a sociology of sexual trauma tales. *Journal of American Culture, 19,* 111–17.

An analysis of the stories of 8 women who appeared on 8 different television talk shows to discuss how they were impregnated in satanic rituals to produce infants for sacrifices shows that despite their horrific plot, these sexual trauma tales do little more than reinforce and replicate dominant cultural discourses about female victimization and helplessness. They are provocative tales about the inevitability of sexual violence in the lives of women, and as such they can be listened to, but not acted upon.

◆ **536** Jenkins, P., & Maier-Katkin, D. (1991). Occult survivors: The making of a myth. In J.T. Richardson, J. Best, & D.G. Bromley (eds.), *The satanism scare* (pp. 127–144). Hawthorne, NY: Aldine deGruyter.

Survivor accounts of ritual abuse are being brought together to create a new synthetic history of cults and satanic activity, but a closer look at the published accounts uncovers contradictions, inconsistencies, and duplicities. These trauma tales actually reveal more about the mental disorders of their authors and the quasi-religious function of therapeutic confessions than they do about ritual abuse or satanic cults.

◆ **537** Schnabel, J. (1994). Chronic claims of alien abduction and some other traumas as self-victimization syndromes. *Dissociation, 7*, 51–62.

Patients' stories of ritual abuse have a thematic resemblance to stories about the experience of having multiple personalities and of alien abductions, with themes of sexual assault, helplessness and rage. There is no convincing evidence that any of these stories are accurate accounts of severe exogenous trauma, therefore it is more useful to view them as examples of self-victimization syndromes.

◆ **538** Wycoff, D.L. (1994). Speaking about life experiences: Personal narrativizing and social constructionism. *Dissertation Abstracts International, 56* (01-A), 0018. (University Microfilms No. AAI95-17098)

Of all of the types of narratives of sexual violence seen on television talk shows and read in first person stories, the ones of ritual abuse are the most horrific, yet paradoxically the most conservative. They defend a Western, Christian, patriarchal world view and provide an enemy for diverse elements of conservative America to attack. While the act of speaking about one's experiences is liberating in many ways, personal narratives of ritual abuse presented in public arenas also impose gender-specific agendas onto what may, should, and ought be said about the experience of sexual violence.

THE CONTROVERSY UNRESOLVED

Nearly two decades of debate leaves unanswered the nagging question of whether recovered memories of childhood ritual abuse are factual reports or fanciful reconstructions. The line between the two is not only clinically relevant, but morally and politically inscribed.

◆ **539** Cook, K., & Kelly, L. (1997). The abduction of credibility: A reply to John Paley. *British Journal of Social Work, 27*, 71–84.

By failing to take into consideration the compelling evidence that ritual abuse is a social problem with real clinical consequences, Paley (see citation 490) contributes to the ruthless backlash against ritual abuse and other more ordinary forms of child abuse. His position that there is no evidence to support accounts of ritual abuse has the status of orthodoxy among skeptics, but leaves unaddressed the question of just how much and what kind of evidence is still needed to convince skeptics of the reality of ritual abuse.

◆ **540** Rogers, M.L. (1991). Evaluating an alleged satanic ritual abuser: What we don't know. *Issues in Child Abuse Accusations, 3*. Retrieved

4-March-01 from the World Wide Web: http://www.ipt-forensics.com/journal/volume3/j3_3_4.htm.

Because allegations of ritual abuse are so horrific and bizarre, the psychological assessment of alleged perpetrators is problematic. Evaluative criteria that distinguish ritual abusers from other types of sexual offenders are needed to facilitate the evaluation process and inform the decision whether to treat or incarcerate.

◆ **541**   Rosik, C.H. (1992). Satanic ritual abuse: A response to featured articles by Shaffer & Cozolino, Gould & Cozolino, and Friesen. *Journal of Psychology and Theology, 20*, 213–216.

The Shaffer and Cozolino (see citation 467), Gould and Cozolino (see citation 503), and Friesen (see citation 501) articles demonstrate that a dialogue between mental health professionals who hold divergent views of ritual abuse must take place in order to heal the rift between believers, skeptics and disbelievers.

◆ **542**   Shaffer, R.E. (1992). Better to investigate ritual abuse than to ignore or deny it: Shaffer responds to Ganaway. *Journal of Psychology and Theology, 20*, 208–209.

Ganaway's (see citation 531) critique of the Shaffer and Cozolino (see citation 467), Gould and Cozolino (see citation 503), and Friesen (see citation 501) articles highlights the need for descriptive studies of ritual abuse that will avoid the kind of reductionism of scientific models that characterizes so much of the literature on ritual abuse, and that has led to such controversial therapeutic interventions.

7

Impact of the Ritual Abuse Controversy on Professionals and Systems

It may be said with little fear of contradiction, clever as the following statement is in satisfying both sides of the debate, that ritual abuse is both the cause and the effect of a paradigm shift in the helping professions. As its cause, ritual abuse reenchanted the secular rationality of the helping professions by suffusing them with a foreboding sense of evil, and in doing so recast the role of professionals from objective outsiders to allies of victims in a moral battle with it. As its effect, ritual abuse emerged from the new trauma model embraced by helping professionals that plumbed the darkest recesses of childhood to discover how the present and the future are contained in the past.

It also may be said with little fear of contradiction, uninspired as the following statement is in declaring the obvious, that whether cause or effect, ritual abuse certainly is a most divisive issue in the helping professions. It cuts deeply and unkindly. It dissevers the professions over its validity, rives them over their role in investigating, treating and adjudicating it, and slices to their collective heart by calling into question whether those they aim to help are, indeed, helped after all.

Over the last twenty years, the issue of ritual abuse has raised the public profile of the helping professions, and has alternately ennobled and denigrated them. If only for its knack in doing just that, ritual abuse indeed is the most diabolical form of abuse after all.

BELIEVERS AND DISBELIEVERS

More for the convenience it offers than anything else, helping professionals often are divided into believers at one end of some chimerical scale of credulity, and disbelievers at the other, with sometimes not more than a passing nod at the many bewildered professionals who gambol somewhere in between. In all fairness, there probably is more than a little movement along this hypothetical continuum, if only for the fact that the definition of ritual abuse, as discussed in Chapter 1, is so slippery. Helping professionals who disbelieve the notion of satanic cultists ritually abusing children in the ceremonial worship of the devil, for example, may believe the notion of other organized groups or rings systematically and stylistically abusing children for entirely profane reasons.

There is little consideration in the following citations of movement along this credulity scale or of inertia in the middle of it. Rather, these citations put believers and disbelievers on the couch, dissect their beliefs and consider the influence of those beliefs, whatever they are, on their professional practice, whatever that might be.

◆ **543**   Grant, C.A. (1995). The assessment and investigation of ritual abuse. In T. Ney (Ed.), *True and false allegations of child sexual abuse: Assessment and case management* (pp. 303–315). NY: Brunner/Mazel.

The issue of ritual abuse contentiously divides child protectionists, criminal justice and mental health professionals into two opposing camps: those who believe the allegations, and those who do not. Regardless of the individual professional's role, his or her belief system will profoundly affect how an alleged case of ritual abuse is perceived, assessed, investigated, treated and resolved.

◆ **544**   Greaves, G.B. (1992). Alternative hypotheses regarding claims of satanic cult activity: A critical analysis. In D.K. Sakheim & S.E. Devine (Eds.), *Out of darkness: Exploring satanism and ritual abuse* (pp. 45–72). NY: Lexington Books.

In regard to claims of ritual abuse, helping professionals can be categorized as nihilists who do not believe the claims; apologists who do; heuristics who are uncommitted; and methodologists who take a wait-and-see stance. The nihilists believe that because they can concoct alternative hypotheses, ritual abuse claims are not true. They uphold no empirical criteria of truth, but demand it of others. The apologists believe that because ritual abuse reports resemble each other in content and are similar to historical accounts of evil, they must be true. Heuristics, most of them mental health professionals, believe they will achieve favorable therapeutic outcomes with self-identified satanic cult survivors if they treat their accounts in a confirming, although not necessarily agreeing, manner. And methodologists believe that in the absence of thorough scientific investigations, it is premature to commit to a position on ritual abuse.

◆ **545**   Holgerson, A. (1995). Professionals as evaluators or indoctrinators in sex abuse cases. *Nordisk Sexologi, 13*, 163–169.

Since the early 1950s, the focus of psychological investigation in legal cases of ritual abuse and sexual abuse in Sweden has shifted from the assessment of the reliability of the person, to the assessment of the reliability of a person's spoken statements. That shift often pits a professional's belief system against a person's disclosure, a clash that is illustrated with descriptions and transcripts from ritual abuse and sexual abuse trials.

♦ **546**   Lotto, D. (1994). On witches and witch-hunts. *Journal of Psychohistory, 21*, 373–396.

In alleging ritual abuse, children express the psychological truth of their childhood in that they feel controlled by powerful adults who sometimes do intrusive and sadistic things to them while preoccupied with their own pursuits. Professionals who believe these accounts do so because the themes of helplessness, rage and fear resonate with their own childhood experiences of being raised by narcissistic, alienating parents. Then when they relentlessly pursue every little detail of the alleged abuse with the children, they re-create for them the psychological truth of their childhood and leave them helpless and victimized.

♦ **547**   Nurston, J., & Smith, M. (1996). Believe or disbelieve? With particular reference to satanist abuse. *Child Abuse Review, 5*, 253–262.

The difficulty of developing a theoretical base of treatment when questions persist as to the veracity of ritual abuse allegations is considerable. The belief system of professionals can and does affect practice.

♦ **548**   Putnam, F.W. (1991). The satanic ritual abuse controversy. *Child Abuse & Neglect, 15*, 175–179.

The issues raised by Jonker and Jonker-Bakker (see citation 312) and Young *et al.* (see citation 474) are fundamental to the controversy currently waging in the child protection field over the issue of ritual abuse. In evaluating reports of ritual abuse it is important to assess the underlying beliefs of the authors; in these 2 articles, the authors clearly are convinced that ritual abuse is real and that the dynamics and effects they are describing are credible features of it. Neither article reaches the standards of empirical research, therefore each is highly impressionistic and naïve in its conclusions. The picture of satanic cults that emerges from these articles is unconvincing, and the lack of evidence presented by the authors to corroborate the allegations renders their depictions unbelievable. These articles are better understood by appreciating how the labyrinthine communication network that links child protectionists around the world operates to transform speculation into science, and rumor into reality.

♦ **549**   Rosik, C.H. (2000). Some effects of world view on the theory and treatment of dissociative identity disorder. *Journal of Psychology and Christianity, 19*, 166–180.

The manner by which mental health professionals approach dissociative identity disorder is strongly linked to their world view. Those who believe in a theological concept of evil and its relationship to individual psychopathology have the most credulous views of ritual abuse, but they often are marginalized by their colleagues whose views are more secular and skeptical.

♦ **550**   Underwager, R., & Wakefield, H. (1991). *Cur alli, prae aliis? Issues in Child Abuse Accusations, 3*. Retrieved 4-March-01 from the World Wide Web: http://www.ipt-forensics.com/journal/volume3/j3_3_5.htm

Why some professionals, and not others, believe in ritual abuse is a product of personality characteristics. "Believers" need self-justification of their nobility, courage and virtuosity in order to enhance their self-concept; they need to define their roles in terms of rescuing innocent children from evil. "Believers" have little ability to tolerate ambiguity and are highly authoritarian.

THE SUBSTANCE OF THE DEBATE

One very good reason why the oft-cited dichotomy between believers and disbelievers should be considered a heuristic is that many helping professionals have never even dealt with an alleged case of ritual abuse. So, given the contentious nature of the debate over the issue, the questions must be asked: just how many cases of ritual abuse are coming to the attention of helping professionals, and is there a profile of the helping professionals who are most likely to encounter them, and believe them to be true?

♦ **551**   Bottoms, B.L., Shaver, P.R., & Goodman, G.S. (1996). An analysis of ritualistic and religion-based child abuse allegations. *Law and Human Behavior, 20,* 1–34.

To ascertain the number and the nature of cases involving alleged ritualistic and religion-based child abuse, a stratified random survey of clinical members of the American Psychological Association was conducted. Findings reveal that only a minority of the 338 responding clinical psychologists have encountered ritual abuse cases, but most believe their patients' accounts despite the lack of corroborating evidence. The influence of the media in shaping the accounts and reinforcing their credibility, and the pressure placed on children by credulous parents and professionals are the major sources for these allegations.

♦ **552**   Brandt, S.J. (1992). An analysis of mental health professionals' response to satanic ritual abuse. *Dissertation Abstracts International, 54* (01-A), 0087. (University Microfilms No. AAG93-12259)

Kansas City mental health practitioners completed a variety of measures to determine if their level of moral development, fundamentalist Christian beliefs, education and type of licensure have any relationship to their belief in ritual abuse. The findings indicate that doctoral level psychologists are significantly more skeptical about ritual abuse than are master level social workers and counselors; respondents with fundamentalist beliefs are more credulous.

♦ **553**   Cole, D.A. (1992). The incidence of ritual abuse: A preliminary survey. *Dissertation Abstracts International, 53* (06-B), 3150. (University Microfilm No. AAG92-32365)

A survey was sent to 1,250 mental health professionals in Los Angeles and Orange counties to determine the incidence of ritual abuse they see in their practices. The findings indicate that 46% of the 250 responding professionals have seen ritual abuse patients or have seen sequelae of ritual abuse in their patients' histories. There is a need to replicate this research on a national sample to assess whether these results are specific to the southern California area.

♦ **554**   Feigon, E.A., & deRivera, J. (1998). Recovered-memory therapy: Profession at a turning point. *Comprehensive Psychiatry, 39,* 338–344.

A survey completed by 154 Massachusetts psychiatrists questioned their opinions on factors plausibly related to the production of false memories of childhood sexual abuse: 69% agree false allegations constitute a real problem that must be addressed by psychiatrists; 37% endorse searching for the childhood roots of presenting complaints; 36% agree the validation of memories is an essential part of therapy; 36% believe inappropriate affect is an indicator truthful memories; 36% believe in the value of abreaction; 26% prefer to refer presumed survivors of sexual abuse to specialists; 18% trust symptom checklists as indicators of sexual abuse; 15% believe memory is a complete record of a person's history; and 18% agree ritual abuse is an important cause of post-traumatic stress disorder and dissociative disorders.

♦ **555**   Lewandowski, C.A. (1995). A comparison of protective service workers' perceptions of ritual and sexual abuse in children: An exploratory study. *Journal of Child Sexual Abuse, 4,* 67–81.

Protective services workers in 4 major cities in Kansas were surveyed to discover if there are differences in their perceptions of ritual and sexual abuse, and to determine their concerns regarding the assessment and treatment of both. Most of the 24 respondents indicate that ritual abuse results in more clinical and spiritual problems for children than does sexual abuse. Most also agree that it is more difficult and stressful to investigate and that they are insufficiently trained in its dynamics.

♦ **556**   McGinn, M.R., & Wade, N.G. (1995). Beliefs about the prevalence of dissociative identity disorder, sexual abuse, and ritual abuse among religious and nonreligious therapists. *Professional Psychology: Research and Practice, 26,* 257–261.

Surveys regarding the prevalence of dissociative identity disorder and ritual abuse in their practices were returned by 497 Christian therapists and 100 members of the American Psychological Association. Although there is a low rate of diagnosing dissociative identity disorder and ritual abuse among all respondents, Christian psychologists are slightly more likely to diagnose ritual abuse than other psychologists. No differences are found in diagnosing ritual abuse or dissociative identity disorder between Christian psychologists, other licensed Christian therapists, nonlicensed Christian therapists, and lay counselors.

♦ **557**   Schuttermaier, J., & Veno, A. (1999). Counselors' beliefs about ritual abuse: An Australian study. *Journal of Child Sexual Abuse, 8,* 45–63.

The beliefs of the Center Against Sexual Assault workers, psychiatrists and psychologists about ritual abuse were examined. Contrary to assertions that there is no consensus definition of ritual abuse, 70% of the staff agreed with a single definition of ritual abuse, and 85% agreed that ritual abuse is indicative of genuine trauma. This Australian program identified 153 cases of ritual abuse between 1985 and 1995. The religious beliefs of staff members were not related to the identification of ritual abuse cases, although the level of training in the recognition and treatment of sexual abuse was.

PROFESSIONAL DISCOURSE ON RITUAL ABUSE

Ritual abuse has a discursive, as well an ideological and material existence. It is discussed, debated, deliberated and, to complete the alliteration, drafted. At conferences and workshops, in academic and professional journals, helping professionals hear and talk about ritual abuse. Both what they are hearing and talking about, and the influence of that discourse on their beliefs and practices, are discussed in the following citations.

◆ **558**　Bucky, S.F., & Dalenberg, C. (1992). The relationship between training of mental health professionals and the reporting of ritual abuse and multiple personality disorder symptomatology. *Journal of Psychology and Theology, 20*, 233–238.

A survey of 433 mental health professionals in the greater San Diego, California, area was conducted to determine whether the disciplines in which they were trained or the state licenses they held have any relationship to their identification of ritual abuse and multiple personality disorder patients. No relationship is found for either, however the number of workshops attended on ritual abuse and on multiple personality disorder is related to the identification of these issues in clinical settings.

◆ **559**　Clapton, G. (1993). *The satanic abuse controversy: Social workers and the social work press*. London: University of North London Press.

Between 1989 and 1992, 149 children from 11 British cities were taken from their families by social workers and put into foster care or made wards of the court because of allegations of ritual abuse. The themes that emerge from an analysis of the reporting on these cases by the social work press include: an emphasis on women as ritual abusers; the rise of a new social work orthodoxy that children never lie; and the intrusion of the irrational into social work practice and reporting. The socioeconomic, ideological and professional forces that give rise to the idea of ritual abuse must be taken into account, and the consequences of involvement in ritual abuse cases for the beleaguered social work profession must be considered.

◆ **560**　deYoung, M. (2000). The devil goes abroad: The export of the ritual abuse moral panic. *British Criminology Conferences: Selected Proceedings, 3*. Retrieved 4-March-01 from the World Wide Web: http://www.lboro.ac.uk/departments/ss/bsc/bccsp/vol03/deyoung.html

An analysis of the ideological recruitment of international child protectionists into the ritual abuse moral panic begins with an examination of the written and spoken discourse of a cadre of American experts who traveled abroad to lecture on ritual abuse. Their discourse found 3 points of resonance with international audiences: it restored the image of the child as innocent victim, occluded the image of the sexual abuser as male, and reenchanted the image of the child protectionist as rescuer. When appropriated, panic discourse has both ideological and material effects, that is, it influences child protectionists to think and act in ways that ends up spreading the ritual abuse moral panic across Europe and Australasia.

◆ **561**　deYoung, M. (1996). Speak of the devil: Rhetoric in claims-making about the satanic ritual abuse problem. *Journal of Sociology and Social Welfare, 23*, 55–74.

A rhetorical analysis of the discourse on ritual abuse by mental health professionals, survivor groups, law enforcement personnel and Christian fundamentalists reveals that the persuasiveness of their claims that ritual abuse is a real and exigent social problem is not a product of the facts they cite or the conclusions they draw, but of the warrants they offer, that is, the statements they make about the threat ritual abuse poses to the social and moral order that resonate with current cultural ideologies.

◆ **562**   Doyle, C. (1996). Current issues in child protection: An overview of the debates in contemporary journals. *British Journal of Social Work,* *26*, 565–576.

An overview of current debates and concerns in the child protection field as reflected in British academic and professional journals reveals that one of the most divisive controversies that has emerged in recent years has to do with ritual abuse.

◆ **563**   Golston, J.C. (1992). The ritual abuse countertransference response and the erosion of clinical scholarship: A review of the *Journal of Child Abuse & Neglect,* v. 15. *Treating Abuse Today,* 2, 4–12.

Clinicians' countertransference responses to horrific reports of ritual abuse have led to polarized debates, flawed scholarship, and a preoccupation with the issue of credibility, as illustrated by the article by Young *et al.* (see citation 474) in *Child Abuse & Neglect,* and by the editorial and commentaries that accompany it.

◆ **564**   Hill, M. (1998). Satan's excellent adventure in the Antipodes. *Issues in Child Abuse Accusations, 10.* Retrieved 4-March-01 from the World Wide Web: http://www.ipt-forensics.com/journal/volume10/j10_9.htm

The importation of the ritual abuse scare to New Zealand is due to American "experts" whose conference presentations and published materials influenced Australasian professionals to start a witch hunt. Notable among them are Kee MacFarlane, of McMartin Preschool fame, and Roland Summit, a psychiatrist who consulted on many of the American day care cases; both gave papers on ritual abuse at the International Conference on Child Abuse and Neglect in Sydney, Australia in 1986. Pamela Klein, an American who was instrumental in starting the ritual abuse panic in England, spoke at a conference in New Zealand. In response to these presentations, the Ritual Abuse Action Network was formed. It was a workshop presented by that group in a Christchurch child abuse conference that fomented the hysteria that led to the Civic Creche case.

◆ **565**   Kelly, L., & Scott, S. (1993). The current literature about organized abuse of children. *Child Abuse Review,* 2, 281–287.

A review of the literature and research studies on ritual abuse, child pornography and prostitution, and pedophile networks, demonstrates that research on ritual abuse tends to be out of the scientific mainstream, although there is increasing acceptance of some related areas of study, such as multiple personality disorder.

◆ **566**   Mulhern, S.A. (1992). Ritual abuse: Defining a syndrome versus defending a belief. *Journal of Psychology and Theology,* 20, 230–232.

A participant observation study conducted between 1987 and 1990 in a variety of ritual abuse workshops for mental health professionals finds that they constitute a form of proselytizing designed to convert skeptical professionals into believing ritual abuse exists. The diagnostic and therapy techniques recommended in these workshops, as well as the explanations given for patients' florid clinical symptoms, presuppose the existence of a network of organized and covert satanic cults.

◆ **567**   Mulhern, S.A. (1991). Satanism and psychotherapy: A rumor in search of an inquisition. In J.T. Richardson, J. Best, & D.G. Bromley (Eds.), *The satanism scare* (pp. 145–172). Hawthorne, NY: Aldine deGruyter.
   The current interest in satanic cults and ritual abuse is the product of changes in the theory and practice of psychotherapy, especially the recent introduction of the trauma/dissociation model, the increased use of hypnosis and the growing interest in the diagnosis of multiple personality disorder. Mental health professionals are being trained in the diagnosis and treatment of ritual abuse in workshops that create an emotional and conceptual context for this belief. An aura of plausibility is created around the idea of satanic cults; patients' art work and journal entries are read to illustrate the process of recovering memories of ritual abuse. These workshops proselytize and attempt to convert attendees to a belief system that is wholly unsupported by evidence.

SYSTEM RESPONSES TO RITUAL ABUSE

It is not just helping professionals who are engaged in the ritual abuse controversy. From psychologists to police, helplines to hospitals, entire professions and whole organizations are engaged in the ritual abuse controversy. Interestingly, the controversy has spawned its own vocations and groups, from hypnotherapists who plumb the depths of the unconscious for long-repressed memories of ritual abuse, to advocacy groups that raise awareness and funds to combat it. It also can be convincingly argued that the ritual abuse controversy has spawned a cottage industry in self-help books, audio and videotapes, and even quite handsomely paid guest speakers. That cottage industry aside, the following citations examine the responses of helping professions and helping organizations, both formal and informal, to the ritual abuse controversy.

◆ **568**   Creighton, S.J. (1993). Organized abuse: NSPCC experience. *Child Abuse Review*, 2, 232–242.
   A survey of 71 British child protection teams conducted by the National Society for the Prevention of Cruelty to Children (NSPCC) finds that teams have encountered 6 ritual abuse cases involving a total of 18 children. In 4 of those cases, the children describe the use of chants, signs and symbols in conjunction with the ritual abuse, the forced ingestion of drugs or potions, and the wearing of costumes. The 18 children, most between the ages of 5 and 9, implicated 50 adults as their ritual abusers, most of them immediate or extended family members, and over 60 other children as victims.

◆ **569**   Fisher, C.B. (1995). American Psychological Association's (1992) Ethics Code and the validation of sexual abuse in daycare settings. *Psychology, Public Policy, and Law*, 1, 461–478.
   The activities of psychologists who validate ritual abuse accusations in day care settings raise pressing ethical concerns. A review of these activities uncovers many disturbing instances of violations of the American Psychological Association's (1992) Ethics Code that prohibits the establishment of multiple relationships with clients and

their families, the use of assessment techniques not grounded in psychological science, the reliance on untested theories, misleading court testimony, and advocacy in the name of assessment.

◆ **570**   Glass, S.L. (1991). An overview of satanism and ritualized child abuse. *Journal of Police and Criminal Psychology, 7,* 43–50.

Police officers must familiarize themselves with satanism's central tenet of gaining power and control over others before they can really appreciate the dynamics of ritual abuse, the unwillingness of victims to disclose, and the disturbing sequelae they experience.

◆ **571**   Kern, T.L. (1994). Satanic ritual abuse: How real? *Issues in Child Abuse Accusations, 6.* Retrieved 4-March-01 from the World Wide Web: http://www.ipt-forensics.com/journal/volume6/j6_1_2.htm.

Law enforcement professionals are unable to validate the belief that ritual abuse is widespread and have found no evidence to corroborate such claims. Mental health professionals, on the other hand, often accept the claim and consider the absence of evidence as proof of a satanic conspiracy. This reversal of the burden of proof has negative consequences for the mental health profession as well as for the alleged ritual abuse victims they treat.

◆ **572**   Lanning, K.V. (1992). A law enforcement perspective on allegations of ritual abuse. In D.K. Sakheim & S.E. Devine (Eds.), *Out of darkness: Exploring satanism and ritual abuse* (pp. 109–146). NY: Lexington.

From a law enforcement view, ritual abuse is seen as a multidimensional sex ring that involves multiple perpetrators and multiple victims and occurs within the context of day care facilities, neighborhoods or family homes. Suggestions for investigating such rings include minimizing the occult nature of the allegations, holding personal religious beliefs in abeyance, listening to the victims, evaluating any contagion that occurs when victims share stories with each other, and communicating with the parents of victims. Investigative contingency plans and multidisciplinary task forces are highly recommended.

◆ **573**   Lanning, K.V. (1991). Ritual abuse: A law enforcement view or perspective. *Child Abuse & Neglect, 15,* 171–173.

From a law enforcement point of view, the assertion that ritual abuse is a real and alarming social problem is suspect. The lack of physical evidence of ritual abuse and the improbability of a successful large-scale conspiracy are compelling reasons to consider alternative explanations for ritual abuse disclosures.

◆ **574**   Merskey, H. (1996). Ethical uses in the search for repressed memories. *American Journal of Psychotherapy, 50,* 323–335.

The legal and ethical implications of repressed memory therapy must be considered in light of the findings of a British Psychological Society survey that reveal that 44% of responding members always or usually believe in the veracity of repressed memories, and 43% always or usually believe allegations of ritual abuse. The belief in ritual abuse which is wholly unsupported by evidence, poses the greatest challenge to the ethical practice of psychotherapy.

◆ **575**   Scott, S. (1993). Beyond belief: Beyond help? *Child Abuse Review, 2,* 243–250.

The barrage of calls made to a national helpline after the 1992 airing of the television documentary *Beyond Belief*, an exposé of ritual abuse in England, illustrates what a pressing concern ritual abuse is and how many lives it touches. The helpline, specially set up for the program and staffed by volunteers recruited through RAINS (Ritual Abuse Information Network and Support) received nearly 200 calls during and immediately after the program, half of them from current victims or survivors of ritual abuse.

WOUNDED HELPERS

It is difficult to say with certainty what is the more traumatizing for helping professionals: a confrontation with evil, or a controversy about it. Certainly ritual abuse offers both, and both leave wounded helpers in their wake.

♦ **576**   Harper, J. (1991, December 12). What about the wounded? *Social Work Today, 99,* 20–21.
Social workers working beyond the boundaries of their knowledge in ritual abuse cases throughout the United Kingdom are experiencing a great deal of stress that adversely affects their health, well-being, work, relationships and world view. Organizations must engage in preventive work and damage limitation by supporting their staff and structuring opportunities for them to talk about their experiences and feelings.

♦ **577**   Martin, S.K. (1992). Working with adult survivors of ritual abuse. *Dissertation Abstracts International, 52* (09-B), 4979. (University Microfilms No. AAD92-06395)
A survey was conducted with 100 mental health professionals who had worked with a total of 533 ritual abuse patients to determine the effects of their work with this newly emerging and controversial clinical population, boundary and safety issues, values and belief systems, and self-care concerns. The respondents are theoretically eclectic and experienced; most find work with ritual abuse patients to be clinically difficult, challenging to their world views, and even personally threatening. The need for additional training in the dynamics and treatment of ritual abuse patients is paramount.

♦ **578**   Rudikoff, E. (1997). Ritual abuse: The experience of therapists working with controversial narratives. *Dissertation Abstracts International, 57* (11-B), 7235. (University Microfilms No. AAM97-12656)
In-depth interviews were conducted with 8 licensed doctoral level psychologists who worked extensively with trauma patients. All of the psychologists find listening to accounts of ritual abuse and working with patients challenging, difficult and disturbing. The theoretical framework of social constructionism assists in analyzing the ways in which accounts of ritual abuse are co-created by the patients and their psychologists to render a subjectively truthful narrative, in the individual, clinical and cultural senses of that term. The interviews also find that psychologists who work with ritual abuse patients experience vicarious traumatization, feel silenced and professionally isolated, struggle to provide treatment in the context of uncertainty, grapple with the concept of evil, and find ways to cope with their experiences.

♦ **579**   Sakheim, D.K. (1995). Allegations of ritual abuse. In L.M. Cohen & J.N. Berzoff (Eds.), *Dissociative identity disorder: Theoretical and treatment controversies* (pp. 327–345). Northvale, NJ: Jason Aronson, Inc.

The phenomenon of psychiatric patients reporting childhood histories of ritual abuse is new and controversial. The allegations of these patients are bizarre and frightening, and psychiatrists are finding that otherwise well received theories and therapies are inadequate to the daunting tasks of explaining ritual abuse and successfully treating it.

♦ **580**   Youngson, S.C. (1993). Ritual abuse: Consequences for professionals. *Child Abuse Review, 2*, 251–262.

The results of a survey of 71 helping professionals who are members of RAINS (Ritual Abuse Information Network and Support) as to the stress they experience as a result of their work are disturbing. Nightmares, loss of appetite, psychosomatic symptoms, depression and/or anxiety are reported by 97%; decreases in social activities by 54%; and increased concerns about personal safety by 86% of the responding professionals. Factors that contribute to these findings include the challenges posed to helping professionals by the clinical complexity of ritual abuse cases, the professional isolation they often experience as a result of working in a controversial area, and the threats and intimidation they encounter by the ritual abusers and even by the survivors they are trying to help.

8

The Ritual Abuse Controversy and American Law

The hard-won reforms in law and in courtroom procedures that had facilitated the prosecution of more common types of sexual abuse, such as incest, also provided the entrée for ritual abuse cases into courts of law. By the time the American day care ritual abuse trials began, many states already had expanded hearsay admissibility, dropped the minimum age for competency to testify, and allowed videotaped or closed-circuit television testimony from children. Other equally hard-won reforms brought ritual abuse cases into the civil courts as well. The statute of limitations had been tolled to allow adults who had recovered memories of sexual abuse to file suits against their abusers; when the memories recovered were of ritual abuse, adults found the path to justice already well-paved. It should be noted that there is a body of excellent scholarship on the legal and social histories of these reforms and their impact on sexual abuse cases. This chapter, however, retains a tight focus on these reforms *vis-à-vis* ritual abuse allegations.

That said, ritual abuse stirs its own controversies in the law and in court. It pushes the envelope of all of these, and other, reforms by raising disconcerting questions. Should there be a law against ritual abuse? If the reality of it is up for grabs, then can there be a science of it to which experts can testify in court, a substance to it upon which juries can render just verdicts? Can children be credible witnesses to it? And if recovered memories of ritual abuse might be false, do they belong in court at all?

In many ways, the law is a barometer of changing professional and public opinion. Although it, and the courtroom procedures that enact it, change slowly, it is remarkably sensitive to the winds of change. And as the new millennium begins, ritual abuse remains on the windy side of the law.

RITUAL ABUSE LAWS

The spectacle of the day care ritual abuse trials, with their young witnesses testifying against those in whose loving care they once were entrusted, raised the question of whether justice could ever be more than just poetic when such unthinkable acts were alleged. That question prompted specially appointed task forces and legislative committees to propose new laws that specifically criminalize ritual abuse and that ratchet up the penalties for it. Few of those efforts actually resulted in new laws, expect in Idaho, Illinois, California, Texas and Louisiana where ritual abuse laws were passed in the late 1980s and early 1990s. To date, none of those laws has resulted in a conviction.

◆ **581**   de Young, M. (1994). One face of the devil: The satanic ritual abuse moral crusade and the law. *Behavioral Sciences and the Law, 12,* 389–407.

The spread of ritual abuse allegations is the product of a moral crusade made up of Christian fundamentalists, mental health professionals, survivor groups and law enforcement professionals. Their claim that ritual abuse constitutes an exigent social problem that must be addressed by the law is persuasive more for its symbolic than empirical content. Its symbolic import is evident in new ritual abuse laws. Most are vaguely written in that they do not define ritual abuse or distinguish it from socially acceptable religious practices, and redundant in that they simply create a context for acts such as sexual abuse that already are against the law.

EXPERT TESTIMONY

Expert testimony is allowed when the technical, clinical or scientific issues raised in a criminal trial are considered beyond the ken of the average juror. Ritual abuse raises those very kinds of issues, and the day care ritual abuse trials featured a parade of experts, some of them clear and convincing, others obtuse and obscurantist, but all of them raising questions about the scientific reliability of ritual abuse testimony.

◆ **582**   Askowitz, L.R., & Graham, M.H. (1994). The reliability of expert psychological testimony in child sexual abuse prosecutions. *Cardozo Law Review, 15,* 2027–2101.

Notorious cases such as the McMartin Preschool ritual abuse case often are set in a context of mass hysteria that increases the likelihood that false allegations will be made. While expert testimony plays an important and legitimate role in child sexual abuse trials, courts must take an active role in ensuring its reliability. High profile ritual abuse cases like McMartin show how easy it is for public abhorrence of a crime to compromise reliability standards.

◆ **583**   Bruck, M. (1998). The trials and tribulations of a novice expert witness. In S.J. Ceci and H. Hembrooke (Eds.), *Expert witnesses in child abuse cases* (pp. 85–104). Washington, D.C.: American Psychological Association Press.

The author, an experimental psychologist, served as a defense expert witness in the Little Rascals ritual abuse trial in Edenton, North Carolina, and the Sterling Day Care ritual abuse trial in Martensville, Canada. She had not fully anticipated the effects the adversarial trial process has on an expert witness: the attempts to impeach credibility, the attacks on the science of psychology, the barrage of questions on topics unrelated to stated expertise, and the long periods on the witness stand of fear, confusion, boredom and fatigue. Despite all that, experts should make themselves available for testimony in controversial cases such as these. In this era of pseudoscience and antiscience, expert court testimony in ritual abuse cases is urgently needed.

◆ **584**   Gambela, F.A., & Serritella, W.J. (1992). Three recent United States Supreme Court decisions for professionals who testify in child sexual abuse cases. *Journal of Child Sexual Abuse, 1,* 15–30.

It is imperative that professionals who are called upon to testify in child sexual abuse trials be familiar with 3 recent U.S. Supreme Court cases, *Maryland v. Craig, Idaho v. Wright* and *White v. Illinois*. These opinions set out the nature and the scope of expert testimony.

◆ **585**   Kiefer, L. (1990). Confrontation clause revisited: Supreme Court decisions *Idaho v. Wright* and *Craig v. Maryland*. An attorney's response. *Issues in Child Abuse Accusations, 2.* Retrieved from the World Wide Web 4-March-01: http://www.ipt-forensics.com/journal/volume2/j2_3_7.htm

Two recent decisions, *Idaho v. Wright* and *Maryland v. Craig* allow for alternatives to children's in-court testimony, but to protect the rights of defendants all investigative interviews with children should be videotaped, and qualified experts should question children in the presence of defendants to determine if they will be too traumatized to give testimony in court.

◆ **586**   Mason, M.A. (1995). The child sex abuse syndrome: The other major issue in *State of New Jersey v. Margaret Kelly Michaels*. *Psychology, Public Policy, and Law, 1,* 399–410.

Testimony from prosecution and defense expert witnesses in the Wee Care ritual abuse case shows the danger of admitting evidence about the so-called "child sexual abuse accommodation syndrome" into trial. The appeals court quite properly rejected that testimony as unscientific.

JURIES

As the day care, family and neighborhood cases presented in Chapters 2 and 3 demonstrate, juries are far from consistent in the verdicts they render in ritual abuse trials. Given that inconsistency, and in light of the fact that many guilty verdicts have been overturned in recent years, the questions remain as to what features of the ritual abuse case, or of jurors as individuals, are more likely to predict a verdict.

◆ **587**   Bottoms, B.L., Diviak, K.R., & Davis, S.L. (1997). Jurors' reactions to satanic ritual abuse allegations. *Child Abuse & Neglect, 21*, 845–859.

Acting as mock jurors, 243 university students rendered judgments on cases involving childhood sexual abuse or ritual abuse allegations either by a 5 year old child or a 30 year old adult. Although jurors are significantly less likely to believe the ritual abuse details than the other case details, they are as likely to vote guilty and believe the alleged victim of ritual abuse as they are to vote guilty and believe the alleged victim of sexual abuse. Victim age has no significant effect on jurors' judgments. In the cases of ritual abuse, religious jurors are more likely to believe the alleged victims than non-religious jurors. Across all conditions, female jurors are more likely to believe the alleged victim and vote guilty than male jurors.

CHILDREN AS WITNESSES

For hundreds of years, American law considered children to be testimonially incompetent. Unobservant, inarticulate and fanciful as they were seen to be, children routinely were denied the opportunity to testify in courts of law. By the 20th century, with its more nostalgic view of childhood, that position moderated somewhat and only children who were very young — two, three and four years old — were kept off the witness stand. By the end of that century, however, it was these very young children who stood before the court and swore to tell the whole truth about ritual abuse. Whether heroes or heretics, the presence of children in ritual abuse cases raises a host of questions and concerns about their truthfulness and credibility.

◆ **588**   McGough, L.S. (1994). *Child witnesses: Fragile voices in the American legal system.* New Haven, CT: Yale University Press.

The problems inherent in using children as witnesses are evident in the McMartin Preschool, Wee Care Nursery and Craig's Country Preschool ritual abuse cases. These cases demonstrate how child witnesses are more prone to suggestibility, memory fade and fantasy than are adult witnesses. Three basic principles of reform should be considered: videotaping of children's testimony according to strict rules that will ensure objectivity and reliability; streamlining the criminal investigation process so that children are not subjected to protracted and multiple interviews; and revising existing evidentiary barriers to the admission of out-of-court statements.

♦ **589**   Montoya, J. (1995). Lessons from *Akiki* and *Michaels* on shielding child witnesses. *Psychology, Public Policy and Law, 1,* 340–369.

The Akiki (Faith Chapel) and Michaels (Wee Care) ritual abuse trials were based on different assumptions about both the value of in-court testimony from children and the value children can accrue from actually confronting their alleged abusers in court. In *Michaels*, the shielding of children impaired the defendant's legal right to confront her accusers, and the court's decision to do so was based on the testimony of parents and therapists who, it can be argued, usually will be biased in the direction of shielding.

♦ **590**   Smith, S.B. (1987). The child witness. In L.F. Michaels (Ed.), *Representing children: Current issues in law, medicine, mental health, and protective services* (pp. 1–10). Denver, CO: National Association of Counsel for Children.

The McMartin Preschool ritual abuse case illustrates the problems inherent in cases involving children as witnesses in court. Although the case has multiple victims and defendants, its real complexity lies in the demands it makes on the criminal justice system to accommodate young witnesses. Court reforms, such as allowing children to testify via closed-circuit television, are long overdue but pose their own problems. Nevertheless, courts must continue to develop ways of decreasing the trauma of testifying for child witnesses.

Taint Hearings

The assessment of the credibility of children as witnesses in courts of law reflects the prevailing view of their suggestibility. There are many excellent historical accounts of how that view has changed over the centuries, but it is the sociopolitical zeitgeist of the end of the millennium that is of interest here. Two opposing views came together to create the controversy over children's credibility as witnesses to ritual abuse. The first, more ideological than scientific, insists that children are resistant to erroneous suggestion, and because they cannot lie about what they have not experienced, are perfectly credible witnesses to ritual abuse. The second, more scientific than ideological, asserts that children are vulnerable to erroneous suggestion when persistently and zealously interviewed, and because of that they are not always credible witnesses in courts of law.

These opposing views noisily clashed in the Wee Care Nursery School ritual abuse case. The conviction of provider Kelly Michaels was overturned with the appellate court ruling that if the state should retry her, a pretrial hearing would have to be held to determine the extent to which the children's testimony was influenced by their interviewers. This so-called "taint hearing," that rests on the scientific view of children's suggestibility, is the stuff of a heated debate over children's credibility as witnesses in cases of ritual abuse.

◆ **591** Anderson, D.D. (1996). Assessing the reliability of children's testimony in sexual abuse cases. *Southern California Law Review, 69,* 2117–2161.

In multi-victim cases like McMartin Preschool and Wee Care Nursery, many children who never disclose or exhibit symptoms of abuse will be vigorously interviewed, often by interviewers who already are certain they have been abused. Skepticism by courts about the reliability of children's statements under these conditions is warranted, but should be tempered by a concentrated approach to reliability assessment in either a hearsay or a taint hearing context.

◆ **592** Bruck, M., & Ceci, S.J. (1995). *Amicus brief* for the case of *State of New Jersey v. Michaels* presented by a Committee of Concerned Social Scientists. *Psychology, Public Policy, and Law, 1,* 272–322.

The *amicus brief* submitted to the New Jersey Supreme Court by 46 members of the Committee of Concerned Social Scientists in the case of Kelly Michaels contends that the interviews conducted with the children were suggestive, leading and coercive. Empirical research shows interviews of this type actually shape children's accounts and decrease their reliability and veracity as witnesses. Transcripts of the interviews illustrate these points.

◆ **593** Ceci, S.J., Bruck, M., & Rosenthal, R. (1995). Children's allegations of sexual abuse: Forensic and scientific issues. *Psychology, Public Policy, and Law, 1,* 494–520.

The intent of *amicus brief* submitted by a Committee of Concerned Social Scientists in *Michaels* is to summarize the findings of well designed and well controlled empirical research on children's suggestibility, and to use those research findings to analyze the interviews conducted with the children in the Wee Care ritual abuse case. The state of knowledge about suggestibility is now so valid and reliable that interviews conducted with children in ritual abuse cases can be weighed against it in pretrial taint hearings.

◆ **594** Dugas, C.M. (1995). *State of New Jersey v. Michaels,* 642 A.2d 1372 (N.J. 1994). *Louisiana Law Review, 55,* 1205–1234.

Evidence from interviews such as those conducted in the Wee Care ritual abuse case should be admitted into trial if found reliable because precedent demonstrates that regardless of how it is obtained, reliable evidence can result in a fair trial.

◆ **595** Dunn, A.R. (1995). Questioning the reliability of children's testimony: An examination of the problematic elements. *Law and Psychology Review, 19,* 203–215.

The McMartin Preschool and the Wee Care ritual abuse cases show how factors such as repetitive and suggestive interviewing can influence children's testimony. Although the courts have considerable discretion in evaluating the truthfulness of children's testimony, including taint hearings, better and more consistent procedures for doing so are still needed.

◆ **596** Jablonski, J.A. (1998). Where has *Michaels* taken us? Assessing the future of taint hearings. *Suffolk Journal of Trial and Appellate Advocacy, 3,* 49–63.

The *Michaels* decision began a nationwide trend in allowing pretrial "taint hearings" to assess child witnesses' reliability before they testify in sexual abuse trials. Those jurisdictions that have declined to allow taint hearings ground their arguments in weak reasoning and fail to follow precedent.

◆ **597** Lyon, T.D. (1995). False allegations and false denials in child sexual abuse. *Psychology, Public Policy, and Law, 1,* 429–437.

The *amicus brief* in *Michaels* ignores the likelihood that abused children will fail to disclose and discuss their abuse unless they are asked direct and even leading questions. The brief overstates the occurrence of false allegations by overlooking the complicated aspects of the *Michaels* case that make it unlike most other sexual abuse cases.

◆ **598** Manshel, L. (1994). The child witness and the presumption of authenticity after *State v. Michaels. Seton Hall Law Review, 26,* 685–763.

Michaels reintroduces archaic stereotypes about children as "the most dangerous of all witnesses." The decision stigmatizes children as a class of citizens especially vulnerable to victimization, and does so with the imprimatur of the state's highest court. By permitting defendants to overcome the presumption of the authenticity of child witnesses, *Michaels* risks closing the doors to many child victims of sex crimes.

◆ **599** Montoya, J. (1993). Something not so funny happened on the way to conviction: The pre-trial interrogation of child witnesses. *Arizona Law Review, 35,* 927–987.

All children's out-of-court statements should be subject to a trustworthiness inquiry that would guide the trial court's determinations, as the McMartin Preschool, Wee Care Nursery and Craig's Country cases attest. Both children and the fact-finding process need protection from relentless reinterviewing. The current videotape legislation, which only invites adult abuses by rehearsing children's testimony, fails to do that. Consequently, only an adversarial testing of children's stories will achieve that goal.

◆ **600** Myers, J.E.B. (1996). Taint hearings to attack investigative interviews: A further assault on children's credibility. *Child Maltreatment, 1,* 213–222.

The attack on interviews in cases of ritual and sexual abuse assumed new dimensions with the *Michaels* decision in which the court created a procedure that allows defense attorneys to request pretrial taint hearings to challenge the investigative interviews conducted with the child witnesses. In these kinds of cases, qualified professionals who can testify as expert witnesses in defense of competent interview practices are urgently needed.

◆ **601** Myers, J.E.B. (1995). New era of skepticism regarding children's credibility. *Psychology, Public Policy, and Law, 1,* 387–398.

Three sources of the growing skepticism about the credibility of children's allegations of abuse are the popular media's skeptical coverage of the ritual abuse day care cases of the 1980s, the writings of some social scientists who portray children in a negative light, and the *Michaels* decision that exaggerates doubts about children's memory and suggestibility.

◆ **602** Myers, J.E.B. (1994). Taint hearings for child witnesses? A step in the wrong direction. *Baylor Law Review, 46,* 873–946.

The *Michaels* decision that allows the use of taint hearings to challenge the investigative interviews conducted with children damages the credibility of child witnesses, creates additional options for appeal, and makes the prosecution of ritual and sexual abuse more difficult to prove. It is recommended that the appropriateness of taint hearings be analyzed under the 6th Amendment confrontation clause rather than the 14th Amendment due process clause.

◆ **603**   Ross, K.L. (1999). *State v. Michaels,* 625 A.2d 489 (N.J. 1993): A New Jersey Supreme Court ruling with national implications. *Michigan Bar Journal, 78,* 32–35.

Suggestive and coercive interviewing of children can lead them into giving false accounts of abuse, as the Wee Care ritual abuse case demonstrates. The New Jersey Supreme Court recognized this problem in a recent ruling on the Michaels case by requiring pretrial taint hearings to establish if potential child witnesses had been properly interviewed.

◆ **604**   Ross, K.L. (1997). *State v. Michaels:* A New Jersey Supreme Court prescription for the rest of the country. *Issues in Child Abuse Accusations,* 9. Retrieved 4-March-01 from the World Wide Web: http://www.ipt-forensics.com/journal/volume9/j9_1_1.htm.

The New Jersey Supreme Court in *Michaels* determined that suggestive and coercive interviews can lead children to give false accounts of abuse. By requiring pretrial taint hearings to determine if children have been interviewed properly, the Court sets a precedence that should be adopted throughout the country.

COURTROOM INNOVATIONS AND THE 6TH AMENDMENT

The 6th Amendment to the U.S. Constitution states that in all criminal prosecutions the accused has the right to be confronted with the witnesses against him or her. This "confrontation right," as it is now known, dates as far back as Roman law and its use in Anglo-American law can be traced to the 17th century treason trial of Sir Walter Raleigh, that colonizer, courtier, tobacconist and poet ("Shall I, like a hermit dwell/ On a rock or in a cell?") who was denied the opportunity to confront his accusers.

When the accusers are abused children, however, the very truth-seeking function of a criminal trial with its adversarial milieu, aggressive cross-examination and scary physical proximity of accused to accuser, seems to many to threaten the psychological well-being of young witnesses and compromise their ability to give an honest and accurate account of their abuse. Reforms to the 6th Amendment were called for and, in reply, technology entered the courtroom. During the 1980s an increasing number of states allowed children to testify outside of the presence of the accused and via videotape or closed-circuit television.

In no other case was technology's clash with the 6th Amendment more evident than in the Craig's Country Day Care ritual abuse case in which the constitutionality of closed-circuit television testimony was decided by the U.S. Supreme Court. In a 1990 decision, the Court ruled that the state's interest in the protection of children may supersede defendants' 6th Amendment right to confront their accusers. The response of legal scholars was swift, some of it sympathetic, some of it savage.

♦ **605**   Barry, K.A. (1990). Witness shield laws and child sexual abuse prosecutions: A presumption of guilt. *Southern Illinois University Law Journal, 15*, 99–121.

Craig prompts both a consideration of other ways that courts can alleviate the trauma of testifying for children, and a call for further research to identity exactly what parts of the trial process are most distressing to child witnesses. Only if actual face-to-face confrontation is identified as the stressor should defendants' 6th Amendment rights be compromised, and then only as a last option.

♦ **606**   Bayardi, M. (1990). Balancing the defendant's confrontation clause rights with the state's public policy of protecting child witnesses from undue traumatization. *Arizona Law Review, 32*, 1029–1050.

Craig raises the basic question of whether defendants have an absolute right to physically confront adverse witnesses and, if they do not, under what circumstances that right must yield to other considerations. It is important to realize that the confrontation clause gives the right to confront, not to intimidate. Because abused children are easily intimidated by the presence of their abusers in court, the available technology of closed-circuit television and videotaped testimony affords a unique opportunity to secure the public policy goal of protecting children and doing so without significant harm to the rights of defendants.

♦ **607**   Besnyl, G. (1991). *Maryland v. Craig:* Defendants' confrontation rights not violated by the use of one-way closed circuit television testimony in child abuse cases. *Western State University Law Review, 18*, 861–872.

Craig demonstrates that widespread public concern about an issue can influence judicial decision-making. The U.S. Supreme Court was wise in choosing to balance the right of face-to-face confrontation with the mandate to protect child witnesses from trauma. Children are uniquely vulnerable, as the public realizes, and deserve the benefits afforded by modern technology in rendering their testimony.

♦ **608**   Bloe, R. (1991). *Maryland v. Craig. Southern University Law Review, 18*, 275–291.

Craig is vulnerable to attack by defense attorneys because of its broad interpretation of constitutional standards. In the decision, the U.S. Supreme Court should have set out specific guidelines for defining the nature and the extent of trauma child witnesses must experience to trigger any exception to the confrontation clause.

♦ **609**   Brannon, L.C. (1994). The trauma of testifying in court for child victims of sexual assault v. the accused's right to confrontation. *Law and Psychology Review, 18*, 439–460.

The *Craig* decision raises significant questions about predicting and characterizing the emotional effects of testifying against the accused for child witnesses in the light of defendants' 6th Amendment rights. Developments in the law after the *Craig* decision are discussed, with special reference to the enactment of the Child Victims' and Child Witnesses' Rights statute.

◆ **610**   Cecchettini-Whaley, G.D. (1992). Children as witnesses after *Maryland v. Craig. Southern California Law Review, 65,* 1993–2037.

The psychological evidence in support of *Craig* that child witnesses are harmed by face-to-face confrontations with defendants in court is unconvincing. A greater degree of proof of considerable trauma to children must be demonstrated before alternative procedures for children's testimony are put into place.

◆ **611**   Chase, C.A. (1993). Confronting supreme confusion: Balancing defendants' confrontation clause rights against the need to protect child abuse victims. *Utah Law Review, 1993,* 407–427.

The 6th Amendment confrontation clause is intended to ensure the reliability of evidence. *Craig* is logically consistent with legal precedent and with the rules of evidence, and will promote the efficient resolution of abuse cases.

◆ **612**   Cotton, T.A. (1994). *Maryland v. Craig:* The Supreme Court clarifies when a child protective statute which allows a child witness to testify outside the presence of the accused will violate the confrontation clause. *Thurgood Marshall Law review, 19,* 309–332.

As both reports of child abuse and the prospect of more criminal trials with children as witnesses increase, taking away defendants' rights to confront their accusers, as *Craig* does, is a grave travesty of justice.

◆ **613**   Cullen, T.F. (1993). *Maryland v. Craig:* The collision of policy and history. *New England Journal on Criminal and Civil Confinement, 19,* 141–173.

Although *Craig* is criticized for infringing on the confrontation rights of defendants, the decision is consistent with the historical and ideological trajectory of U.S. Supreme Court decisions on the 6th Amendment.

◆ **614**   Cusik, T. (1991). Televised justice: Toward a new definition of confrontation under *Maryland v. Craig. Catholic University Law Review, 40,* 967–1000.

Craig leaves many crucial questions unanswered about the level of evidence needed to invoke an exception to face-to-face confrontation and about the characteristics of the class entitled to protection. The exception actually may overreach its limited purpose of protecting child witnesses from trauma.

◆ **615**   Delaney, H.J. (1990). Witnesses: Child sexual abuse victims not categorically prohibited by confrontation clause from testifying via one-way closed circuit television. *North Dakota Law Review, 66,* 735–741.

The *Craig* decision is sensitive to the special vulnerabilities of children who must testify in court to their own victimization. The used of closed-circuit television as a means of testimony does not severely jeopardize defendants' 6th Amendment confrontation rights.

♦ **616**   Draddy, G.C. (1998). Special courtroom seating arrangement fails to meet confrontation clause requirements—*Commonwealth v. Amirault*, 677 N.E. 2d 652 (Mass. 1997). *Suffolk University Law Review, 32,* 161–168.

In the Fells Acres ritual abuse day care trial, child witnesses were allowed to sit at a small table, facing the jury. Because they had their backs to the defendants, the defendants were unable to see their facial expressions and successfully argued that their right to confrontation was denied.

♦ **617**   Emerson, P.K. (1990). Protecting sexually abused children: *Maryland v. Craig. Thurgood Marshall Law Review, 16,* 109–125.

Craig raises the question as to whether the 6th Amendment requires an actual face-to-face meeting between a child witness and a defendant before a closed circuit television procedure is used. The importance of *Craig* is its acknowledgement that affirmative exceptions to confrontation do exist.

♦ **618**   Evans, S.H. (1991). Criminal procedure — Closed circuit television in child sexual abuse cases: Keeping the balance between realism and idealism —*Maryland v. Craig. Wake Forest Law Review, 26,* 471–502.

There are problematic areas in *Craig*, including the lack of guidelines as to when closed circuit television procedure should be invoked, the defendant's right to presence, and the presumption of innocence. While the closed circuit television procedure is not perfect, it does balance the traditional purpose of the confrontation clause with the state's interest in protecting child witnesses from trauma.

♦ **619**   Fields, B.J. (1990). *Maryland v. Craig:* The constitutionality of closed circuit testimony in child sexual abuse cases. *Georgia Law Review, 25,* 167–197.

In *Craig*, the majority opinion held that face-to-face confrontation is not an absolute guarantee under the 6th Amendment. The exception recognized in *Craig* is a departure from the U.S. Supreme Court's previous focus on the truth-finding function of the clause. By locating the confrontation clause exception in the state's interest in protecting child witnesses, the Court risks undermining its purpose.

♦ **620**   Fields, G.A. (1992). *Maryland v. Craig:* Suffering children to testify via closed circuit television. *Howard Law Journal, 35,* 285–301.

In permitting children to testify via closed circuit television, *Craig* balances the scales of justice by assuring that young victims, who otherwise would not have a voice in the court system, will be allowed to testify in such a way that they do not suffer further emotional trauma.

♦ **621**   Fisher, G.P. (1991). Constitutional law — Restricting an accused's Sixth Amendment right to confront child witnesses in child abuse cases— *Maryland v. Craig*, 110 S. Ct. 3157 (1990). *Suffolk University Law Review, 25,* 1224–1232.

The U.S. Supreme Court's ruling in *Craig* is consistent with the philosophy underlying previous rulings on the 6th Amendment, but in the face of a growing number of child sexual abuse cases being heard in courts across the country, is destined to raise major questions about defendants' confrontation rights.

◆ **622**   Francis, K.A. (1992). To hide in plain sight: Child abuse, closed circuit television, and the confrontation clause. *University of Cincinnati Law Review, 60,* 827–856.

The protections guaranteed by the confrontation clause and the implications posed by *Craig* are in conflict. The decision risks undermining the original purpose of the confrontation clause.

◆ **623**   Gassner, S. (1993). Child witness statutes. *Journal of Juvenile Law, 14,* 227–233.

In light of *Craig,* state laws may override federal laws regarding the degree of confrontation rights.

◆ **624**   Goodhue, G.K. (1991). *Maryland v. Craig:* Balancing the Sixth Amendment confrontation rights with the rights of child witnesses in sexual abuse trials. *New England Law Review, 26,* 497–528.

Provided the reliability of a child's testimony is otherwise assured and the court makes an early and specific finding that the child will be emotionally traumatized by face-to-face testimony, the use of alternative methods for taking the child's testimony, such as that set out in *Craig,* does not violate the defendant's 6th Amendment confrontation rights.

◆ **625**   Goodman, A.C. (1995). Two critical evidentiary issues in child sexual abuse cases: Closed circuit testimony by child victims and exceptions to the hearsay rule. *American Criminal Law Review, 32,* 855–882.

Craig is an example of a tough case making bad law by jeopardizing defendants' constitutionally protected 6th Amendment confrontation rights.

◆ **626**   Kamego, A.L. (1991). The confrontation clause does not prohibit a child witness in a child abuse case from testifying via one-way closed circuit television when face-to-face confrontation would cause trauma to the witness. *University of Detroit Law Review, 68,* 555–564.

Craig overlooks the fact that there are few empirical studies that conclusively prove that children are traumatized by the experience of testifying in court; exceptions to face-to-face testimony must be considered in some cases, and the use of closed circuit television is only one of several alternative methods that should be considered.

◆ **627**   King, R.H. (1992). The molested child witness and the Constitution: Should the Bill of Rights be transformed into the bill of preferences? *Ohio State Law Journal, 53,* 49–99.

Craig is the most recent of a several U.S. Supreme Court decisions on the confrontation clause, but it is inconsistent with the legal logic informing previous decisions.

◆ **628**   Kohlmann, R.H. (1996). The presumption of innocence: Patching the tattered cloak after *Maryland v. Craig. St. Mary's Law Journal, 27,* 389–421.

The special treatment *Craig* affords child witnesses sends an unspoken but compelling message to juries that judges have determined child witnesses need protection from defendants. This message erodes the practical value of the presumption of innocence.

◆ **629** McCarvill, T.J., & Steinberg, J.M. (1992). Have we gone far enough? Children who are sexually abused and the judicial and legislative means of prosecuting the abuser. *St. John's Journal of Legal Commentary,* 8, 339–368.

Despite recent judicial and legislative initiatives, barriers to the successful prosecution of child sex abusers remain. The kind of flexible approach to the confrontation clause afforded by *Craig* is not enough to ensure successful prosecution. What still is needed is uniform legislation that tolls the statute of limitations when the victim is 23 years old.

◆ **630** McNeil, W.K. (1991). *Maryland v. Craig:* The demise of face-to-face confrontation. *Loyola Law Review,* 36, 1137–1155.

In its zeal to protect children, the U.S. Supreme Court in *Craig* eliminates the historically recognized safeguard of face-to-face confrontation.

◆ **631** Metz, J.K. (1995). Child molestation and the confrontation clause: Has the Supreme Court gone too far? *Journal of Juvenile Law,* 16, 15–168.

In *Craig,* the U.S. Supreme Court fails to consider recent research on the psychological benefits to children who face defendants in court and testify against them, as well as research on the difficulties in accurately predicting whether children will be traumatized by testifying in front of defendants.

◆ **632** Miller, L.R. (1990). Allowing a child abuse victim to testify via one-way closed circuit television does not violate a criminal defendant's Sixth Amendment confrontation clause right if the trial court specifically finds such a procedure necessary to protect the child's welfare. *St. Mary's Law Journal,* 22, 555–577.

The confrontation right is not absolute, as the U.S. Supreme Court correctly ruled in *Craig.* The closed circuit television procedure for children's testimony, therefore, is a perfectly logical way to address an exception to the clause in that it protects children without completely denying defendants' confrontation rights.

◆ **633** Montoya, J. (1992). On truth and shielding in child abuse trials. *Hastings Law Journal,* 43, 1259–1319.

The social science data offered in support of *Craig* is compelling, but the implications of compromising courtroom confrontations between child witnesses and defendants are insufficiently considered by the U.S. Supreme Court.

◆ **634** Moore, E.A., Howitt, P.S., & Grier, T. (1991). Child witness testimony: Is it sufficiently reliable to justify the protective procedures sanctioned by *Maryland v. Craig? Juvenile and Family Court Journal,* 42, 1–9.

Psychological studies uphold the *Craig* decision, showing that children are sufficiently reliable witnesses as a class to justify the use of protective measures.

◆ **635** National Center for the Prosecution of Child Abuse (1991). *State legislation regarding the use of closed-circuit television testimony in criminal child abuse proceedings.* Alexandria, VA: American Prosecutors Research Institute.

Craig brings attention to alternative methods for the presentation of children's testimony in abuse cases. State statutes allowing or mandating the use of closed circuit television testimony are summarized according to the crimes specifically listed by the statute, the specified age of the victim, the factors courts must consider in determining the need for closed circuit television testimony, and the individuals who may be present during the testimony.

◆ **636**   Parise, A.S. (1991). *Maryland v. Craig:* Ignoring the letter and purpose of the confrontation clause. *Brigham Young University Law Review,* 2, 1093–1106.

Videotapes of sessions between children and their counselors should be used as an alternative to closed circuit testimony when children are unable to testify in the presence of defendants. The tapes would provide accurate information while protecting defendants from coached testimony.

◆ **637**   Pershkow, B.I. (1991). *Maryland v. Craig:* A child witness need not view the defendant during testimony in child abuse cases. *Tulane Law Review,* 65, 935–943.

In *Craig,* the U.S. Supreme Court properly allows an exception to defendants' right to physical confrontation with their accusers, and in doing so protects child witnesses from further trauma.

◆ **638**   Rittershaus, M.A. (1991). *Maryland v. Craig:* Balancing the interests of a child victim against the defendant's right to confront his accuser. *South Dakota Law Review,* 36, 104–119.

The *Craig* decision is consistent with both the spirit of the confrontation clause and legal precedent.

◆ **639**   Ruddock, E.M. (1991). Confrontation clause. *Thomas M. Cooley Law Review,* 8, 389–409.

In trying to balance the welfare of child witnesses against the clearly established constitutional right of defendants, *Craig* harkens the beginning of a well-intentioned reconstruction of the Star Chamber.

◆ **640**   Sanders, J. (1991). Protecting the child victim of sexual abuse while preserving the Sixth Amendment confrontation rights of the accused: *Maryland v. Craig. Saint Louis University Law Journal,* 35, 495–509.

There is well documented legal precedence for partially denying defendants' face-to-face confrontations with their accusers. *Craig* is consistent with those cases.

◆ **641**   Schwalb, B.L. (1991). Child abuse trials and the confrontation of traumatized witnesses: Defining confrontation to protect both children and defendants. *Harvard Civil Rights–Civil Liberties Law Review,* 26, 185–217.

There are compelling questions as to whether *Craig* convincingly proves that testimony via closed circuit television advances the protection of child witnesses. The decision inadequately considers the impact of closed circuit television on a trial's ability to fairly and reliably pursue the truth. *Craig* may become a springboard from which the confrontation clause can be used to test the qualitative fairness of criminal trials.

◆ **642** Small, M.A. (1994). Constitutional challenges to child witness protection legislation: An update. *Violence and Victims, 9,* 369–377.

The U.S. Supreme Court's landmark *Craig* decision creates uncertainty about the state constitutionality of child witness protection legislation.

◆ **643** Stokes, J.B. (1990/1991). *Maryland v. Craig* and the conflict clause: When does "confront" mean confront? *American Journal of Trial Advocacy, 14,* 363–387.

U.S. Supreme Court Justice Scalia was correct in his scathing dissent in *Craig* when he asserted that current beliefs about the terrible consequences of child abuse hardly justify a retreat from 200 years of constitutional law.

◆ **644** Tomlinson, K.L. (1991). *Maryland v. Craig:* Televised testimony and an evolving concept of confrontation. *Villanova Law Review, 36,* 1569–1610.

Over the years, the U.S. Supreme Court has struggled with the protections that should be given under the confrontation clause, taking into consideration the changing times, circumstances and purposes served by the right to confront. *Craig* is consistent with the evolving concept of face-to-face confrontation.

◆ **645** Underwager, R.C. (1990). Confrontation clause revisited: Supreme Court decisions. *Idaho v. Wright,* and *Craig v. Maryland.* A Psychologist's Response. *Issues in Child Abuse Accusations, 2.* Retrieved from the World Wide Web 4-March-01: http://www.ipt-forensics.com/journal/volume2/j2_3_8.htm

No mental health professional is able to predict with accuracy whether any given child will be traumatized by giving testimony in court in the presence of a defendant. The *Craig* decision is bad law in that it establishes requirements for the assessment of children that psychologists simply cannot meet.

◆ **646** Walton, E. (1994). The confrontation clause and the child victim of sexual abuse. *Child and Adolescent Social Work Journal, 11,* 195–207.

For social workers interested in the testimony of children, *Craig* foregrounds the clash between the 6th Amendment rights of those accused of sexual abuse and the state's interest in protecting child witnesses from trauma, and reveals the necessity of improving social workers' interactions with children before they testify.

◆ **647** Wendel, P.T. (1993). A law and economic analysis of the right to face-to-face confrontation post *Maryland v. Craig:* Distinguishing the forest from the trees. *Hofstra Law Review, 22,* 405–494.

A macro-analysis of *Craig* suggests that at some point the benefits of face-to-face confrontation in terms of the low possibility of erroneous conviction will be exceeded by the greater possibility of erroneous conviction due to the high cost of witness refusal to testify because of anticipated trauma. In the light of that analysis, *Craig* poses only a narrow intrusion on the right to face-to-face confrontation, and one that is necessary to achieve the efficient and effective enforcement of child abuse laws.

◆ **648** Whitlock, C.A. (1991). Admissibility of video-taped testimony: What is the standard after *Maryland v. Craig* and how will the practicing defense attorney be affected? *Mercer Law Review, 42,* 883–905.

A total of 37 states now permit closed circuit testimony in child abuse cases, but possible infringements on the rights of defendants still must be considered, especially by defense attorneys.

◆ **649** Wolf, M.J. (1991). *Maryland v. Craig:* Electronic testimony and the confrontation clause. *Journal of Juvenile Law, 12,* 145–150.

The conflict between trial procedures designed to lessen the trauma of testimony for child witnesses and protect the rights of defendants to confront their accusers at trial is difficult to resolve, although the *Craig* decision makes some progress towards resolution.

REPRESSED MEMORIES OF RITUAL ABUSE AND THE LAW

Over the last fifteen years or so, over 800 civil suits against alleged abusers have been filed in the United States by adults who have recovered memories of abuse. Only some of these cases involve recovered memories of ritual abuse, of course, but many of them faced statutes of limitations in place to prevent surprises through renascent claims made long after evidence has been lost, witnesses have disappeared, and memories have faded, that stood in the way of any civil action that could be pursued against alleged abusers.

But a recent, and heatedly debated theory, that memories of both ritual abuse and sexual abuse often are repressed and may not be recovered as memories until years, even decades, after the alleged abuse occurred, changed all of that. Invoking a unique application of the delayed discovery doctrine that states that the statute of limitations does not begin to run out until the person has discovered the facts that are essential to any legal action, a majority of states tolled the statute of limitation, making it possible for alleged survivors of childhood abuse, including ritual abuse, to sue for recovery of damages.

Over very recent years, and in reaction to the "false memory syndrome" debate, some states have reconsidered. What has further reduced the number of recovered memory civil suits is the 1993 *Daubert* decision in which the U.S. Supreme Court raised the bar of expert testimony by declaring that its reasoning and methodology must be based on scientific knowledge and that it must be properly applied to the facts in the case before it will be admitted into court.

◆ **650** Schutte, J.W. (1994). Repressed memory lawsuits: Potential verdict predictors. *Behavioral Sciences and the Law, 12,* 409–416.

Two case vignettes, one about the recovered memory of ritual abuse and the other about the recovered memory of incest, were presented to 251 students who had to determine whether to side with the plaintiff or the defendant. Demographic variables are more predictive of verdicts than the nature of the case, with religious, authoritarian females more sympathetic to the plaintiff.

◆ **651**   Spadaro, J.A. (1998). An elusive search for the truth. *Connecticut Law Review, 30,* 1147–1198.

The Ingram case illustrates the challenges that repressed memories pose to the court. It is unlikely that all of his recovered memories of ritual abuse are true and equally unlikely that all of them are false. To determine the truth of such memories courts must evaluate their reliability in a pretrial hearing. Employing the criteria set out in the *Daubert* case facilitates that assessment. For recovered memories to be introduced at trial, they must be judged reliable, helpful, and based on scientifically valid reasoning and methodology.

9

Ritual Abuse Reports

Ritual abuse has left in its wake quite a human toll around the world but not a particularly long paper trail. The absence of official commentary, whether from professional organizations or government bodies, certainly contributes to the persistence of interest in ritual abuse even in the face of disconfirming evidence and reasonable alternative hypotheses for claims and cases of it. Official reports, after all, have a disconcerting tendency to rationalize, intellectualize, bureaucratize and even trivialize the topic at hand. Had a stack of them been written and filed, it probably would have depleted the power of the idea of ritual abuse to continue to boldly mark the contours of the controversy over it.

REPORTS ON RITUAL ABUSE CASES

Since 1983, over a hundred American day care centers and preschools, a dozen or more neighborhoods, and an inestimable number of families have had encounters with ritual abuse allegations. Each encounter, in turn, has taken its own toll that can be measured, in part, by arrests and convictions, civil suits, won and lost reputations, conflict and sometimes uneasy reconciliation. Yet, despite that, the number of official reports on the American day care, neighborhood and family ritual abuse cases can be counted on two hands.

Few of those reports have ever been made the subjects of professional discourse. The opportunity for professionals of various stripes and beliefs to meet on common ground to discuss facts, figures and findings, therefore, has been largely missed. Missed, too, is the opportunity for professionals to critically examine their work on ritual abuse and analyze the scaffold of beliefs that supports it.

In Europe and Australasia where helping professionals are differently and, arguably, better organized, official reports on ritual abuse cases are widely circulated and discussed. The reports, too, tend to be more thorough than their American counterparts, dissecting not only the case in question but the larger social, ideological, political and professional forces that are its context. The recommendations these reports set out, then, tend to find their way into practice.

American Day Care
Ritual Abuse Case Reports

♦ **652** Juliar, D.S., & Harshbarger, S. (1996). *Report on the Fells Acres day care cases.* Boston, MA: Office of the Attorney General.

The trials of Gerald Amirault, Violet Amirault and Cheryl LeFave in the Fells Acres day care ritual abuse case, the decision to have the children sit in the courtroom with their backs to the defendants, and the challenges that seating arrangement poses to the defendants' 6th Amendment confrontation rights are explained.

♦ **653** Mowbray, C.T., & Bybee, D. (1990). *Sexual abuse in a day care setting: The community investigation response.* Lansing, MI: State of Michigan Department of Mental Health.

An investigation conducted in Niles, Michigan, to assess community response to the Small World ritual abuse case shows that this small, rural, conservative community, although deeply divided over the truthfulness of the allegations, responded to them with the provision of a wide range of services and support for the accusing children and their families. Recommendations for improving community and agency responses to allegations of ritual abuse in day care settings are presented.

♦ **654** Rubenstein, A.M. (1990). *Report: Investigation into Breezy Point Day School.* Doylestown, PA: Office of the District Attorney.

A report filed by the Bucks County District Attorney on the year long investigation into the Breezy Point ritual abuse case chronicles the case, examines the children's allegations and the findings of their medical and psychological examinations, looks into the backgrounds of the 2 accused providers, and into the dubious credentials and criminal record of James Stillwell, founder of the National Agency Against the Organized Exploitation of Children and consultant to the parents. The report details the process and the rationale for the decision to not prefer criminal charges against the 2 accused providers.

American Family and Neighborhood
Ritual Abuse Case Reports

♦ **655** ACLU of Washington (1997, October). When child protection investigations harm children: The Wenatchee sexual abuse cases. Retrieved

9-February-01 from the World Wide Web: ftp://ftp.calweb.com/users/j/
jmprice/satanic-ritual-abuse/wenatchee-report-aclu-wa

The Wenatchee ritual abuse case reveals 8 ways in which the Washington child protection system harms children: it hospitalized children in an out-of-state psychiatric facility until the allegations were proved; it allowed the lead detective in the case to be an alleged victim's foster parent; it allowed the police to dictate when children's mental health therapy should be terminated; it allowed the records of interviews with the children to be destroyed; it allowed coercive interviews with children to occur; it failed to require that all interviews in the case be well documented; it failed to clarify the proper roles of police and state social workers in the interviews; and it failed to provide a mechanism for quality control and accountability during the investigation.

◆ **656** Commission Established by Executive Order No. 85-10. (1985, October). *Report to Governor Rudy Perpich concerning Kathleen Morris, Scott County attorney*. St. Paul, MN: Author.

The investigation into the conduct of Kathleen Morris, Scott County District Attorney, finds 2 acts of malfeasance: she kept exculpatory evidence from the Bentz defense team about children's stories of murder and mutilation that raise questions about their credibility; and she violated a court order to sequester witnesses in the Bentz trial by housing child witnesses in the same hotel and allowing them to discuss their testimony with each other. Five additional charges are supported by clear and convincing evidence but do not reach malfeasance: she dismissed the charges for 21 cases that could have been prosecuted; lied to the media by saying the children had not been interviewed on multiple occasions; lied to the presiding judge in the Bentz trial by saying the defense never asked for the notes she had already told them did not exist; failed to inform the judge that the children were housed together during the trial; and physically and verbally abused her employees. The commission does not recommend her removal from office.

◆ **657** Humphrey, H.H. III (1985, February 12). *Report on Scott County investigations*. St. Paul, MN: Office of the Attorney General.

The Minnesota Attorney General's investigation into the Jordan ritual abuse case determined that the recantation of the accusing children was sufficient reason to doubt the veracity of their allegations of ritual murder; the lack of evidence corroborating the children's accounts of ritual abuse is sufficient reason to not bring charges or reinstate charges against any of the accused; the mistakes made by the police and the district attorney destroyed any opportunity to prosecute those who may have sexually abused children; and those same mistakes caused the suffering of those who were falsely accused. In this case, too many people interviewed the children on too many occasions, created too many opportunities for the children to share stories and contaminate each other's accounts, and kept too few written notes and records. Criminal charges were filed before comprehensive investigations were conducted, thus little corroborating evidence was ever collected. Background checks were rarely performed and family, friends and neighbors were rarely interviewed before arrests were made. There is reason to believe that some of the children in this case actually were sexually abused, but there is no evidence to support the belief that sex rings were engaging in ritual abuse. The report can be found at the internet URL: http://www.a-team.org/scottco.html.

◆ **658** Lyon, K. *The Wenatchee report update*. Retrieved 9-February-01 from the World Wide Web: http://user.aol.com/DougHSkept/witchhunt/wen1_report.txt

Between September and December 1995, charges against some Wenatchee ritual abuse case defendants have been dropped, and the sentences of others have been overturned as the national media bring publicity to the case and advocacy groups are successful in soliciting support for the accused.

♦ **659** Lyon, K. (1995). *The Wenatchee report*. Retrieved 9-February-01 from the World Wide Web: http://user.aol.com/DougHSkept/witch-hunt/wen_report.txt

By September 1995, 24 people in the Wenatchee ritual abuse case are still in prison and 40 children are still separated from their parents. The community is deeply divided by the course of events that has escalated beyond anyone's imagination and, apparently, beyond everyone's control. The anatomy of the investigation is dissected, from the initial allegations through the trials and guilty pleas.

♦ **660** Van de Kamp, J. (1986, September). *Report of the Attorney General on the Kern County child abuse investigation*. Sacramento, CA: Office of the Attorney General.

The Kern County Sheriff's Department had no policies on investigative procedures and no interview protocols. Some deputies had attended a satanic crime seminar but never took the state-mandated training on child sexual abuse. Working without supervision, they deferred to the district attorney and social workers. The 3 agencies involved in the investigation shared no plan and their opposing philosophies about the reliability of children's disclosures hampered their investigation. Interviews were leading, suggestive and reinforcing; only 28 of the 134 interviews were tape-recorded; only half of the written reports of the interviews were signed by a supervisor and many reports paraphrased the interviews incorrectly. Nine searches produced no evidence; no medical tests were conducted on children who claimed they had been drugged and sexually abused. The ritual abuse allegations seriously eroded the credibility of the children and their ability to testify about sexual abuse. Carolyn Heim, the lead therapist working with the children housed in a county shelter, was dismissed from the center but continued to counsel the children on her own. She interviewed them in groups, kept spotty records, and summarized her contacts to avoid discovery motions by the defense.

♦ **661** Wallen, V. (1998). *OFCO 1998 review of the Wenatchee child sexual abuse investigations*. Tukwila, WA: Washington State Office of the Family and Children's Ombudsman.

A review of the procedures used by the State Division of Children and Family Services and local law enforcement officials to investigate allegations of ritual abuse in Wenatchee was prompted by complaints of poorly conducted and improper interviews with the alleged victims and their alleged abusers. An examination of case files, police reports, court transcripts, interviews and media materials in this case finds that: current documentation policies do not adequately facilitate a review of interview techniques to establish their appropriateness and the risk they pose for factual distortion; neither the child protective service workers nor the mental health professionals who conducted interviews in this case were trained in sexual abuse; and child protection services workers also were not trained in how to establish a working relationship with law enforcement agencies. The Ombudsman's Office recommends that both state law and child abuse policies be modified to require proper documentation and adequate training for child protective service workers. The report can be found at the internet URL: http://www.wa.gov/governor/ofco.

European and Australasian Ritual Abuse Case Reports

◆ **662** Clyde, J.J. (1992). *The report of the inquiry into the removal of children from Orkney* in February 1991. Edinburgh, Scotland: HMSO.

The £6 million inquiry into the Orkney Islands ritual abuse case details the chronology of the case and sets out 194 recommendations for improving child protection in Scotland, social work intervention in complicated and controversial cases, foster care involvement, and reform of the Children's Panels.

◆ **663** Miller, C.B. (1994). *In the Sheriffdom of South Strathclyde, Dumfries and Ayr: Report.* South Strathclyde, Scotland: Author.

The inquiry ordered into the Ayrshire ritual abuse case by the Court of Session took 152 days to complete and heard testimony from 103 witnesses. The 450 page report of the inquiry sets out a chronology of the case and discusses the legal grounds for referring it to the Children's Panel, the findings in fact, the evidence presented by the child witnesses, their social workers and the expert witnesses. It indicts the social workers for conducting leading and suggestive interviews with the children, and for pursuing single-mindedly the ritual abuse idea. The inquiry concludes that the evidence in this case was so ineptly collected and so contaminated that it is impossible to decide whether any of it is credible; on balance, the case had not been proven. The inquiry concludes that the children should be returned to their families.

◆ **664** Nottinghamshire County Council (1990). *The revised joint enquiry (JET) report.* Nottingham, England: Author.

The summary of the 5 volume Joint Enquiry Report on the Broxtowe Estate ritual abuse case concludes there is no evidence to substantiate the ritual abuse claims in this case, and that the claims were the result of both leading and suggestive questioning and the cross-germination occurring when the children, foster parents and social workers interacted with each other. The inquiry recommends: social workers and police develop a process to effectively manage joint inquiries; social workers immediately end their reliance on information on ritual abuse; therapeutic/disclosure interviews by social workers be rigorously examined for their ability to elicit reliable information; foster parents not be used to gather information on ritual abuse; care be taken in recruiting outside experts and consultants; and caution be exercised in eliciting the services of the media. The summary of the report can be found at the internet URL: http://samsara.law.cwru.edu/complaw/jetrep.htm.

◆ **665** Werkgroep Ritueel Misbruik (1994). *Report of the Ritual Abuse Workgroup.* The Hague, Netherlands: Ministerie van Justitie.

The investigation of the Ritual Abuse Workgroup formed after the Oude Pekela case finds no compelling evidence to corroborate alleged cases of ritual abuse in the Netherlands. The Workgroup proposes that more productive lines of inquiry are to examine the role the belief systems of investigators' and clinicians' play in generating and shaping ritual abuse allegations, and to assess the role that American experts play in generating European cases. The English translation of the report can be found at the internet URL: http://www.skepsis.NL/rimi.html.

◆ **666** Wood, J.R.T. (1996). *Royal Commission into the New South Wales Police Service.* Sydney, Australia: Royal Commissioner.

This 6 volume inquiry examines police corruption and pedophilia investigations in New South Wales, Australia. Chapter 5 of volume 4 discusses the difficulties posed by ritual abuse allegations. Chapter 7 of volume 4 discusses the Mr. Bubbles case. The report concludes that the case was "a debacle," due to the lack of training of investigating officers, the use of a probationary constable as an interviewer, the multiple interviews conducted with the children, the use of parents as interviewers, the unauthorized use of hypnosis in an interview with a 3 year old, inattention to the discrepancies in the children's accounts, and the failure to assess the role the consulting psychiatrist played in generating the ritual abuse details. The Commission makes no finding of guilt or innocence in the Mr. Bubbles case, concluding that "the trail is too old, the evidence of the children too contaminated, and there was nothing the Commission could find to independently corroborate or disprove the matters raised." The report can be found at the internet URL: http://www.premiers.nws.gov.au/pubs.htm.

FUNDED STUDIES AND RITUAL ABUSE TASK FORCE REPORTS

In both the United States and Europe, there have been several initiatives to examine ritual abuse as a social issue. Rather than analyzing individual cases, these funded studies and task force reports take a wider perspective by assessing the incidence of ritual abuse within defined geographical areas, investigating the characteristics and sources of allegations, and analyzing its real and potential impact on local and national resources.

Funded Studies on Ritual Abuse

◆ **667**   LaFontaine, J.S. (1994). *Extent and nature of organised and ritual abuse. Research findings.* London, England: HMSO.

A survey of police and social service agencies, commissioned by the Department of Health, finds 967 cases of organized abuse in England and Wales over a 4 year period; 85 of those involve allegations of ritual abuse. While substantiated cases of organized abuse comprise only a small percentage of all cases of child abuse, the ritual abuse cases garner the most attention and concern. This is especially problematic because no evidence corroborating these allegation has ever been discovered, and a review of the case files of children made wards of the court shows that their ritual abuse disclosures were influenced and shaped by their adult interrogators. The roles that British evangelical Christians and American experts play in spreading the ritual abuse myth across Great Britain are considered, and the types of cultural axioms the myth resonates with are discussed.

◆ **668**   Lloyd, D.W. (1990). *Ritual child abuse: Understanding the controversies.* Washington, D.C.: Clearinghouse on Child Abuse and Neglect Information.

Ritual abuse is best defined as the "intentional physical abuse, sexual abuse, or psychological abuse of a child by a person responsible for the child's welfare, when such abuse is repeated and/or stylized and is typified by such other acts as cruelty to animals, or threats of harm to the child, other persons, or animals, and is performed to reinforce the cult's religious cohesion." The controversy over whether it exists is largely a product of its previously imprecise definition, the lack of a central registry for ritual abuse reports, and the failure to distinguish the post-traumatic reactions of survivors from mental illness.

♦ **669** Goodman, G.S., Qin, J., Bottoms, B.L., & Shaver, P.R. (1994). *Characteristics and sources of allegations of ritualistic child abuse* (Grant no. 90CA1405). Chicago, IL: National Center on Child Abuse and Neglect.

Five studies explore the characteristics and sources of allegations of ritual abuse. The first finds that 31% of the surveyed clinical members of the American Psychological Association, the American Psychiatric Association, and the National Association of Social Workers had encountered at least one case of either ritual or religion-related abuse; 1.4% had encountered more than 100 cases. The second finds that 23% of surveyed state social workers, prosecuting attorneys and police encountered at least one case of each type of abuse. In both the first and second study, respondents who encountered ritual abuse cases believed the allegations although they could offer no evidence to corroborate them. The third involved a subset of cases from the first study that involved claims of repressed memories of ritual or religion-related abuse. The alleged ritual abuse repressed memory cases began earlier and lasted longer, are more likely to involve a diagnosis of multiple personality disorder, and are based on weaker corroborative evidence than are other cases. The fourth examined children's knowledge of satanic abuse. This laboratory-based study finds that although children have stereotypic knowledge about the devil and satanism, they are not likely to invent stories of ritual abuse on their own. Finally, the fifth study details 3 types of religion-related abuse and finds that there is more convincing evidence for it than there is for ritual abuse. The findings of these 5 studies have a great deal of implication for forensic evaluation, clinical practice, and future research. The report can be found at the internet URL: http://home.rica.net/rthoma/nccansra.htm.

♦ **670** Waterman, J., Kelly, R.J., McCord, J., & Oliveri, M.K. (1990). *Reported ritualistic and non-ritualistic sexual abuse in preschools: Effects and mediators. Executive summary.* Washington, D.C.: Clearinghouse on Child Abuse and Neglect Information.

The report describes a study that analyzed the effects on children and their families of ritualistic and non-ritualistic sexual abuse in day care centers, and identifies the factors that mediate those effects. A group of children alleging ritual abuse was compared to a group alleging sexual abuse and to a nonabused control group. Children reporting ritual abuse have more fears, negative attitudes and behavior problems, and exhibit more sexual acting out than either sexually abused or nonabused children. A 5 year follow-up of the ritual abuse group shows that although most of the children improved significantly, a small percentage continues to have significant emotional and behavioral problems. The study also finds that ritual abuse affects the parent-child relationship, impairs parental marital and sexual relationships, and leads to distrust of social institutions. These and other family factors are found to be the most significant mediators of the children's functioning.

Ritual Abuse Task Force Reports

◆ **671**   Lloyd, D.W. (Ed.) (1989). *Investigating allegations of ritualistic sexual abuse: Proceedings of a think-tank.* Huntsville, AL: National Children's Advocacy Center.

A think-tank, put together by the National Children's Advocacy Center comprising Susan J. Kelley, Abigail Sivan, Kathleen C. Faller, Linda Meyer Williams, Kenneth Lanning, Beth Dickinson, Larry Hardoon, Chris Hatcher, Sandra Baker and Charles Wilson discussed ritual abuse with moderator David Lloyd. Discussants debate the definition of ritual abuse, its sequelae, the complications of investigating cases of it, the dynamics of cult mind control, and the reasons for professionals' belief in ritual abuse.

◆ **672**   Ritual Abuse Task Force (1991). *Ritual abuse: Definitions, glossary, the use of mind control.* Los Angeles, CA: Los Angeles County Commission for Women.

A task force composed of professionals from various fields, adult survivors and parents of abused children was constituted in 1988 to examine ritual abuse. It defines ritual abuse as physical, sexual and psychological abuse in the context of cult rituals, the purpose of which is to indoctrinate victims into the cult belief system, intimidate them into silence, and/or detract from their credibility as witnesses. Ritual abuse involves such acts as human and animal sacrifice; forced ingestion of feces, urine and semen; isolation in cages and coffins; mind control through hypnosis, drugs and programming; ingestion of blood and human flesh; sleep deprivation and starvation; and participation in such rituals as the "birthing ritual" in which the child is placed within the carcass of a dead animal or the body of a dead person and is "born" into membership in the cult, and the "marriage ritual" in which the child is wed to the devil. Little is known about the ritual abusers except that they often include women and they are more sadistic than pedophiles. They carry out the ritual abuse according to a satanic calendar, and play specific roles in the ceremonies. The sequelae of ritual abuse includes multiple personality disorder and post-traumatic stress disorder. Ritual abuse is widespread. The prognosis for ritually abused children is guarded. The report can be found at the internet URL: http://www.witchhunt.org/articles/states/laratf.htm.

◆ **673**   San Diego County Grand Jury (1991/1992). *Child sexual abuse, assault and molest issues.* San Diego, CA: Author.

The grand jury reviewed expert testimony and case studies to determine San Diego County's legal response to cases of incest, sexual abuse and ritual abuse. In regards to the latter, the grand jury interviewed a cadre of social workers, mental health professionals and police who have been involved with alleged ritual abuse cases, and who have pressured the legal system to respond to them. While each of the interviewed professionals insists ritual abuse is a significant problem in the county, none could provide any factual evidence to corroborate that claim. Ritual abuse allegations tend to increase after professionals attend conferences where it is discussed and where alleged survivors give personal testimony. The grand jury concludes there is no evidence to support the contention that ritual abuse is a problem in the county, and the contention itself is tantamount to a contemporary myth. The grand jury vigorously opposes Senate Bill 1771 that would set up a state wide task force on ritual abuse and that inevitably would spread the myth over the state. The report can be found at the internet URL: http://www.vix.com/pub/men/falsereport/satanic/sandiego.html.

♦ **674**   Task Force on Ritual Abuse (1992). *Report of Utah state task force on ritual abuse.* Salt Lake City, UT: Author.

The Utah Task Force on Ritual Abuse was created in 1990 with the purpose of gathering information about ritual abuse in the state, sponsoring responsible education for professionals and the public, and suggesting needed programs to address the problem. The task force defines ritual abuse as a "brutal form of abuse ... consisting of physical, sexual and psychological abuse... It usually involves repeated abuse over an extended period of time." Survivors report sexual assault, bestiality, acts of torture including burning, cutting, burial in coffins, forced ingestion of blood, urine and feces, and infant sacrifice. The reports are strikingly similar in nature and resemble reports of survivors in other states and countries. The task force finds the present criminal code sufficient to address the most serious aspects of ritual abuse, but specially trained police are needed to investigate cases; although no courtroom procedures should be changed to accommodate cases of ritual abuse, prosecuting attorneys should be trained in its dynamics. Finally, the task force also strongly recommends that mental health professionals be trained in ritual abuse dynamics, especially those working in public agencies. A recent survey of Utah citizens finds that 90% believe ritual abuse is a problem, and 68% want the state Attorney General to provide more funds for its investigation.

INVESTIGATIVE GUIDES

Several guides for investigating alleged cases of ritual abuse also have been published. Most of these treat ritual abuse as one manifestation of "cult crime" that includes such disparate acts as cemetery desecration, animal mutilation, satanic graffiti and ritual murder. The following citations, however, are of investigative guides that focus exclusively or significantly on ritual abuse.

♦ **675**   Lanning, K.V. (1992). *Investigator's guide to allegations of "ritual" child abuse.* Quantico, VA: Federal Bureau of Investigation.

Historically there have been many threats to children, but the contemporary concern about ritual abuse is a reworking of the "stranger danger" threat, made all the more plausible by the interchangeable use of terms like "ritualistic," "satanic," and "occult." It is important for investigators to realize that rituals can be sexual, as they are alleged to be in ritual abuse, but they also are cultural and spiritual; therefore the injudicious use of the term "ritual abuse" could apply to abuse of children in cultural groups or religious settings that are not cultic or satanic. The confusion about these terms and their implications is perpetuated in law enforcement training sessions, and by first person accounts by alleged survivors. It is advisable to drop the term "ritual abuse" altogether and replace it with "multidimensional sex rings." Such rings have multiple abusers, multiple victims, engage in repetitive rituals and maintain silence through threat and intimidation. Investigators looking into such rings are advised to minimize the satanic implications, hold their own religious beliefs at abeyance, listen to the alleged victims and objectively evaluate their disclosures, assess the degree of contagion from overzealous interviewers or the media that may influence disclosures, develop a contingency plan should the case require it, and use multidisciplinary task forces for assessment, evaluation and investigation. The report can be found at the internet URL: http://www.religioustolerance.org/ra_rep03.htm.

◆ **676** Multi-Victim and Multi-Perpetrator Ritualistic Abuse Task Force (1990). *Investigative protocol.* San Diego, CA: San Diego County Commission on Children and Youth.

The strategy for investigating multi-victim/multi-perpetrator ritual abuse cases emphasizes the formation of a multidisciplinary investigative team, the development of a planning strategy with timelines, the assessment of the role of each agency involved in the investigation, and the creation of linkages between the agencies as well as between the investigating team, the community and the media.

◆ **677** State Technical Assistance Team (1994). *Basic guide for evaluation-investigation of sexual and ritualistic abuse.* Jefferson City, MO: Missouri State Department of Social Services.

The guidelines advocate a multidisciplinary team approach to ritual abuse investigation and evaluation. Specific guidelines for coordinating the collection of evidence, conducting forensic examinations, organizing information, and interviewing victims, witnesses, and suspected perpetrators must be set out. Prosecution, treatment and mental health services for ritual abuse victims also must be carefully coordinated.

10

Ritual Abuse Narratives

Sexual tales about the erotic, the gendered, the relational and the perverse have cluttered the cultural landscape for generations. They also have played a central role in the history of social thought. To anthropologists, sexual tales reveal something about the culture of which they are constitutive; to historians they are tropes for making sense of the past; to psychologists they expose the infrastructure of character; and to sociologists they bridge the gap between individual lives and social forces and political structures.

It is only within quite recent years that sexual tales have been eclipsed by sexual *trauma* tales. These first-person narratives of sexual suffering, secrecy, shame and surviving, once the most personal and private of stories, lately have become the most public of properties. Whether told in mass marketed self-help books, on television talk shows, in the tabloids or in autobiographies, sexual trauma tales have become the story of contemporary culture. When those trauma tales are in the form of first-person narratives about ritual abuse, how they link to culture is more than a little controversial.

SURVIVOR NARRATIVES

In the sociological imagination, power has three dimensions: the ability to influence the outcome of a specific decision; the ability to influence the agenda from which a specific decision is made; and the ability to influence consciousness. It is that last dimension of power — the ability to influence consciousness, and thereby to frame an issue and set a standard of proof for evaluating claims—that is the most relevant to the topic of ritual abuse survivor narratives.

A sexual trauma survivor narrative can be subversive. It can have the power to challenge the dominant cultural discourse about sex and the power relations that support it, and thus can prefigure social change. Certainly that is the case with rape survivor narratives. By describing rape as a gendered act of violence so common in women's lives that the fear of it has always functioned to keep women in their place, the survivor narratives reveal the relationship between biography and history, the personal and the political. In doing so, they set the agenda for a whole generation of subversive sexual politics.

Can the same be said of ritual abuse survivor narratives? Do these narratives, the products of recovered memories, the stories of fragmented personalities, the reactions to deeply disputed cases, have the power to influence consciousness, to frame the issue of ritual abuse, and to set a standard of proof for claims of it? Herein lies the controversy. If they do not, then ritual abuse survivor narratives are just Grand Guignol stories that can be read with pity, revulsion, bemusement or even titillation, but can never be acted upon.

First-Person Survivor Narratives

♦ **678** Beckylane. (1995). *Where the rivers join: A personal account of healing from ritual abuse.* Vancouver, B.C., Canada: Press Gang.

The author, a Canadian college instructor, recovered memories of ritual abuse in therapy. She began therapy with intact memories of an unhappy childhood during which her mother frequently and painfully catheterized her for chronic bladder and kidney infections. She then slowly began recovering memories of ritual abuse she experienced from infancy until she was 7 years old. The ritual abuse was conducted by a cult that had paid her parents for access to her. Although the nature and dogma of the cult are not clear to her, she recalls participating in rituals that included human sacrifices and cannibalism. When the cult no longer needed her for its rituals, she was incestuously abused by her own father for several more years.

♦ **679** Buchanan, L. (1994). *Satan's child: A survivor tells her story to help others heal.* Minneapolis, MN: CompCare.

During therapy, the author began recovering memories of childhood ritual abuse by a satanic cult that practiced blood-drinking, cannibalism and infant sacrifice. Virtually every aspect of her life was negatively affected by the ritual abuse and, for a time, by the memories of it. Through her own determination and the help of a mental health professional, she was able to recover the past and establish mastery over it. She offers advice to others who are, or worried they might be, survivors of ritual abuse.

♦ **680** Dragon, J., & Popp, T. (Eds.) (1999). *Multiple journey to one: Spiritual stories of integrating from dissociative identity disorder.* Santa Rosa, CA: Dancing Serpents Press.

The personal accounts of 8 people, all once diagnosed with multiple personalities and now successfully integrated, are presented by two editors who also are recently integrated. Most of the accounts deal with childhood histories of ritual abuse, and all consider the development of dissociation and of multiple personalities as mechanisms for coping with extreme childhood abuse. The integration process for all of the survivors was slow and at times extremely difficult; each survivor benefited from a strong spirituality that sustained him or her during the integration process.

♦ **681**   Fisher-Taylor, G. (1992). Ritual abuse: Towards a feminist understanding. *Herizons, 6,* 19–21.

Feminist therapy, with its validation of memory and of female identity, helped the author to recover memories of childhood ritual abuse. Her involvement with a network of women ritual abuse survivors who met to discuss their experiences and to support each other was a helpful adjunct to therapy.

♦ **682**   Hoffman, W. (1994). *Ascent from evil: The healing journey out of satanic abuse.* Liguori, MO: Liguori Press.

The author recovered memories of ritual abuse during sessions with a Christian counselor. Abused by a satanic cult, she experienced a lifetime of psychological problems but discovered that she was better able to successfully heal from them only after she had dealt with the spiritual problems caused by the ritual abuse.

♦ **683**   Jadelinn (1998). *Spirit alive: A woman's healing from cult ritual abuse.* Toronto, Canada: Women's Press.

The author, diagnosed with multiple personality disorder, came to terms with her diagnosis and the childhood ritual abuse that caused it. Her successful therapy helped her appreciate how multiple personalities emerged to help her survive the ritual abuse and cope with its sequelae.

♦ **684**   Joe, S. (1991). *Out of hell again.* Rocky River, OH: State of the Art Publishing.

During years of participation in a 12-Step group, the author made significant progress in dealing with his codependency, but still had the feeling that he had deeper and more serious problems to address. One evening he accidentally drove over a rabbit and was suddenly filled with fear followed by fits of rage over which he had no control. During subsequent sessions with a mental health professional, he began recovering memories of childhood ritual abuse by a satanic cult. When he finally recovered the most deeply buried memory of being forced, as a 4 year old, to stab an infant to death as part of a sacrifice, his real healing commenced.

♦ **685**   Ladd, J. (1991). Logotherapy's place for the ritually abused. *International Forum for Logotherapy, 14,* 82–86.

A personal account from an adult survivor of childhood ritual abuse and incest whose exposure to logophilosophy through participation in logotherapy strengthened her will to work through her childhood experiences and pursue her life goals.

♦ **686**   Lorena, J.M., & Levy P. (Eds.). (1998). *Breaking ritual silence: An anthology of ritual abuse survivor stories.* Gardnerville, NV: Trout and Sons.

The first-person accounts of ritual abuse from female and male survivors, ranging in age from 20 to 60 and living in the United States, Canada and Europe, that comprise this anthology are disturbingly similar. While they vary somewhat in specific details, such as dates on which cult rituals were conducted and the nature and purpose of the rituals, they are consistent in their depiction of sexual abuse, helplessness and terror. All of the accounts also are testimony to the resilience of the human spirit that empowers and enables survivors to work through the devastating psychological, physical and spiritual sequelae of childhood ritual abuse.

◆ **687**   Oksana, C. (1994). *Safe passage to healing: A guide for survivors of ritual abuse.* NY: Harper Perennial.

The author, who recovered memories of childhood ritual abuse during therapy, offers a guide to recovery. Plaiting her own personal narrative with interviews of other ritual abuse survivors and with research findings, she explains how survivors can deal with the kind of body memories, flashbacks, recovered memories, distortions in self-image and self-control, spiritual problems, and threats to safety that she experienced. Her own recovery of memory was not hurried and she recommends that survivors take their time and find their pace in recovering their own memories. She gives advance warnings of words and phrases that trigger dissociative and suicidal responses for her and that may do the same for other survivors. She concludes that to recover from ritual abuse, survivors need 3 qualities: courage, creativity and commitment.

◆ **688**   Pike, P.L., Mohline, R.J., Hart, A. & Ellison, K.L. (1995). Ritual abuse and recovery: Survivors' personal accounts. *Journal of Psychology and Theology, 23,* 45–55.

The personal accounts of 2 ritual abuse survivors illustrate how successful therapy must take into account the emotional, psychological, interpersonal and spiritual sequelae of ritual abuse. Written in the first person, the accounts weave memories with specific aspects of the therapeutic encounter.

◆ **689**   Reid, G.R. (1997). *Nobody's angel.* El Paso, TX: Youthfire Publications.

After recovering memories of childhood ritual abuse in a satanic cult, the author went on to establish a ministry for other victims of satanic cults. His ministry is based on the belief that participating in satanism, as a victim, a dabbler or cultist, leaves the soul vulnerable to possession by evil spirits and demons, and that the possession often manifests itself in addiction, violence and mental illness. The recovery of the soul, therefore, is the first step to healing.

◆ **690**   Richardson, A. (1997). *Double vision: A travelogue of recovery from ritual abuse.* Pasadena, CA: Trilogy Books.

The author, a ritual abuse survivor, interweaves observations and information about ritual abuse with excerpts from the journal she kept during the 3 years of counseling with a Congregationalist minister during which she recovered memories of ritual abuse. Although she remembers the details of the ritual abuse, and the horrific rituals in which she was compelled to participate, she is not certain about the dynamics or the dogma of the cult that abused her.

◆ **691**   Rose, E.S. (1996). *Reaching for the light: A guide for ritual abuse survivors and their therapists.* Cleveland, OH: Pilgrim Press.

After recovering her own memories of ritual abuse in a matrilineal satanic cult, the author developed a step-by-step guide for other survivors and the mental health professionals who treat them.

◆ **692**   Rose, E.S. (1993, January/February). Surviving the unbelievable. *Ms. Magazine*, pp. 40–45.

The personal account of childhood ritual abuse by a pseudonymous free-lance writer whose mother was a member of a matrilineal satanic cult that engaged in cannibalism, blood-drinking and infant sacrifice, including the sacrifice of her own sister who was decapitated by cultists immediately after her birth. Upon his return from the Vietnam War, the author told her father of her ritual abuse but he passed off her allegations as childhood nightmares. His denial, coupled with cult death threats, forced her to repress many memories of her ritual abuse. She is now speaking out to break the intergenerational cycle of ritual abuse.

◆ **693**   Smith, M., & Pazder, L. (1980). *Michelle remembers*. NY: Pocket Books.

This *New York Times* bestseller is the first personal account of ritual abuse ever published. The pseudonymous Michelle Smith sought counseling from Lawrence Pazder for emotional problems following a miscarriage. Over the next 14 months, and in daily sessions that often lasted 6 hours, Smith began recovering memories of ritual abuse by a Canadian satanic cult of which her mother was a devotee. Some of the rituals were performed in a local cemetery where Smith was injected with stupefying drugs and forced to lie in an open grave; other ceremonies were held in an old house where she was confined within a statue of the devil with live snakes and the dismembered limbs of sacrificed babies. Her ritual abuse culminated in an 81 day Black Mass during which she was tortured by electrical shocks, tooth extractions, and the surgical implantation of a tail on her spine and horns on her head. A personal intercession with the Virgin Mary saved her from the cult.

◆ **694**   Stratford, L. (1993). *Stripped naked*. Gretna, LA: Pelican.

Part 3 of the autobiography of a woman who endured years of ritual abuse by a satanic cult and who was forced to become a "breeder," supplying the cult with infants for sacrifice. Feeling that she has not recovered all of the memories of her ritual abuse, she enters therapy and is diagnosed with multiple personality disorder. As she comes to know the alter personalities and becomes aware of the memories of ritual abuse each of them holds, she appreciates the ways in which they have contributed to her emotional, physical and spiritual survival.

◆ **695**   Stratford, L. (1992). *I know you're hurting*. Gretna, LA: Pelican.

Part 2 of the autobiography of a woman who endured years of ritual abuse by a satanic cult and who, as a "breeder" for the cult, participated in the sacrifices of 3 of her infants. After recovering memories of ritual abuse, the author continues to struggle with its emotional, physical and spiritual sequelae. She travels around the country speaking in churches and to organizations, and appears on Christian television and radio talk shows to discuss her own problems and to encourage other ritual abuse survivors to come forward.

◆ **696**   Stratford, L. (1988). *Satan's underground: The extraordinary story of one woman's escape*. Eugene, OR: Harvest House.

Part 1 of the autobiography of a woman who as a child was adopted into a middle class family and offered for sexual abuse by her mother to various men who did work around the house. After her father left, her mother accelerated her own physical and emotional abuse of the author and involved her in pornography. Battling bouts of elective mutism and hysterical paralysis, the author ran away at 15 only to be returned by the authorities to her mother, who then set her up in a pornography ring run by a satanic high priest. She then endured years of ritual abuse by black-robed satanists who skinned babies alive in rituals. As a "breeder" for the cult, the author was forcefully impregnated on 3 occasions and made to participate in the sacrifices of her own infants. After fleeing from the cult, she repressed all memory of the ritual abuse which she later recovered in counseling sessions with evangelist Johanna Michaelson.

◆ **697**   WaterWomon, C. (1992). Surviving ritual abuse. *Matriart, 2,* 10–12.

The author's art work expressed her memories of childhood ritual abuse long before she recovered them. She believes that her artistic expression allowed her to deal with the ritual abuse in her own time, and when much of its horror had been artistically expressed, she was cognitively and emotionally ready to deal with the memories.

First-Person Narratives of Parents of Ritually Abused Children

◆ **698**   Bander, J. (1997). *A mother's story: The Civic Creche child sex trial.* Auckland, New Zealand: Howling at the Moon.

An account by the pseudonymous mother of a 6 year old who was one of the key witnesses in the Civic Creche ritual abuse trial. She tells about how her son began to unfold a story of ritual abuse, including torture, confinement and human sacrifice, his experiences at the trial, and both his and her own dissatisfaction with the 10 year sentence imposed on Peter Ellis.

◆ **699**   Crowley, P. (1990). *Not my child: A mother confronts her child's sexual abuse.* NY: Doubleday.

The mother of one of the children who accused Kelly Michaels of ritually abusing her at the Wee Care Nursery School describes the impact of the abuse and the trial on her daughter, and the devastating effects the case had on her family.

◆ **700**   Hill, J. (1996). Believing Rachel. *Journal of Psychohistory, 24,* 132–146.

The pseudonymous mother of a 4 year old girl allegedly ritually abused by the janitor and some of the day care providers at the Rogers Park Jewish Community Child Care Center in Chicago offers her account of the case. Her child experienced severe emotional and behavioral problems after her disclosure; the problems were exacerbated by her mother's initial unwillingness to believe she had been ritually abused. Her mother reluctantly changed her mind when other children enrolled in the center confirmed her daughter's account. Her belief in her daughter was a significant factor in the child's recovery from the ritual abuse.

Children's Narratives

◆ **701**   Newsome, M. (1999, November). My lie sent my father to jail. *Redbook,* pp. 88–90.

The only evidence against Jeffrey Modahl in the Kern County ritual abuse case was the testimony of his 10 year old daughter who had been subjected to intensive interviews. Medicated with Thorazine at the time of her trial testimony, and under the erroneous impression that nothing untoward would happen to her father, the 10 year old told the court about sexual abuse in the context of satanic rituals. Her father was convicted, and although she wrote him a letter admitting she had lied and apologizing for it, his conviction was not overturned until 15 years later. From the age of 10 until 16, she was in 15 different foster homes. Now 25, she is divorced with 2 children. She knows her father forgives her, but she is unable to forgive herself.

Accused Ritual Abusers' Narratives

◆ **702**   Buckey, P., Buckey, R., & Buckey, P.A. (1990). After the McMartin trials: Some reflections from the Buckeys. *Issues in Child Abuse Accusations, 2.* Retrieved 4-March-01 from the World Wide Web: http://www.ipt-forensics.com/journal/volume2/j2_4_6.htm.

Raymond Buckey, his mother Peggy and sister Peggy Ann discuss the toll the McMartin Preschool ritual abuse case took on them and their family. For Raymond and his mother, the years in jail awaiting trial were particularly difficult; each was threatened and assaulted by other inmates, shunned by neighbors and friends, and demoralized by the increasingly bizarre accounts of ritual abuse made by a growing number of children. Peggy Ann lost her license to teach and had to initiate a civil suit for its restoration. They take comfort in their religious beliefs and in their knowledge that they are innocent of all charges.

◆ **703**   Michaels, K. (1993, Sept. 6). Eight years in Kafkaland. *National Review,* pp. 36–37.

Kelly Michaels gives her personal account of her 8 year legal battle in the Wee Care ritual abuse case and her amazement that an ordinary person like herself could be the target of such an irrational panic over ritual abuse.

◆ **704**   Michaels, M.K. (1993, November). I am not a monster. *Mademoiselle,* pp. 126–133.

Kelly Michaels maintains her innocence in the Wee Care ritual abuse case. She describes herself as a naïve, trusting young woman who believed, when she was arrested, that the police had made a terrible mistake and that she would be completely vindicated at trial. Disillusioned after her conviction, she spent several years in solitary confinement before her conviction was overturned. Although the prosecutor intends to retry her, she is confident she will be completely exonerated once the jury understands how the children were browbeaten by their interviewers into making the bizarre ritual abuse allegations against her.

HELPERS' NARRATIVES

Over the decades during which sexual abuse colonized Western consciousness, highly publicized scandals— of sexually abused children not believed while falsely accusing ones were, of children removed from their abusive families only to be returned and abused again, of innocent fathers carted off to jail and guilty ones using their cultural capital to resist punishment — rocked the child protection, mental health and allied fields. Pro-family and anti–child-saving pressure groups coalesced in response to these scandals and exerted increasing influence over public perception and policy. As a result, intervention with sexually abused children was forced to become more procedural and bureaucratic, that is, less intuitive and risk-taking.

But ritual abuse demands something else entirely of professionals. It calls out for imaginativeness, audacity, willingness to believe and a moral commitment to stand by those beliefs. As the following citations illustrate, meeting those demands often comes with both a personal and a professional price.

Mental Health Professionals' Narratives

◆ **705**   Feldman, G.C. (1993). *Lessons in evil, lessons from the light: A true story of satanic abuse and spiritual healing.* NY: Crown.

The successful therapy of the pseudonymous patient Barbara Maddox is presented. She entered therapy for sexual dysfunction and unwarranted anger at her daughter, and through hypnosis recovered memories of ritual abuse by her mother, grandparents and other satanic cultists. The author, her treating psychologist, examines her own journey from skepticism to belief in her patient's memories. Once the author had expanded her own world view to accept the reality of evil, she became so preoccupied with understanding evil that her already difficult marriage became even more troubled, and she became fearful about the safety of her own children. In an attempt to discover her own encounters with violence, she participated in past life therapy and recovered memories of being an 18th century Indian girl struggling to free herself from a patriarchal culture. She maintains a friendship with Maddox whom she considers an inspiration.

◆ **706**   Johnson, M. (1994). Fear and power: From naivete to a believer in cult abuse. *Journal of Psychohistory, 21,* 435–441.

The personal narrative of a psychotherapist who came to believe that satanic cults are engaging in ritual abuse and that cult leaders perceive any therapeutic intervention with their victims as a threat to their power. The author's change of mind about ritual abuse was prompted by his work with an adult male inpatient, diagnosed with multiple personality disorder, who had an alter personality that was luring him back to the cult. When the author successfully intervened, he was harassed by anonymous telephone calls, attempted break-ins, and intrusions on his private property by strangers he believed were leaders of the cult.

◆ **707**   Mayer, R.S. (1991). *Satan's children.* NY: Avon Books.

Five patients, all diagnosed with multiple personality disorder, recover memories of ritual abuse in satanic cults during the course of therapy. All were successfully treated and integrated by the author, a psychologist, who examines his own growing awareness of ritual abuse acquired through extensive reading of psychological and popular literature and consultations with colleagues. These patients challenged everything he knew about treating multiple personalities, forced him to expand his world view to accommodate a specific vision of evil, and made him fear for his own and his family's safety. Although the author still is not convinced there is a national satanic conspiracy targeting children, as his patients believe, he finds it impossible to reject the notion of ritual abuse altogether, especially in the face of his patients' profoundly fractured personalities.

◆ **708**   Perlman, S.D. (1995). One analyst's journey into darkness: Countertransference resistance to recognizing sexual abuse, ritual abuse, and multiple personality disorders. *Journal of the American Academy of Psychoanalysis, 23,* 137–151.
Recognizing sexual abuse, ritual abuse and multiple personality disorder may overwhelm psychoanalysts and threaten their basic assumptions. Once psychoanalysts and their patients come to believe in ritual abuse, their fear can become so compelling that they see danger and threat everywhere. The author's treatment of a woman with multiple personalities and a childhood history of both incest and ritual abuse is discussed to illustrate the journey both took to recognizing and treating the abuse.

◆ **709**   Rockwell, R.B. (1995). Insidious deception. *Journal of Psychohistory, 22,* 312–327.
After years of attending meetings of the International Society for the Study of Dissociation and Multiple Personality the author, a psychiatrist, has come to believe that ritual abuse is a reality and that it is widespread. He is alarmed at attempts by others to discredit that belief, particularly Wright (see citation 259) in his examination of the Ingram ritual abuse case. Wright relies too much on the opinion of Ofshe (see citation 252) whom the judge did not find a credible witness because he has no expertise in sexual abuse and his experiment in which he created pseudomemories for Ingram was not scientific.

◆ **710**   Rockwell, R.B. (1994). One psychiatrist's view of satanic ritual abuse. *Journal of Psychohistory, 21,* 443–460.
The author recounts his first encounter with an adult ritual abuse patient who was diagnosed with multiple personality disorder. The patient had an alter personality that had memories of ritual abuse by a cult. The author suggests that Jungian theory be used to analyze cults and ritual abuse.

Advocates' Narratives

◆ **711**   Core, D. (1991). *Chasing Satan.* London: Gunther Press.
The author, the director of the Childwatch, documents her personal crusade to alert a skeptical British society about the nature and extent of ritual abuse. Her investigation reveals that ritual abuse is an exigent threat, affecting tens of thousands of children across the country. The author has lectured widely and consulted on several sensational British ritual abuse cases.

◆ **712**   Nathan, D. (1995, June). Sweet justice: My fight to free Kelly Michaels. *Redbook,* pp. 84–87, 122, 124.
The author, a freelance reporter, first met Kelly Michaels in 1988 when she was awaiting sentencing on her conviction in the Wee Care ritual abuse case. Although

she was shunned by other reporters who referred to Michaels as "The Demon Seed," and by the parents of the Wee Care children, she did review the evidence in the case and listened to the tapes of the interviews with the children. Convinced that Michaels was innocent, she began a campaign that led to the formation of the Kelly Michaels Defense Committee, and culminated in overturning of Michael's convictions.

Researchers' Narratives

◆ **713**   Scott, S. (1999). Dancing to a different tune: A reply to responses to "Here be dragons." *Sociological Research Online, 4.* Retrieved from the World Wide Web 9-February-2001: http://www.socresonline.org.uk/4/2/scott_sara.html.

The responses of Wise (see citation 775) and Huntington (see citation 757) to "Here be Dragons" share a common concern: the article's assertion that ritual abuse claims are true serves the needs of social workers and police officers, but avoids the responsibility of feminist sociologists to analyze the social construction of discourse. When the discourse is the subject of heated public debate, as ritual abuse is, suspending concern about the lived experiences of the women the author interviewed was ethically, politically and practically problematic.

◆ **714**   Scott, S. (1998). Here be dragons: Researching the unbelievable, hearing the unthinkable. A feminist sociologist in uncharted territory. *Sociological Research Online, 3.* Retrieved 2-February-01 from the World Wide Web: http://www.socresonline.org.uk/3/3/1.html.

The author, a feminist sociologist, describes the ways in which the dominant societal response to allegations of ritual abuse as untrue affected her research. She conducted life history interviews with 11 women and 3 men who identified themselves as ritual abuse survivors, and then offers a reflexive, feminist account of knowledge production that strives to make visible the social and political context of the research that shaped her engagement with her subjects, her choice of subjects, the questions she asked and her interpretation of their responses. The nexus between her own experiences, that of her subjects whose accounts she asserts are true, and the "discourse of disbelief" surrounding those accounts consumed her. The "disembedding" process by which her research moved from specific, emotional and embodied encounters to academic articles was particularly problematic and distressing.

ADDITIONAL CITATIONS

Although not first-person narratives, the following sources take unique approaches to ritual abuse for specialized audiences.

◆ **715**   Sanford, D. (1990). *Don't make me go back, mommy: A child's book about satanic ritual abuse.* Portland, OR: Multnomah Press.

This 24-page illustrated book on ritual abuse for children between the ages of 5 and 11 tells the story of a 5 year old whose worried parents take her to therapy when they notice changes in her behavior. During therapy, she discloses that she was ritually abused in her day care center by providers and strangers dressed in hooded black robes. The child works through the horror of the ritual abuse with her therapist and recovers with the support of her parents. The book is intended for use by mental health professionals, parents and child protectionists to assist children in disclosing ritual abuse.

♦ **716**   StarDancer, L.J. (1989). *Turtle Boy and Jet the Wonderpup. A therapeutic comic for ritual abuse survivors*. Kelseyville, CA: H.P.L. Publishing.

This cartoon storybook for ritual abuse survivors of all ages tells the story of a boy alter in a multiple personality system and his fantasy of triumphing over the ritual abuse that fractured the host personality. The book is intended for use as an adjunct to ritual abuse and recovered memory therapy for children, adolescents and adults.

11

Anthropological, Folkloric and Sociological Perspectives on Ritual Abuse

The study of childhood trauma has a frustrating history. Periods of insight and interest alternate with much longer periods of indifference and insensitivity. At each historical moment at which assiduity is reclaimed, however, the very notion of childhood trauma unfolds just a little more from the view that it is an individual event bound to soma and psyche, to the view that trauma, its experience, meaning and resolution are continuously shaped by the cultural context.

This unfolding view provides an entrée for social scientists into a field preponderated by mental health professionals and child protectionists. Arguably, when the childhood trauma under consideration is ritual abuse, they have not always been warmly welcomed. For a field already rancorously divided into "believers" at one extreme, "disbelievers" at the other with many others, bewildered and uncertain somewhere in between, social scientific discourse on contemporary legends, demonologies, social structures and moral panics seems to offer only dusty answers to a field hot for certainties.

What social scientists can, and do, contribute to an understanding of ritual abuse, however, is an analysis of *why* it is late-modern strains and sensibilities that form the cultural crucible for allegations of it, and *how* the controversy over it has retained its polemical strength for so long.

THE ANTHROPOLOGY OF RITUAL ABUSE

From an anthropological perspective, allegations of ritual abuse represent a contemporary reworking of age-old and transcultural legends about good and evil, innocence and depravity. Legends wrap a cultural narrative around social strains and the anxieties and uncertainties they produce. By naming the threat to stability and order, they have the cathartic effect of channeling anger and moral rectitude, thereby creating at least an illusion of control and stasis. Legends, then, serve an inherently conservative function. Although they can become institutionalized and can instigate collective reactions, most have a lively, if only discursive, existence in folklore, that is, in the stories, tales and admonitions that ordinary folks share and circulate outside of social institutions.

◆ **717**   Brion, D. (1993). The hidden persistence of witchcraft. *Law and Critique, 4,* 227–252.

The American day care ritual abuse cases strongly resemble the 17th century Salem witchcraft cases in that both are responses of psychic communities to perceived threats to their cohesiveness. Holders of a communitarian cosmology tend to interpret these threats in terms of a supernatural evil of some kind, and are not dissuaded from that belief by lack of evidence.

◆ **718**   Campion-Vincent, V. (1995). Descriptions of sabbaths and rituals in contemporary anti-satanic fears. *Cahiers Internationaux de Sociologie, 98,* 43–58.

Popular cultural descriptions of satanic cult rituals are derived largely from Christian anticultist images of evil threats to vulnerable children. These images, which draw on deep cultural axioms and symbols about evil and innocence, are both legitimated and institutionalized by the Catholic church, Christian fundamentalists and child protectionists. Sensationalized by the mass media, as well as by the hypnotically produced testimonies of self-identified survivors, they erroneously suggest that a satanic menace to children is pervasive.

◆ **719**   Doland, V. (1992). Satanic ritual abuse and determinate meaning: A reply to Professor Ellis. *Journal of Psychology and Theology, 20,* 278–280.

The article by Ellis (see citation 722) convincingly argues that ostension can create a reality of its own, including ritual abuse. The zeal to interpret a "text," or series of accounts of ritual abuse in a way that privileges one's own ideologies about evil can destroy the lives of children and the people they accuse.

◆ **720**   Ellis, B. (1995). Kurt E. Koch and the "Civitas Diaboli": Germanic folk-healing as satanic ritual abuse of children. *Western Folklore, 54,* 77–95.

Kurt E. Koch, a Lutheran minister and mental health counselor who in the 1950s created a "demonic" clinical psychology derived from Germanic folk legend and folk healing practices, saw demonic possession as the cause of mental illness. His theory supported a growing Christian mental health movement in the United States and Great

Britain that focused on demonology and that contributed to the ideological and professional contexts of the contemporary ritual abuse moral panic.

◆ **721**   Ellis, B. (1993). The Highgate Cemetery vampire hunt: The Anglo-American connection in satanic cult lore. *Folklore, 104*, 13–39.

A cyclical exchange of folklore traditions between Great Britain and the United States contributed to the each country's cultural context that, in turn, gave rise to ritual abuse allegations. A good example of that exchange begins with the hunt for vampires in London's Highgate Cemetery in the early 1970s by a newly formed faction of the British Occult Society that speculated that a coven of satanists had resurrected the King Vampire of Wallachia who was buried there. The well-publicized hunt expanded into allegations of ritual abuse by the satanists during Black Masses held in the cemetery. Widely reported in the United States, the case legitimated pernicious rumors in that country that satanic cults were ritually abusing children.

◆ **722**   Ellis, B. (1992). Satanic ritual abuse and legend ostension. *Journal of Psychology and Theology, 20*, 274–277.

Folklorists use the term "ostension" to label real-life actions that are guided by preexisting cultural legend. In the case of ritual abuse, ostension would refer to the rather unlikely scenario of child abusers changing their *modus operandi* to incorporate elements of the ritual abuse legend. The more likely scenarios are pseudo-ostension, or false ritual abuse allegations; quasi-ostension, or the interpretation of evidence as being corroborative of ritual abuse; or proto-ostension, or the appropriation of ritual abuse claims by those who have not been ritually abused.

◆ **723**   Hunter, J. (1998). Interpreting the satanic legend. *Journal of Religion and Health, 37*, 249–263.

If the ritual abuse cases that have been cropping up across the United States are indeed the product of a moral panic, then it is imperative to find the source of the panic. The source can be found in the anxiety created by the growing awareness that sexual feelings between adults and children are ubiquitous, powerful and mutual. The satanic ritual abuse legend is the embodiment of the fear that if society gives up the myth of the sexless child and the companion myth of adults unattracted to children, then people will descend into the kind of evil that is metaphorically represented in ritual abuse accounts.

◆ **724**   Johnson, R.C. (1994). Parallels between recollections of repressed childhood sex abuse, kidnapping by space aliens, and the 1692 Salem witch hunts. *Issues in Child Abuse Accusations, 6*. Retrieved 4-March-01 from the World Wide Web: http://www.ipt-forensics.com/journal/volume6/j6_1_4.htm.

The way repressed memories of ritual abuse are recovered and treated is similar to the way memories of alien abduction are recovered and treated, and both of those are similar to the way memories of witchcraft were dealt with in 17th century Salem. In all of these cases, distressed people blame real or imagined folk devils for their victimization, learn their symptoms from books, other victims and purveyors of popular culture, and have their beliefs reinforced and validated by folk beliefs and legends.

◆ **725**   LaFontaine, J.S. (1998). *Speak of the devil: Tales of satanic abuse in contemporary England.* Cambridge, England: Cambridge University Press.

During the late 1980s, reports of ritual abuse began spreading across England and culminated in several sensational cases. Despite the fact that no evidence corroborating the allegations has been found, the belief that diabolical devil worshippers pose a threat to English children persists. There are striking parallels between the present day social movement to uncover ritual abuse and historic and contemporary witch hunts throughout history and in different cultures. While the roots of the current concern about ritual abuse are found in the unsettling socioeconomic and ideological changes in English culture, the themes of ritual abuse — devil worship, sexual violation, cannibalism, infant sacrifice — are deeply historic and universal.

◆ **726**   Stevens, P. (1992). Universal cultural elements in the satanic demonology. *Journal of Psychology and Theology, 20,* 240–244.

The motifs in satanic demonology, including human sacrifice, cannibalism, and ritual sex abuse, represent universal cultural fears deeply rooted in human evolutionary biology. The cultural bases of these motifs help explain the widespread allegations of ritual abuse, and the testimonies of alleged survivors.

◆ **727**   Victor, J.S. (1998). Social construction of satanic ritual abuse and the creation of false memories. In J. deRivera, T.R. Sarbin (Eds.), *Believed in imaginings: The narrative construction of reality* (pp. 191–216). Washington, D.C.: American Psychological Association Press.

The collective belief in stories about imaginary ritual abusers becomes false memories of ritual abuse through the social process of ostension by which social scripts from folk legend and popular culture are internalized by individuals as cognitive schema for organizing fragments of memory.

◆ **728**   Victor, J.S. (1996). How should stories about satanic cults be understood? *Harvard Mental Health Letter, 12,* p. 8.

Psychotherapy patients often claim they were ritually abused in childhood in satanic cults. These fantastic accounts must be examined on 3 levels: the sociological, that treats them as examples of contemporary legends that resonate with current cultural fears and anxieties; the interpersonal, that treats them as a product of the interaction between suggestible patients with the mass media and/or with mental health professionals who hold strong beliefs in ritual abuse; and the psychological, that treats them as confabulated mixtures of real and imagined events

◆ **729**   Victor, J.S. (1993). Sexual attitudes in the contemporary legend about satanic cults. *Issues in Child Abuse Accusations, 5.* Retrieved 4-March-01 from the World Wide Web: http://www.ipt-forensics.com/journal/volume3/j3_3_1.htm.

Historically, tales about satanic cults and their threats to children tend to arise during periods of unsettling social change. These legends provide convenient scapegoats for social anxieties about the stability of the moral order and the prospects for the future. The predominate themes of these legends is that children are being perversely abused by satanists. That children figure prominently as victims is testimony to the changing position of the child *vis-à-vis* changes in gender roles, parenting styles, and sexual attitudes.

THE DEMONOLOGY OF RITUAL ABUSE

From an anthropological point of view, a demonology is an institutionalized ideology about an evil force that is threatening society's most cherished values and human resources. Unlike folklore that warns more than it controls, a demonology has both ideological and material effects in that it influences how people think and act. Because the contemporary satanic demonology that is both the cause and the effect of allegations of ritual abuse resonates with other institutionalized beliefs, especially religious beliefs, anthropologists and other social scientists are particularly interested in religious beliefs in, and religionists' reactions to, allegations of ritual abuse.

◆ **730**   Passantino, B., & Passantino, G. (1992). Satanic ritual abuse in popular Christian literature: Why Christians fall for a lie searching for the truth. *Journal of Psychology and Theology, 20,* 299–305.

Ritual abuse survivor stories are particularly appealing to Christians because of their congruence with their beliefs in human depravity, the existence of Satan and demons, and the reality of evil. Christians are urged to guard against gullibility by determining if the ritual abuse survivor story is verifiable, reliable, consistent with a biblical world view, and written without vested interest before believing it is true.

◆ **731**   Pengelly, J., & Waredale, D. (1992). *Something out of nothing.* London: The Pagan Federation.

One of the consequences of widespread yet unsubstantiated claims of ritual abuse is that people professing minority religious beliefs are suspect. This guide, written for child protectionists, explains Pagan and Wicca beliefs, two alternative philosophies that have come under attack during the ritual abuse moral panic that is sweeping across Great Britain.

◆ **732**   Rogers, M.L. (1992). A call for discernment — natural and spiritual: An introductory editorial to a special issue on satanic ritual abuse. *Journal of Psychology and Theology, 20,* 175–186.

Ritual abuse is considered a form of systematic physical, emotional and sexual abuse ritualistically perpetrated by cults engaged in devil worship or ceremonies. Christians find the notion of ritual abuse consonant with their belief system, but they must be careful not to unthinkingly embrace this controversial notion. They must exercise their freedom to explore ideas without first pushing them through a theological filter and then accepting them or not solely because of their consistency with Christian beliefs. They must be more critical of those, many of them Christians themselves, who capitalize on fear by asserting that all ritual abuse allegations are true; and they must embrace survivors of abuse while at the same time realizing their disclosures can be truthful, inaccurate or, in some cases, completely false.

◆ **733**   Underwager, R., & Wakefield, H. (1992). The Christian and satanism. *Journal of Psychology and Theology, 20,* 281–287.

The belief that a satanic conspiracy is targeting young children actually is against Christian faith, excluded by Christian doctrine, and should not be supported, encouraged or approved by Christians. Scripture and theological scholarship prove that Satan is a wholly vanquished foe whose sole remaining capacity is to lie about the relationship between behavior and its consequences. Christians who are caught up in this ritual abuse belief are inadvertently furthering the cause of Satan because their behavior has consequences inimical to the very principles of Christianity.

♦ **734** Woodman, J. (1997). Psychologising Satan: Contemporary satanism, satanic-abuse allegations and the secularisation of evil. *Scottish Journal of Religious Studies, 18,* 129–145.
The notion of "satanic" has been a dominant trope within Western folk conceptions of evil. Ritual abuse allegations occupy the nexus of traditional religious notions of external evil in the form of satanists who horrifically abuse children, and secular notions of internal evil in the form of the sequelae of ritual abuse — multiple personalities and dissociation — which represent a form of spirit possession. This dynamic interplay between religious and secular notions of evil within the concept of ritual abuse suggests that the continuity of religious beliefs in secular societies both compensates for the failure of secular discourse to construct a viable concept of evil, and enables individuals and societies to achieve a sense of orientation in rapidly changing and unsettling social environments.

THE SOCIOCULTURAL CONTEXT OF RITUAL ABUSE

From a sociological perspective, the cultural crucible from which legends and demonologies arise is of considerable interest. In its examination of the unexpected and unsettling social changes occurring across cultures during the anxious couple of decades before the start of the new millennium, it sheds some analytical light on the questions of why the ritual abuse legend, albeit real or imaginary, arose when it did, and what social, ideological, political and professional forces shape its content and directs reactions to it.

♦ **735** Bottoms, B.L., & Davis, S.L. (1997). The creation of satanic ritual abuse. *Journal of Social and Clinical Psychology, 16,* 112–132.
The belief that ritual abuse is widespread is the outcome of a complex skein of sociocultural, professional and individual forces that came together in the 1980s in the United States. The belief is not without consequence. For therapists, it leads to inappropriate interactions with clients, including suggestive interviewing and memory recovery efforts; for patients, it is associated with psychological and interpersonal deterioration. The belief also poses challenges to mental health professionals and researchers to more closely examine the kinds of interactions that produce false allegations of ritual abuse, as well as the kinds of therapeutic interventions that are needed to deal with them.

♦ **736** Brenner, I. (1994). A twentieth-century demonologic neurosis? *Journal of Psychohistory, 21,* 501–504.
Allegations of ritual abuse require an appreciation and understanding of determining factors such as history, mythology, anthropology, theology, sociology,

psychology, law and forensic pathology. The cynical backlash against the "growth industry" of ritual abuse cannot be idly dismissed, for it is likely to spill over into other more common types of sexual abuse. At the same time, the backlash is instructive for it cautions against the contagious nature of group hysteria that can be generated by fears of ritual abuse.

♦ **737**   deYoung, M. (1996). A painted devil: Constructing the satanic ritual abuse of children problem. *Aggression and Violent Behavior, 1,* 235–248.

The social construction of ritual abuse into a social problem follows a fairly predictable sociological trajectory. It begins with persuasive yet wholly unsubstantiated claims by various interest groups that the problem is real and threatening; those claims then prompt agencies and organizations to develop initiatives, programs and laws to address the threat. This routinization of ritual abuse as a problem then evokes criticism from those unpersuaded by the claims, and adjustments then are made both in the programs put forth to deal with it and in the ideology and belief system that sustains those efforts.

♦ **738**   Robbins, S.P. (1998). The social and cultural context of ritual abuse allegations. *Issues in Child Abuse Accusations, 10*. Retrieved 4-March-01 from the World Wide Web: http://www.ipt-foresics.com/journal/volume10/j10_8.htm.

The many interrelated and converging sociocultural factors in the United States during the 1980s that gave rise to widespread allegations of ritual abuse and sustained professional and public belief in their credibility include: the demonization of cults and alternative religions, the occult "crime wave," media sensationalism, the recovered memory movement, and feminist theory with its abuse survivor ideology. Those forces, coupled with economic insecurity and changing family forms, rendered the culture ripe for such a compelling rumor panic about ritual abuse that otherwise reasonable people came to believe in fantastic and unfounded accounts of ritual abuse.

THE RITUAL ABUSE MORAL PANIC

From a sociological perspective, a moral panic is a collective reaction resulting from unsettling social strain and incited and spread by interest groups, towards persons who are actively transformed into "folk devils" and then treated as threats to dominant social interests and values. Through the use of emotive rhetoric, a moral panic tends to orchestrate cultural consent that something must be done, and quickly, to deal with this purported threat. The increased moral authoritarianism and social control that typically follow in the wake of a moral panic end up preserving and reaffirming the very interests and values that supposedly are being undermined by the folk devils.

To sociologists, the contemporary concern about ritual abuse has all of the hallmarks of a moral panic. It arose from social strain, is being spread by interests groups of different stripes, has variously named day care providers, parents and others as its folk devils, and new laws, policies, procedures and practices that are intended to protect the social and moral order as well society's most vulnerable citizens, have followed in its wake. From a sociological point of view, the ritual abuse moral panic, like all moral panics before it, is serving as a stabilizing function during a protracted period of disquieting social change.

♦ 739   Bravos, Z. (1991). Child abuse and witchcraft? Perspectives on the 15th and 20th centuries. *Issues in Child Abuse Accusations, 3.* Retrieved 4-March-01 from the World Wide Web: http://www.ipt-forensics.com/journal3/j3_3_2.htm.

The witchcraft moral panic of the 15th century has much in common with the ritual abuse moral panic of the 20th century: a compelling cultural ideology that children do not lie, an equally compelling presumption of the guilt of the accused, the reliance on special techniques of prosecution to deal with secularized evil, and a scientifically invalid search for behaviors that are indicative of the abuse.

♦ 740   de Young, M. (2000). The devil goes abroad: The export of the ritual abuse moral panic. *British Criminology Conferences: Selected Proceedings, 3.* Retrieved 4-March-01 from the World Wide Web: http://www.lboro.ac.uk/departments/ss/bccsp/vol03/deyoung.html.

An analysis of the ideological recruitment of international child protectionists into the ritual abuse moral panic begins with an examination of the written and spoken discourse of a cadre of American experts who traveled abroad to lecture on ritual abuse. Their discourse found 3 points of resonance with international audiences: it restored the image of the child as innocent victim, occluded the image of the sexual abuser as male, and reenchanted the image of the child protectionist as rescuer. When appropriated, panic discourse has both ideological and material effects, that is, it influences child protectionists to think and act in ways that ends up spreading the ritual abuse moral panic across Europe and Australasia.

♦ 741   de Young, M. (1998). Another look at moral panics: The case of satanic day care centers. *Deviant Behavior, 19,* 257–278.

A sample of 15 American day care ritual abuse case illustrates how a moral panic foments and spreads, and what kind of often contradictory and largely symbolic social and legal changes it can bring about. The day care ritual abuse moral panic also reveals that the providers use whatever power available to them to resist their stigmatization as ritual abusers, and the battle to restore their reputations further divides the public, professionals, and communities into believers, skeptics and disbelievers.

♦ 742   de Young, M. (1998). Sociological views on the controversial issue of satanic ritual abuse: Three faces of the devil. *Trauma Response, 4,* 22–24.

From a sociological perspective, the prevailing notion that ritual abuse is an exigent social problem can be analyzed as an example of a subversion ideology, that is, a culturally constructed myth about a conspiratorial group that is undermining the core values of a rapidly changing society; a moral panic, or collective reaction to a real or imaginary threat that escalates over time as it attempts to protect threatened values; or a contemporary legend, that is, a collective metaphor that expresses a society's anxiety about its changing social and moral order. The article can be found at the internet URL: http://www.aaets.org/arts/art26.htm.

◆ **743**   Henningsen, G. (1996). The child witch syndrome: Satanic child abuse of today and child witch trials of yesterday. *Journal of Forensic Psychiatry, 7,* 581–593.

The 17th century witch trials among the Basques and in northern Sweden are reasons to be attentive to contemporary ritual abuse trials. The child witch syndromes are remarkably similar: both are associated with moral panics, the breakdown of social solidarity, a conviction that the targeted crimes cannot be prosecuted without relaxing extant legal procedures, the use of witch signs, the absence of physical evidence, and suggestive and leading interviews of alleged victims. Mental health professionals, social workers, lawyers and judges will learn a great deal about the contemporary ritual abuse moral panic through examining historical examples of witch hysteria.

◆ **744**   Jenkins, P. (1992). *Intimate enemies: Moral panics in contemporary Great Britain.* Hawthorne, NY: Aldine deGuyter.

The changing socioeconomic, political and ideological climate of Great Britain during the 1980s generated beliefs that children were being ritually abused. The moral panic that belief generated culminated in several infamous ritual abuse cases in England and Scotland. Far from an isolated event, the British ritual abuse moral panic is discursively and ideologically linked to recent moral panics about pedophiles and serial killers.

◆ **745**   Nathan, D. (1991). Satanism and child molestation: Constructing the ritual abuse scare. In J.T. Richardson, J. Best, & D.G. Bromley (Eds.), *The satanism scare* (pp. 75–94). NY: Aldine deGruyter.

Historically, when Western societies experience the strains produced by rapid social change, moral panics about the safety of children tend to unfold. This occurred during the 1980s in the United States when economic shifts and changes in the status of women and in the nature of the family, combined with feminist concerns about sexual abuse and religious concerns about satanism to form a moral panic about ritual abuse. The moral panic had such a hold on the thinking of child protectionists and mental health professionals that the absence of evidence corroborating claims was only met by them with ever-changing theories about the origin, nature and dynamics of ritual abuse. Without thoughtful public and professional discourse about ritual abuse and the forces that make it real, the moral panic will continue to ruin the lives of those falsely accused and those who falsely identify themselves as victims.

◆ **746**   Sjoeberg, R.L. (1997). False allegations of satanic abuse: Case studies from the witch panic in Rattvik 1670–71. *European Child and Adolescent Psychiatry, 6,* 219–226.

A 17th century outbreak of witch hysteria in Sweden is analogous to the contemporary ritual abuse moral panic. In each case, the moral panic arose during a period of rapid social change, was fomented by interest groups and by the allegations of children that were coaxed and shaped to conform to the prevailing image of the folk devil.

◆ **747**   Sjoeberg, R.L. (1995). Child testimonies during an outbreak of witch hysteria: Sweden 1670–1671. *Journal of Child Psychology and Psychiatry and Allied Disciplines, 36,* 1039–1051.

The testimonies of 809 children to local priests and to the Royal Commission of Inquiry that looked into the 17th century witch hunt in Rattvik, Sweden, reveal that the children's capacity to distinguish fantasy from reality, their tendency to give stereotyped testimony, and their degree of suggestibility to the influences of interviewers are related to their age, sex and degree of peer influence. The findings are particularly relevant to the contemporary ritual abuse moral panic because these same factors seem to both prompt and problematize it.

◆ **748**   Victor, J.S. (1998). Moral panics and the social construction of deviant behavior: A theory and application to the case of ritual abuse. *Sociological Perspectives, 41*, 541–565.

The American day care ritual abuse cases illustrate the nature of the moral panic that swept over the United States in the 1980s. Originating in the unsettling changes in the nature of the family, women's roles and the economy, the moral panic was spread by child-savers whose claims were legitimated by various social institutions.

◆ **749**   Victor, J.S. (1991). The satanic cult scare and allegations of ritual abuse. *Issues in Child Abuse Accusations, 3*. Retrieved 4-March-01 from the World Wide Web: http://www.ipt-forensics.com/journal/volume3/j3_3_1.htm.

The international ritual abuse moral panic is a product of collective behavior and the emotions associated with it — fear, outrage and vindictiveness — are legitimated by interest groups and in conferences. The ritual abuse scare persists because it resonates with cultural and professional belief systems, as the Langley Estate case in Rochdale, England, illustrates.

12

The Ritual Abuse
Controversy Continues

Whatever ritual abuse reflects about real or imagined threats, in this cultural hall of mirrors no image of it goes unchallenged.

Modern Debate

◆ **750** Cook, K., & Kelly, L. (1997). The abduction of credibility: A reply to John Paley. *British Journal of Social Work, 27*, 71–84.

By failing to take into consideration the compelling evidence that ritual abuse is a social problem with real clinical consequences, Paley (see citation 490) contributes to the ruthless backlash against ritual abuse and other more ordinary forms of child abuse. His position that there is no evidence to support accounts of ritual abuse has the status of orthodoxy among skeptics, but leaves unaddressed the question of just how much and what kind of evidence is still needed to convince skeptics of the reality of ritual abuse.

◆ **751** Frankfurter, D. (1994). Religious studies and claims of satanic ritual abuse: A rejoinder to Stephen Kent. *Religion, 24*, 353–360.

Kent's (see citations 20 and 21) position that the truth about ritual abuse will be found only by religious scholars is as specious as the interviews he conducted with self-identified "survivors," and the outrageous conclusions he draws from them.

◆ **752** Ganaway, G.K. (1992). Some additional questions: A response to Shaffer and Cozolino, to Gould and Cozolino, and to Friesen. *Journal of Psychology and Theology, 20*, 201–205.

Shaffer and Cozolino (see citation 467), Gould and Cozolino (see citation 503), and Friesen (see citation 501) draw *a priori* conclusions about satanic cults and ritual abuse in the absence of any corroborating evidence. Their approach is more a leap of faith than a scientific inquiry, and their articles would be rejected for publication by any reputable peer-reviewed academic journal. While it is important to be sensitive to the needs of trauma patients, the suspension of clinical judgment on the part of mental health professionals, which they advocate, has deleterious effects and is one of the most significant contributing factors to the growing cottage industry in ritual abuse assessment and treatment.

◆ **753**   Golston, J.C. (1992). The ritual abuse countertransference response and the erosion of clinical scholarship: A review of the *Journal of Child Abuse & Neglect*, v. 15. *Treating Abuse Today, 2*, 4–12.

Clinicians' countertransference responses to horrific reports of ritual abuse have led to polarized debates, flawed scholarship, and a preoccupation with the issue of credibility, as illustrated by the article by Young *et al* (see citation 474) in *Child Abuse & Neglect*, and by the editorial and commentaries that accompany it.

◆ **754**   Goodman, G.S., Levine, M., & Melton, G.B. (1992). The best evidence produces the best law. *Law and Human Behavior, 16*, 244–251.

Contrary to the position taken by Underwager and Wakefield (see citation 136), the *amicus curiae* brief submitted by the American Psychological Association in *Craig* recognizes both the seriousness of defendants' interest in confronting their accusers, and the importance of protecting child witnesses from harm. The psychological evidence, as the studies cited in the brief demonstrate, supports the conclusion that children may be so traumatized by testifying in the presence of defendants as to render their testimony unreliable.

◆ **755**   Harshbarger, S. (1995, May 12). The Amiraults are not the victims [Letter to the Editor]. *Wall Street Journal*, p. A-13.

The State Attorney General who brought charges in the Fells Acres ritual abuse case criticizes reporter Rabinowitz (see citations 92–94) for a misleading and selective portrayal of the defendants as the real victims in this case.

◆ **756**   Herman, J. (1994). Presuming to know the truth. *Nieman Reports, 48*, 43–44.

To Wright (see citation 259), the Ingram ritual abuse case represents an archetype, a modern equivalent of the Salem witch trials. His sweeping generalizations about an epidemic of false allegations by children would never pass as science, and should not be allowed to pass as journalism. Although trendy, his account of the case rests on unverifiable assumptions: that false allegations are common and increasing; recovered memories are spurious; and quack psychotherapists, religious zealots and survivor groups are fomenting mass hysteria. By privileging Ingram's position in his account and denigrating his daughters', Wright perpetuates the age-old advantage that abusive parents, especially fathers, have over their victimized children.

◆ **757**   Huntington, A. (1999). A critical response to Sara Scott's "Here be dragons: Researching the unbelievable, hearing the unthinkable. A feminist sociologist in uncharted territory. *Sociological Research Online, 4*. Retrieved 9-February-2001 from the World Wide Web: http://www.socresonline.org.uk/4/1/huntington.html.

In her article, Scott (see citation 714) reflects on her research and asserts that acceptance of a "subtle" realist epistemological stance offers an adequate base from which to assert claims of ritual abuse are true. In making that assertion she abandons the obligation of the feminist sociologist to focus on sense-making, not truth-asserting, and the attendant recognition that "sense" is always historically, socially and cultur-ally contingent.

◆ **758** Jonker, F., & Jonker-Bakker, I. (1992). Reactions to Benjamin Rossen's investigation of satanic ritual abuse in Oude Pekela. *Journal of Psychology and Theology, 20,* 260–262.

Rossen's (see citation 316) conclusion that the Oude Pekela case is an example of mass hysteria is specious, especially given the fact that he had no direct contact with the victimized children, their parents or other key players involved in the case. His dubious credentials further weaken the integrity of his conclusion.

◆ **759** Jonker, F., & Jonker-Bakker, I. (1992). Safe behind the screen of "mass hysteria": A closing rejoinder to Benjamin Rossen. *Journal of Psychology and Theology, 20,* 267–270.

The persistence of the idea that the Oude Pekela ritual abuse case is nothing more than an example of mass hysteria can be traced directly to the allegations of Rossen (see citation 316) who in choosing not to believe the children's disclosures is able to maintain a safe distance from the devastating implications of a ritual abuse case.

◆ **760** LaFontaine, J.S. (1994). The current literature about organized abuse of children [Letter to the Editor]. *Child Abuse Review, 3,* 4–5.

Kelly and Scott's (see citation 565) review of the literature on organized abuse should be criticized for presenting a pro–ritual abuse point of view. Their review cites as authorities Stratford (see citation 696) whose alleged autobiography of childhood rit-ual abuse has been debunked on every detail and whose publisher withdrew the book when she was exposed as a fraud; Boyd (see citation 368) whose account of ritual abuse in Great Britain is riddled with factual inaccuracies; as well as other American "experts" whose cited work has none of the rigor required of scientific scholarship.

◆ **761** LaFontaine, J.S. (1994). Allegations of sexual abuse in satanic rituals. *Religion, 24,* 181–184.

Kent (see citations 20 and 21) undermines his own premise that ritual abuse can only really be analyzed by scholars of religion by his uncritical acceptance of the nar-ratives of a few ritual abuse survivors and his rejection of scholarly work in the field that calls into question the credibility of those narratives.

◆ **762** Matzner, F.J. Does satanism exist? *Journal of the American Acad-emy of Child and Adolescent Psychiatry, 30,* 848.

Nurcombe and Unutzer's (see citation 410) article is completely unscientific in its presentation and alleged assessment of a case of ritual abuse. Their conclusion that satanic cults are ritually abusing children is wholly speculative.

◆ **763** Middleton, W. (1994). Further comments on multiple person-ality disorder. *Australian and New Zealand Journal of Psychiatry, 28,* 154–156.

Gelb (see citation 502) overlooks the clinically documented association between childhood abuse, especially ritual abuse, and multiple personality disorder.

◆ **764** Mulhern, S.A. (1991). Patients reporting ritual abuse in child-hood: A clinical response. *Child Abuse & Neglect, 15,* 609–611.

Young *et al.* (see citation 474) fail to consider that their own beliefs in ritual abuse and the introspective therapeutic techniques they employed with their sample patients could be the major factor that contributes to the similar stories of ritual abuse by the patients.

♦ **765**   Noll, R. (1989). Satanism, UFO abductions, historians and clinicians: Those who do remember the past.... *Dissociation, 2*, 251–253.

The Hill and Goodwin (see citation 18) article is based on a highly selective reading of historical documents. It is this kind of naïve approach to history that perpetuates the ritual abuse myth.

♦ **766**   Nurcombe, B. (1991). Does satanism exist? A response. *Journal of the American Academy of Child and Adolescent Psychiatry, 30*, 848–849.

Matzner (see citation 762) is overly critical of Nurcombe and Unutzer (see citation 410) about the diagnosis of ritual abuse for a young child. The conclusion of that article that ritual abuse is a real problem is predicated upon police suspicions about the workings of covert satanic cults, the various satanic practices well documented in Christian literature, and the corroborated cases of child sex rings that show that covertly organized groups of people can abuse children for long periods of time without detection.

♦ **767**   Nurcombe, B. (1991). Ritual abuse of children: Reply. *Journal of the American Academy of Child and Adolescent Psychiatry, 30*, 1024–1025.

Shopper's (see citation 773) critique of the Nurcombe and Unutzer (see citation 410) article is an insensitive response to the case of a 5 year old ritually abused girl. The clinical assessment of the girl was carried out according to standard procedures, and the findings of the assessment ruled out alternative explanations for her behavioral and emotional problems.

♦ **768**   Olio, K., & Cornell, W.F. (1998). The façade of scientific documentation: A case study of Richard Ofshe's analysis of the Paul Ingram case. *Psychology, Public Policy, and Law, 4*, 1182–1197.

A review of the original documents and interview transcripts in the Ingram case reveals that Ofshe's conclusions (see citation 252) are based on errors of fact, methodological flaws, and other confounding factors. Therefore, his conclusion that Ingram was inadvertently hypnotized and as a result confessed to ritually abusing his daughters is incorrect. Ofshe's imperfect narrative of this case and his pseudoscientific conclusions are being uncritically accepted and repeated in the literature, becoming an academic version of an urban legend.

♦ **769**   Passantino, G., Passantino, B., & Trott, J. (1989). Satan's sideshow. *Cornerstone, 18*, 23–28.

The claims Stratford (see citation 696) makes in her autobiography about childhood ritual abuse and being forced to serve as a "breeder," producing babies for a satanic cult to sacrifice, are completely false. A thorough investigation of her background fails to find any evidence to support her story, and a great deal of evidence to support the conclusion that she is a chronic liar. Her story can be disputed on every detail, including the most minor and she, herself, changes the details constantly according to her audience. Harvest House, her religious publishing house, should have confirmed the details of her story before publishing the book and Christians, who comprise the primary readership, should be aware that the book is fiction. The article can be found at the internet URL: http://www.answers.org/Satan/SatanSideshow.html.

◆ **770** Putnam, F.W. (1991). The satanic ritual abuse controversy. *Child Abuse & Neglect, 15,* 175–179.

The issues raised by Jonker and Jonker-Bakker (see citation 312) and Young *et al.* (see citation 474) are fundamental to the controversy currently waging in the child protection field over the issue of ritual abuse. In evaluating reports of ritual abuse it is important to assess the underlying beliefs of the authors; in these 2 articles, the authors clearly are convinced that ritual abuse is real and that the dynamics and effects they are describing are credible features of it. Neither article reaches the standards of empirical research, therefore each is highly impressionistic and naïve in its conclusions. The picture of satanic cults that emerges from these articles is unconvincing, and the lack of evidence presented by the authors to corroborate the allegations renders their depictions unbelievable. These articles are better understood by appreciating how the labyrinthine communication network that links child protectionists around the world operates to transform speculation into science, and rumor into reality.

◆ **771** Rossen, B. (1992). Response to Oude Pekela incident and the accusations of Drs. F. Jonker and I. Jonker. *Journal of Psychology and Theology, 20,* 263–266.

The *ad hominen* attacks of Jonker and Jonker-Bakker (see citation 310) deflect from the real argument about whether the Oude Pekela case is an actual case of ritual abuse or an example of mass hysteria.

◆ **772** Scott, S. (1999). Dancing to a different tune: A reply to responses to "Here be dragons." *Sociological Research Online, 4.* Retrieved from the World Wide Web 9-February-2001: http://www.socresonline.org.uk/4/2/scott_sara.html

The responses of Wise (see citation 775) and Huntington (see citation 757) to "Here be Dragons" share a common concern: the article's assertion that ritual abuse claims are true serves the needs of social workers and police officers, but avoids the responsibility of feminist sociologists to analyze the social construction of discourse. When the discourse is the subject of heated public debate, as ritual abuse is, suspending concern about the lived experiences of the women the author interviewed was ethically, politically and practically problematic.

◆ **773** Shopper, M. (1991). Ritual abuse of children. *Journal of the American Academy of Child and Adolescent Psychiatry, 30,* 1023–1024.

Nurcombe and Unutzer's (see citation 410) conclusion that the 5 year old girl they assessed was ritually abused is more than a little dubious given the fact they used anatomically correct dolls in the assessment, failed to evaluate the girl's reality testing, refused to check the details of her story against other sources, and apparently never even considered more appropriate alternative diagnoses.

◆ **774** Siano, B. (1993, April/May). All the babies you can eat. *Humanist,* pp. 40–42.

Rose's (see citation 692) account of childhood ritual abuse offers no evidence to support her claim. That an article like this should appear in *Ms. Magazine,* that has played such a role in revitalizing the feminist movement, is disgraceful. Rose tries to give her story a feminist slant by linking ritual abuse with male domination, yet in her story it is females — her mother, aunt and grandmother — who are her tormentors. Rose also seeks to avoid the controversy over the role of satanism in ritual abuse by not using the word, yet the acts she describes are stereotypically satanic in nature. One of the many worthy efforts of the feminist movement has been its success in increasing public awareness of sexual violence. This is why *Ms. Magazine*'s embrace of the ritual abuse moral panic, and the ludicrous account of Rose, is so infuriating.

◆ **775** Wise, S. (1999). Reading Sara Scott's "Here be dragons." *Sociological Research on Line, 4.* Retrieved 9-February-2001 from the World Wide Web: http://www.socresonline.org.uk/4/1/wise.html

Scott's (see citation 714) dilemmas encountered in her research on ritual abuse parallel the dilemmas the author encountered a decade before in her own research on child abuse. The two diverged in their approach to the problem, however. The author maintained her focus on the analysis of the social, political, ideological and moral forces that constructed child abuse into a social problem; Scott, on the other hand, got stuck in the middle of those forces by asserting that ritual abuse claims are true, and in doing so, can offer no real analysis of these claims.

13

Conclusion

In the preface to this book I resisted the temptation to use the word "stuff" to describe much of the material on ritual abuse. Now, in the conclusion, I resist a more tantalizing temptation to dissect the arguments, analyze the patterns, compare and contrast the findings, and reveal the ideological underpinnings of the sources in this book that contribute so much more than just "stuff" to the ritual abuse controversy. More bluntly stated, I resist that temptation to tell the reader what to believe about ritual abuse and, in doing so, try to make the controversy go away.

The early 20th century writer and social critic Ambrose Bierce, who, by the way, never had a thing to say about ritual abuse, although the title of his *Devil's Dictionary* (1911) hints that he had at least an intellectual encounter with the precisian, once defined controversy as "a battle in which spittle or ink replaces the injurious cannonball and the inconsiderate bayonet." Whether waged with words or weapons, he warns, controversy is to be avoided.

As a sociologist, not to be confused with a social critic, although one would be forgiven for doing so, I disagree. I believe there is value in controversy. When stripped of the "stuff" that obfuscates, alienates and opinionates, what remains prompts us to reflect, reexamine and reassess. The citations in this book, whether of scientific inquiries, investigative reports or personal reflections, provide both the analytic tools and the empathic understanding to reexamine the questions raised in the Preface. Is ritual abuse a clandestine form of abuse only emerging at last into the harsh light of public scrutiny, a culture-bound fiction that symbolizes the anxieties and ambiguities peculiar to late-modern societies, or perhaps a contemporary reworking of ancient legends and myths about innocence and evil? What implications for justice are there when professionals and social institutions respond, or for that matter fail to respond, to allegations of ritual abuse? Should children's accounts and adults' recovered memories of it be believed, or are they formed in conversational partnership with their confidantes? What are the sequelae of such horrific abuse, and if allegations and memories of it are not genuine, then what are the consequences for children and adults of usurping their own autobiographies by believing they are?

These questions remain at the heart of the ritual abuse controversy and they lie ready for reflection, reexamination and reassessment. After two decades of cannonballs and bayonets, spittle and ink, it seems a propitious time do so.

Databases

AHSearch
Alt-Health Watch
Anthropological Literature via Eureka
British Library Inside
CINAHL
ComAbstracts
Contemporary Women's Issues
COPAC
DARE
EBSCO
Electric Library
Emerald
ERIC
Gender Watch
General Reference Center Gold
Humanities Abstracts
Ingenta
International Political Science
Abstracts
ISI Basic Indexes
LawRunner
LEXIS-NEXIS Academic Universe
LLBA

Lois Law
Medline
National Criminal Justice Reference
Service
National Data Archive on Child Abuse
and Neglect
National Library of Medicine
Newslibrary
OPAC
PAIS International
PILOTS
PsychFirst
Readers Guide Abstracts
Research Library
Social Science Abstracts
Social Science Plus
Social Work Abstracts
SocioCite
Sociological Abstracts
UnCover Web
Wilson Select Plus
WorldCat

Author and Title Index

219

Name and Subject Index